D1710606

Whether uncovering the social order of a specific time and place, or addressing the grand questions of social history, we often find ourselves doing archaeology. While other fields (ethnography, primatology and women's studies) have much to offer, especially in developing models of what life in the past might reasonably have entailed, archaeology's contribution is distinctive in addressing more directly what life *was* like. Such a claim does not just depend on lots of data, but on reliable means of discerning hierarchy from this data.

This book contends that despite traditional doubts, practical limitations, and contemporary critiques, a rigorous social archaeology is indeed possible. The early chapters outline what a productive social archaeology might look like, covering such issues as the possibility and prospect of cross-cultural social inference, the central importance of archaeological theory and of social models, the nature of inequality, and the extraordinary effects rules for arranging statuses have on the character of life. The following section of the book offers a systematic review and critique of cross-cultural correlates of inequality. For example, the ways in which residential buildings can vary are summarized and examined for how they might yield insight into a former status system. In the final chapter these correlates are used to help answer the question, "Was Çatal Hüyük a *ranked* Neolithic town in Anatolia?"

NEW STUDIES IN ARCHAEOLOGY

Series editors
Colin Renfrew, *University of Cambridge*
Jeremy Sabloff, *University of Pittsburgh*
Clive Gamble, *University of Southampton*

Archaeology has made enormous advances recently, both in the volume of discoveries and in its character as an intellectual discipline: new techniques have helped to further the range and rigour of inquiry, and encouraged inter-disciplinary communication.

The aim of this series is to make available to a wider audience the results of these developments. The coverage is worldwide and extends from the earliest hunting and gathering societies to historical archaeology.

For a list of titles in the series please see the end of the book.

The archaeology of rank

PAUL K. WASON

Bates College

The archaeology of rank

 CAMBRIDGE
UNIVERSITY PRESS

Published by the Press Syndicate of the University of Cambridge
The Pitt Building, Trumpington Street, Cambridge CB2 1RP
40 West 20th Street, New York, NY 10011-4211, USA
10 Stamford Road, Oakleigh, Victoria 3166, Australia

First published 1994

Printed in Great Britain at the University Press, Cambridge

A catalogue record for this book is available from the British Library

Library of Congress cataloguing in publication data

Wason, Paul K.
The archaeology of rank / Paul K. Wason.
  p. cm. – (New studies in archaeology)
Includes bibliographical references and index.
ISBN 0 521 38072 3
1. Social archaeology. 2. Social classes – History. 3. Social
structure – History. I. Title. II. Series.
CC72.4.W37 1994
930.1–dc20 93-42094 CIP

ISBN 0 521 38072 3 hardback

TO NINA

CONTENTS

FIGURES AND TABLES

Figures

Tables

ACKNOWLEDGMENTS

Like you, I often read the front matter of books. Here I find authors saying they could never acknowledge everyone, so here are a few and let's hope the rest don't feel left out. Why not just list them all, I would ask. Can there be so many? When it came my turn, I decided to save the disclaimers for why I haven't used someone's favorite book and simply list everyone who made a difference. But I soon discovered how large the circle really is, and that just as in tracing genealogies, it is hard to know where to begin. Should I mention the college professors who had a special hand in teaching me how to think – Lou Pitelka, Joseph D'Alphonso, Robert Chute, Bruce Bourque – or go even further back to those evenings when my father read to us from his own favorite authors – Lewis, Tolkien, Conan Doyle – imaginative thinkers who, perhaps, have helped me become a little more flexible and a little less dull in thought and expression. Probably not. A better case can be made for starting much later with graduate school mentors like Bill Arens, Pedro Carrasco and Lou Faron, or with those who taught me archaeology – Bruce Bourque, Ed Lanning, Mike Gramley, Mike Moseley, Bob Feldman, Elizabeth Stone, Phil Weigand.

And then we come to those who helped directly with the book as it grew from digressions in term papers, through a dissertation, and on to more drafts than I or those I am about to acknowledge care to remember. The text in final form owes much to Jeremy Sabloff, Colin Renfrew, Bruce Bourque, and an anonymous Cambridge reviewer, while Phil Weigand, Elizabeth Stone, and Ed Lanning had an early influence. Also early on (and at a formative stage of her own writing career) Gina King offered enthusiastic editorial assistance. She has continued to encourage my interest in writing, which is much appreciated. I have not perhaps come as fully to my senses as these scholars would have liked, but if they care to read this book again, they will discover how much I have learned from them. I must also thank those I work with at Bates College (even Sheila) who have encouraged the efforts of that curious hybrid – a member of the College's administration who nevertheless is engaged in serious scholarship (well, pretty serious). I am pleased to say that even as many small liberal-arts colleges are just getting used to the teacher-scholar, Bates is already taking steps to support the administrator-scholar. Yet in the broader academic world, the historical suspicion that such a person is not strictly legitimate, a dabbling hobbyist with untoward pretensions, will for some time keep this a role that must be fashioned anew each time rather than an office to be filled. Which only reinforces how crucial is the support of real people, including the lineage chiefs and paramounts (if you will) of the academy. Gina Tangney and Martha Crunkleton in particular have appreciated and supported my efforts, and several Bates faculty members have also followed the progress of my work. This has been heartening, even fortifying. I wish to thank Jessica Kuper, Peter Richards, and those at Cambridge University Press who have helped me learn something about how to turn a great wad of scribblings into a book. Thanks also to Jennifer Wood for creating the artwork for the cover and frontispiece, block prints based on a figurine and mural from Çatal Hüyük.

Finally I offer thanks to my friends and family (even Don) for their support and encouragement. Thanks to Kate and Carolyn who have spent too much of their four and two years wondering, in Carolyn's words, "Where mine Daddy?", and to my wife Nina, who has seen this through with me. She has expressed admiration for my ability to go back to work each evening and put in a few hours' writing. (She also counsels holding out for the music video, when friends seem to think they might want to read it – but we needn't go into that just now.) Yet if the scheduling has not always been ideal, I have, of course, enjoyed the work itself, and should say rather that I admire her ability – and appreciate her willingness – to take up what I let slip while I had the pleasure of doing archaeology – er, I mean, while I undertook the arduous task of finishing this work.

I

The present study of past society

From the playground bully to Rameses the Great, it is striking how freely, and with what zeal, we indulge the spirit of inequality. Having experienced unequal relationships of many kinds, we do not wonder at the immense range of sizes, shapes, and, of course, colors inequality has taken through the ages. By force of personality, by brute force, by natural law and divine right – not to mention hard work and a winning smile – everywhere we turn, some people are held up as better than the rest. There may be no one alive today who has not known institutionalized social hierarchy; perhaps no human has *ever* lived unaffected by the thought that one was superior to another.

It is hard to pin down just what we ought to mean by "egalitarian" (and so also with "inequality," "hierarchy," "ranking"), but a society of full equality may be an ideal never realized. Quite likely there has everywhere been a tendency for some people to accrue favor, prestige, and a recognized superiority. But while we can all attest to the weight of informal personal distinctions, hierarchy that derives from the ongoing structure of society is of a very different character, and from this has arisen one of the most enduring controversies of our intellectual tradition. In one view, both informal inequality and formal social hierarchy have shadowed us throughout our species' history, while the alternative envisions a long epoch in which all peoples passed their lives free of this institutionalized kind of inequality. The latter view is probably the one most favored by archaeologists of this century, and it is the inspiration for many questions of longstanding importance to prehistorians. When did inequality first appear? When did it become institutionalized? How? Why? Can we discern patterns among its myriad forms, broad *kinds* of hierarchy? Do our models of social inequality (ranking, socio-economic stratification, casteism, slavery) describe real and significant variation in the past? And how should we value them as ways of characterizing the world today? These are among the central questions of evolutionary anthropology, and (in this form) make little sense apart from the assumption that human society has evolved from a non-hierarchical condition. Was this the case? Inspired by primate and feminist studies, scholarship of the past decade has seen an extraordinary upsurge in appreciation for the view that institutional hierarchy has been a feature of human society from the beginning. Of course, many standard evolutionary questions remain important just the same. Any number of specific regional histories do suggest increasing hierarchy over time, which, however we conceive the primal state, raises a number of questions. How smooth was the development? Over what time scale? Was it prone to reversals? (Is it still?) And, do these long-term histories show movement through similar changes from region to region? In addition, this view of the history of social inequality raises its own questions. Is even human "social" inequality, then, essentially biological? Can we discern patterns concerning which individuals are likely to be high or low in the hierarchy? But ultimately, the origins of human social inequality may be the most interesting and most important question of all.

There are at least two things all of these questions have in common. They hold an irresistible fascination for archaeologists and reflective people generally (quite a few of whom in my experience are archaeologists at heart). And second, their answers depend on our ability to recognize inequality from archaeological data. Since the past cannot be observed directly (the *raison d'être* of all historical disciplines), whatever we know about a former time must be traced from its enduring effects, from its mark on the present. Any attempt to answer one of these questions, or for that matter to learn anything at all about a society no longer functioning, will depend on some combination of written documents, speculation on the origin of present customs, and inferences drawn from material remains and their contexts. This last approach is archaeology, of course – social archaeology. Yet, only recently has it become accepted that archaeology can yield insight on so non-material a thing as social organization. But if complete skepticism is no longer warranted, caution certainly is, and its best expression is neither temerity nor reluctance but an insistence on solid methodology: the development of archaeological correlates of social features, soundly based on the inferential process actually involved. A decade ago Colin Renfrew remarked on the youthful (embryonic?) status of our field:

> It is too early ... to write a satisfactory manual of social archaeology ... The subject is still at an exploratory stage, and the most which we can hope for is a number of insights, some of which may prove helpful in the construction of a coherent methodology for the study of the social organization of early societies, and in the development of a relevant body of archaeological theory.
> (Renfrew 1984a:19)

This is still true as I write, and my purpose is to further the archaeological study of society by improving one branch, the inference of status hierarchy. I have drawn together a number of these insights of which Renfrew speaks, and in hopes of moving beyond the "exploratory stage," have organized them into an outline of a "coherent methodology." These means of studying inequality are approached in the context of a model of social inference, given systematic arrangement, and often significantly refined. The challenge of social archaeology is using the static archaeological record to infer the life of a once-functioning society. Success demands understanding what separates the two, and methods adequate to bridge this gap. In the present ferment, how we view society, the archaeological record, and a range of epistemological issues are all in dispute, and with understandings differing both on what we are looking for and on the character of our data and tools, it is little wonder views diverge on how best to connect the present record with past society.

The gap to be bridged

Archaeological inference of social organization requires a model of society, archaeological data, and a reliable connection between them. While different models (social types, scaler measures, bundled continua) each have advantages and disadvantages, and while in any instance data may be inadequate, a major hindrance to reliability is insufficient regard for the nature of the gap between archaeological data and social model. The diagram (Fig. 1.1) is my attempt at outlining what is involved in bridging this gap.

Social inference does not so much identify a fact that has lain hidden for ages, as help us make use of a model of social life; we are explicitly seeking a contemporary social-theoretical understanding of life in the past. A reliable inference requires a good connection between each "step" separating the conclusion from the organization of the former society, although, of course, social inference is not in reality the mechanical process a diagram like this suggests. The approach outlined here, and elaborated in the next few chapters, consists largely of points useful for establishing a reliable connection at each "step" in this model.

The logical possibility of social inference

In recommending caution rather than skepticism, I brushed over the question of in what sense social archaeology is possible. This may not seem a pressing issue, yet agreement on just *what* is possible has never been universal, and with the epistemological issues raised by post-processual archaeology, reservations are, if anything, deeper and more prevalent than ten years ago. Clearly I do not believe the skeptic ultimately prevails, but these objections do alert us to fundamental and not entirely avoidable problems which must be overcome for social inference to give a reliable picture of former status systems.

Grahame Clark may have been the first to incorporate social inference into a theoretical model of archaeology. My undergraduate memory of *Archaeology and Society* is of an excellent introductory essay on what archaeology should be. In part this is because of its readability and good sense, but it is also because I was grounded in the texts of the sixties and seventies; to the reader in 1939 it was striking and original, "a milestone in the history of the discipline" (Trigger 1989a:264). Clark's functionalist view of society led him to the conclusion that archaeology should be (and so, presumably, could be) the study of life in the past, including social and political organization. Clark also held that when relying on archaeological data alone we are likely to learn more about economies than social structures and belief systems, and in practice he did concentrate for some years on the economic and technical aspects of social life (e.g. Clark 1952). V. Gordon Childe also helped move social inference to the realm of the possible, particularly in *Social Evolution* (1951). Yet he was ever pessimistic about social inference, and his work can as easily be read as a catalog of qualifications and limitations.

In Trigger's view, it was Gordon Willey who set the stage for the serious

Models of society
Features of social organization

Observation and
analysis in ethnography;
social theory

Human actions & their meanings
to others

Middle
range
research
including
ethnoarchaeology
and/ or
interpretive
procedures

Material expressions of
activities, non-material
behaviors, ideology

Archaeological record of material
consequences of activity

Observation and
analysis in
archaeology

Reconstructed view of activities
and their meanings

Archaeological and
social theory
(e.g. use of middle
range theory)

Present description of past
social organization

S
o
c
i
a
l

a
r
c
h
a
e
o
l
o
g
y

Figure 1.1 A model of the archaeological inference of social organization

archaeological study of social organization with his 1953 *Prehistoric Settlement Patterns in the Viru Valley, Peru* (Trigger 1980:161). Yet, it was not until the early 1960s that the mood really began to swing toward optimism about recovering social life. Advocating a holistic view of cultural systems, Lewis Binford "repudiated the idea that it was inherently more difficult to reconstruct social organization or religious beliefs than it was to infer economic behavior" (Trigger 1989a:298), and many archaeologists associated with the "New Archaeology" movement worked with the confidence that we could study virtually any aspect of culture open to ethnography. The "ladder of difficulty" in archaeological inference was seen as essentially a practical problem, to be overcome with the explicit application of methodology. But while skepticism nearly disappeared with the dominance of processual archaeology in the 1960s and 1970s, the field still has its critics. Most recent critiques are essentially philosophical, arguing (on the basis of one epistemological perspective or another) either that archaeological data *cannot* yield information about society (e.g. Leach 1973) or that the cross-cultural generalizing approaches used by most social archaeologists are not valid (e.g. Shanks and Tilley 1987a, 1987b; Hodder 1990b).

Illuminating the black box

In 1973 Edmund Leach argued that we cannot learn about society from archaeological materials; it is logically not possible. These comments were offered as the "Concluding Address" to the Sheffield "Research Seminar in Archaeology and Related Subjects," the published proceedings of which (Renfrew, ed. 1973) remain an important document of processual archaeology. And while he was referring specifically to social types, Leach's objections are meant to apply broadly to social inference. Indeed, if valid, Leach's concerns would be an inditement of all processual archaeology.[1]

Human nature, Leach argues, is not fully governed by natural law, so even a thorough knowledge of conditions previous to an action will not allow us to predict that action (Leach 1973:764). Archaeologists do not observe human activity directly, only "residues of the past." Since behavior is not predictable and archaeologists cannot observe it, they cannot possibly know about it. Ethnographic parallels offer little help. They may illustrate possibilities, but cannot demonstrate which was most probable.

> My point is that the task of the archaeologist is to dig up and analyse residues of the past ... But do please recognize the limitations of the archaeologist. As soon as you go beyond asking "What" questions, such as: "What is the nature of my material?" and start asking "How" and "Why" questions, such as ... "Why does my series of deposits change over time?" ... then you are moving away from verifiable fact into the realm of pure speculation.
> (Leach 1973:764)

Archaeology can never be more than the physical description of things dug from the ground and assumed to have been made by humans. The prehistoric social system is a "Black Box," that is, "any imaginary mechanism, the workings of which cannot be investigated" (p. 765). Assuming there may be any number of social configurations represented by a set of data, it is an illusion to suppose we can validly infer one of them. Hence his response to Renfrew's (1973b) inference of chiefdom social organization for the Neolithic of Southern England.

> As we have seen the social anthropologists in this audience were quite unimpressed by the second half of Renfrew's suggestion; ... ethnographic parallels suggest at least half a dozen alternative possibilities and none of them need be right. That does not mean that they should not be used as guesses; but the highly speculative nature of such reconstructions needs to be appreciated.
> (Leach 1973:767)

We might argue that Renfrew did not provide strong evidence for chiefdoms, but Leach's point is different; any such conclusion, if based on archaeological data, must be "pure speculation." This is important, but there are other factors which, while not eliminating the problem (a fact with its own implications for method) show it to be a great exaggeration. Consider what it means to study social organization. A social system is a model, an abstraction; we do not see social organization even in a living society, but infer it from observations of specific actions. In a sense it is always in the black box. The archaeologist must infer actions, then use these to infer social organization. But while ethnographers observe actions directly, they must still infer social organization.

Just because this is an inferential process does not make it speculative, but a common result is that there will often be alternate possible conclusions. Leach's concern is that archaeological data may not suffice to choose among them. This is important for often a social situation may be expressed in varied ways materially, while a configuration of material culture might be associated with any of several social features. There is no real basis for assuming a one-to-one correspondence between material and social features, and in fact some work indicates considerable flexibility. Based on the occurrence of specific social features in New World societies, for example, Feinman and Neitzel conclude for one set of associations: "The complexity of these relationships suggests that although certain correlations do exist, no single attribute can be used to predict the values of all the rest" (Feinman and Neitzel 1984:67). Clearly this sets limits on our ability to infer one feature of social life from evidence of another, yet it does nothing to abolish the possibility generally. Reliable connections between configurations of material culture and features of social organization, such that you can use the one to recognize the other, *can* be found, even though the nature of the connection and the domain of its validity require more careful definition than is often recognized.

Many connections for example, work only one way. Major burial differences will not be found unless there were substantial status differences, but even highly differentiated statuses will not always be marked by major burial differences, much less specific kinds of mortuary variation. As with material–social connections we can sometimes "assume" certain correlations among two aspects of social organization, although these are bound to be uncommon since our only way of knowing that one will not occur without the other is by knowing that it cannot. Thus redistribution cannot exist at a significant level without some centricity in the structure of the society. This in turn requires status inequality since centralized leadership presupposes personal status differences. Any evidence for redistribution, and any for central leadership, is at the same time evidence for personal ranking. But the connection does not work both ways; ranking can (at least in theory) occur without either redistribution or central leadership, just as it can exist without being marked by the placement of large golden statues in graves. Leach *does* have a point. The fact that we cannot assume, and can rarely demonstrate, an invariant correspondence among features does make correlations harder to find and all too often less reliable, but in the next few chapters I present what I believe to be reliable means for reducing the number of alternatives, or at least for better choosing among them.

Our supposed inability to postulate cross-culturally valid (sometimes caricatured as "invariant") connections among features of social life is also at the heart of more recent critiques. These typically are broad objections to processual archaeology in that propositions basic to most post-processual archaeologies undermine the validity of social inference as well. The issues are complex and intertwined, but I distinguish two important strands which are primarily epistemological objections to processual archaeology. It is largely by extension that they are also "subversive" of the archaeological inference of social organization.

The presentist problem

The goal of social archaeology is describing former social life in terms of contemporary social theory: the explicit pursuit of a contemporary understanding of the past. But if the social models we try to "identify" are abstractions and contemporary constructs, they are meant to express something real about past society. Do they? Shanks and Tilley argue that much archaeology is deeply enmeshed in the appropriation of the past, not in describing the past itself:

> The past is never safe, never divorced from the present ... The past is colonized and appropriated by a narcissistic present.
> (1987a:28)

> The past, then, is gone; it can't be recaptured in itself, relived as object. It only exists now in its connection with the present, in the present's practice of interpretation.
> (1987b:26)

They expect no more from archaeological data than "resistances." These data may constrain our purulent desire to say what we please about the past and represent it as truth, they may keep us from total subjective skepticism, but they will never actually direct our thoughts. Nevertheless,

> The intention is not to sacrifice objectivity and replace it with an extreme and disabling relativism with archaeologists locked into the present. In the works that archaeologists write there can be no simple choice between fictional creations and objective copies of the past.
> (Shanks and Tilley 1987a:7–8)

We can debate whether or not Shanks and Tilley's approach leaves us in disabling relativism,[2] and it is also clear than not all post-processual archaeologists are in agreement with Shanks and Tilley's "strong program" of revisionism, but certainly we must discard anything like a positivist view of objectivity. They have not sacrificed objectivity so much as recognized that we never had it, and deceive ourselves to think our view of the past is an objective reconstruction of the way it was.

Our models depend on beliefs about human nature, beliefs which derive from sources other than archaeology (thankfully, for otherwise they would be pallid, lifeless things indeed). These models in turn affect what we look for and influence what we will find. But, does anyone seriously maintain that we find only what we were looking for, much less all of what we were looking for? Have the spade and trowel never revealed a surprise? Are theories so unrelated to empirical concerns that we will not change our view of the past no matter what is found? Even those espousing the most radical epistemologies stop short of this conclusion, yet some do invoke this argument whenever it becomes tactically useful for subverting an established approach of processual archaeology. With Hodder I find this too "presentist." To the contrary, our present understanding is "partly built out of the reality of the past" (Hodder 1991b:188).

One problem is that of scale: not maintaining the same level of specificity throughout a critique. It may be true that we can never know the past as it was in itself, never experience it as those who lived it the first time around. We may even acknowledge that this has sometimes been a goal of archaeology.

> Traditional and new archaeology represent a desire for the past in itself; a desire for an objective past, for primary original objectivity, the essence of the past, the essential meaning, the ideal presence of the past. The past is to be perceived by the autonomous archaeologist whose subjectivity is to be marginalized in a simple immediate experience of the past.
> (Shanks and Tilley 1987b:13)

Cunningly overdrawn (and of characteristically indeterminate meaning), this contains nonetheless a plausible representation of what many of us wish archaeology could be. But when they raise their objections in the very next sentence, Shanks and Tilley depend on a shift in the "scale" of the argument. The processual view has become a bizarre fantasy unrelated to anything any archaeologist has ever believed possible.

> This is idealist fiction. The past cannot be exactly reproduced. Exact reproduction is repetition, tautology, silence. The archaeological past is not re-created as it was or in whatever approximation.
> (Shanks and Tilley 1987b:13)

Every scholar who has worked with archaeological data has recognized – and regularly bemoaned – our limits in knowing about the past. And we have had to acknowledge that these limitations are rather more severe than many of us used to assume. We tend to talk about practical limitations which we hope to overcome (and so progress toward a more objective view of the past) but if Shanks and Tilley have a lesson worth attending, it is that our understanding of the past will remain constrained regardless of preservation, and regardless of improved methodology.

Nevertheless, the last sentence is a gratuitous addition, unrelated to the preceding argument. Yes, it is absurd to believe we can know everything about the past without distortion, but this does not mean we can learn nothing of a real objective past. This divide between processual and post-processual archaeology, both the importance given to the issue and the inclination toward polar views on it, is, I believe, a consequence of enlightenment thinking. Central to, and very much the glory of the enlightenment, is the belief that through human reason alone we can acquire for ourselves truth, all truth. This idea has shaped modern Western science, and whatever we may say of such faith in reason, science is not all fluff; airplanes *do* fly. There is little wonder students of humanity have sought similar success, and processual archaeology is explicitly meant to be scientific, applying the "best" of human reason to the study of the past. But the shame of the enlightenment is the belief that through human reason alone we can appropriate for ourselves truth, all truth. There have always been dissenters, arguing that it is not for our finite minds to grasp reality in its essence and complexity, and that to forsake revelation from God is to choose the wrong path from the start. Although not generally advocating revelation, post-structuralists similarly warn of enlightenment hubris, and a host of radical epistemologies have come to the same conclusion; we cannot know for sure.

This is like a gust of fresh, bracing air to a world too long shut up in Descartes' heated-chamber, but it is easy to continue the same mistake of taking ourselves and our discoveries too seriously. I do not object to the conclusion itself, but to the post-modern implications so often drawn from it, for it is necessarily a limited statement. It cannot mean that we can never know anything in whatever approximation. Many of us have found that even in this post-Enlightenment era, airplanes still fly. And it is limited, too, in that it is inherently tentative. Too often people make this claim with an incongruous spirit of absolutism, as if to say, "this we know for sure: 'We cannot know for sure.'" Some have even gone so far as to say – perhaps in a last-ditch effort to avoid accepting our finitude – there is no one world to know, but many "different pasts" each valid in its way.

The self-centeredness of relativism may well drive us to the conclusion that nothing is real save our own thoughts. But rather than recognize this as a *reductio ad absurdum*, some take it as reason to doubt there ever was such a thing as the past. Shanks and Tilley find it strange that archaeology has not been more dramatically altered by the realization that data are theory-laden. "There is still a wide consensus in the belief in 'objective reality' or the archaeological record" (Shanks and Tilley 1987b:9). But even their strong view of theory-ladenness questions only our ability to *know* the real past objectively, not the *existence* of an objectively real past. This conflation of epistemology and ontology may be common enough in the current academic world, but it is devoid of substance. It is nothing more than a singularly aggressive form of intellectual imperialism.

Furthermore the theory-ladenness of our conclusions may not be the great trap some make out. Shanks and Tilley state: "If all observation is to a certain extent theoretical ... it is illogical to maintain that theories can be independently tested against observation" (1987a:40–41), and Hodder says: "Although ... the real world does constrain what we can say about it, it is also clear that the concept of 'data' involves both the real world and our theories about it. As a result, the theories one espouses about the past depend very much on one's own social and cultural context"

(1991b:17). Allowing flexibility in how we read "very much," this is a reasonable caution. Yet Hodder rejects middle range theory on essentially these grounds; these theories are not objective tests, "independent instruments of measurement," because what we choose to measure depends on perception, and because like all methods, this is itself theory dependent (Hodder 1991b:17).

But "object theory," the theories affecting perceptions, are different theories from those used in analysis (e.g. middle range theories), and as Peter Kosso points out, they are logically independent. While we need to make assumptions "to break into the circular association between theory and observation" (Kosso 1991:626) these assumptions can be revised, and we are not caught in a fruitless cycle of testing theories against themselves and so retaining bias throughout. Our conclusions must also be consistent with other aspects of human knowledge, which while theory-laden as well, are based on yet different theories. This takes us some way. I am not convinced that these lines of theory are *completely* independent, for most will derive from the same cultural milieu, but their *logical* independence is essential to the possibility of meaningful encounter with archaeological data, to the chance to let the past speak to us.

If we accept that there is something real out beyond our subjective selves, then perhaps we can do better or worse at coming to know it. Even though "knowing subjects introduce distortions into their accounts," the conclusion is not radical subjective skepticism, for "[i]t is their accounts of the past, not the past realities themselves, that are subjective" (Patterson 1989:561). On the surface, the result is much the same; no description I produce of the past will express a complete objective reality. But the implications for how we go about archaeology are profound; here we are encouraged to find ways of making our accounts accord better with a past that really was, rather than just revising them to serve more conveniently our political agenda. Interestingly, much later in the same book, Shanks and Tilley turn around and reject radical subjectivism. "A real past," they now tell us, "exists but the pure essence of the objectivity of that past, i.e. how it really was, eludes us in that to begin to deal with the past involves us in decisions or choices as to how we might conceive it" (1987a:110).

We must face our finitude from both directions; that reason alone will not lead us to complete objective truth, but that at the same time we are not each alone in the universe, our personal thoughts unsullied by decisive contact with external reality. This is a persistent tension in social archaeology; our methods may not yield all detail, but it does not follow that what they yield is untrue, meaningless, useless. We *can* be responsive to our data in such a way as to constrain the number of plausible descriptions of the past. Yet (at the proper scale) this critique does make a point, for this is not the same as saying we can know the past, in detail, as an objective fact in itself. We cannot recite the refrain of far too many scientists and popularizers, "we used to *believe* that, but now we *know* this." If we are not condemned to wallow forever in a post-modern slough of despond, a relativist present, isolated from whatever else (if anything) is or was out there, neither can we buy the enlightenment-style objective truth hawked at the vanity fair of easy scientism. Our progress into the past is a complicated journey demanding whatever means we can devise to separate real encounters with a former way of life from projections of our own way of life. Interestingly, Shanks and Tilley make their way to essentially this same view.

> It is entirely misleading to pose the problem of understanding and explaining the past in terms of either a purely factual representation tied to the past and purged of subjective "bias," or a presentist quest for liberation from the dogmatic burden of the archaeological record through unrestrained fictionalizing and mythologizing. Interpretation is an act that cannot be reduced to the merely subjective. Any archaeological account involves the creation of *a* past in *a* present and its understanding.
> (Shanks and Tilley 1987a:103–104)

These are problems faced by all attempts at knowing beyond "cogito, ergo sum." While they do become more acute in social archaeology – because of how far removed it is from raw data – I contend that with care we can be more responsive to the past than otherwise. A "good" social inference requires an openness to the possibility that our model is *not* an appropriate description of former social relations. For example, we must control the tendency toward premature closure, to construct, say, either/or propositions for testing (e.g. Was this a chiefdom or a state?) or in some other way make it harder rather than easier to discover a social configuration we have not already imagined.

The contextual critique of cross-cultural methodology

The second line of post-processual thought said to undermine social inference is its recognition of the importance of "contextualization." Hodder believes there are no universally applicable correlations between material culture and social organization, no correlations we can depend on apart from an in-depth understanding of the historical context of each example. Material culture is not a direct reflection of human relations; symbolic meanings intervene, and we must understand these if we want to read what is recorded in material culture. While he does not actually rule out social inference – his objection is to cross-cultural methods which attempt to bypass meaning – he does believe that this problem "throw[s] doubt on the usual assumption that variations in social ranking can be monitored using archaeological evidence" (Hodder 1990b:309).

The contextual critique is important, and since development of cross-cultural methodology for social inference is the primary goal of this book, I review these arguments more carefully in chapter 2. But for the moment it is sufficient to observe that this critique, too, resolves largely to a question of scale; I agree that there are limits to the depth of knowledge we can gain through cross-cultural correlates alone. Hodder argues, both reasonably and importantly, that "the relationship between behaviour and material culture depends on the actions of individuals within particular culture-historical contexts" (1991b:13). But the consequence he identifies does not really follow: "There is thus no direct, universal cross-cultural relationship between behaviour and material culture. Frameworks of meaning intervene and these have to be interpreted by the archaeologist" (Hodder 1991b:14; see also Shanks and Tilley 1987a:105). At the most detailed level this may be true, and certainly the interpretation of meaning, when possible, is valuable in any case. Nor do I take issue with the need for context, only with the assumption that we must define it as the local culture and its unique history. A cross-cultural relationship between a configuration of material culture and an aspect of social organization can also be a valid context for understanding a specific assemblage of material remains.

This, of course, assumes that cross-culturally valid relationships really do exist, despite the local, historically contingent symbolic manipulation of material-culture that intervenes between social organization and material culture patterning. I think they do. To sketch one possible example, someone could have a large house built because of being a legitimate chief, and someone else might build a large house to bolster a claim to high status not otherwise widely recognized. It would be hard, perhaps impossible, to tell what the large house meant in this specific sense without a fuller cultural context. Details of form, including decoration, could be very important in the representation of status through architecture, and cross-cultural generalizations would not help us read these architectural statements. But at a much grosser level we now know – excuse me, there is reason to believe – that, quite apart from this context, a person could not build a much larger house than anyone else without access to more resources, without some status difference with economic implications.[3] Yes, for fullest understanding we need the historically-particular context, but a cross-cultural generalization about the relationship between a pattern of material culture and an aspect of social organization can yield the information that inequality was present.

The plan

"Theory," said George Santayana, "helps us bear our ignorance of fact." Indeed. But it also helps us bear the overload of facts that would smother us, had we no means of focusing our attention on just a few, no theory to bring order (if necessarily artificial) to our picture of reality. And if well used, might theory (including social theory, models of society) also be a means of reducing our ignorance of fact?

The rest of this book roughly follows the model of social inference presented in the Fig. 1.1 – describing what is involved; defending the possibility of each task; and applying the model to one aspect of society, the status system. In chapter 2 I review the value of theory (specifically social models) for archaeological inference. Likewise with the theory most central to social inference, middle range research and ethnographic analogy, I discuss how the archaeological study of social organization depends on (and can otherwise make use of) these two key aspects of social inference. Thus I develop a framework for using archaeological data to infer social organization.

As the first step in *using* the model of social inference just developed, chapter 3 covers social inequality and its implications for real life. Following an overview of inequality and its manifest forms, I use the models of Service, Fried, and Johnson and Earle (particularly the big man, chiefdom, stratified society, and state types) to move from an abstract to a more operationalized description of ranking. These models are particularly helpful for understanding how different structural rules for arranging statuses can lead to very different cultures. I focus on just a small number of variables – presence or absence of ranking, achieved versus ascribed ranking, and non-stratified ranking versus socio-economic stratification – and use the type models as a means of determining how these differences might play out in real life.

Sometimes the mere mention of words like "type" and "chiefdom" elicits a well-choreographed reflex of resistance. And because this attitude is not without justification I must offer some explanation for my procedure. I remain convinced that these models reveal important aspects of status, important in terms of what it would be like to live under these social conditions. It may be neoevolutionary theory that critics reject with such vehemence, so I must add the disclaimer that while these models of inequality derive from specific evolutionary typologies, by advocating their use for understanding social life I am not requesting that you accept a *process* of unilinear evolution. Johnson and Earle used the typological approach in their recent analysis of the evolution of society. As examples of one of the types, the archaic state, they discuss France and Japan in the middle ages, drawing attention to the incongruity of putting the two side by side.

> Our two examples are widely separated both spatially and culturally. Yet when the layers of aesthetic, technological, social, and philosophical differences are stripped away – when all that remains is the small set of variables that forms the core of our model of social evolution – we find astonishing similarities between the two societies.
> (Johnson and Earle 1987:248)

The point is not that you can strip away these layers and what is left will be a good description of Japan in the middle ages. Nor will we arrive at a "central core" in the sense that all else is historically-particular epiphenomena. The point is that this core is real and important in that these structures for ordering social relations will affect the overall character of life, and will affect it in similar ways for medieval France, despite the also real and important differences.

Approaches to the archaeological recognition of inequality (and to distinguishing among these few variables), are the concern of chapters 4 through 7. The cross-cultural correlates of inequality reviewed are organized for presentation based on the kind of evidence used: data on mortuary practices, artifacts, and settlements. I review, for example, a range of ways in which residential buildings can vary, considering if, and how, each variable might be made to yield insight into the status system.

And then, at last, an example. The final chapter is devoted to a "case study" in which I apply the archaeology of rank to Çatal Hüyük, asking, essentially, whether it was a *ranked* Neolithic town in Anatolia. Not bound by space or time in choosing an example, I set out to find a case that would allow me – using the correlates discussed – to demonstrate ranking conclusively yet not so easily as to give the idea that this is all a grand program for proving the obvious; Karnak, Ur, ChanChan, and Teotihuacan were right out. I imagine that such an "ideal" example does exist, but I did not find it before falling under the spell of Çatal Hüyük. Still, if my conclusions are less compelling than I wanted, a good case can be made, and the exercise usefully illustrates important aspects of the inference of social organization, yields specific questions that can be addressed in future excavations, and ably fulfills the basic purpose of a case study in a book of this sort – providing a "down to earth" illustration of what has been a largely abstract discussion.

In 1978 Colin Renfrew warned of the "operational difficulty" (Renfrew 1978:99) faced by social inference, and twelve years later Pam Crabtree again made much the same point: "[t]he identification of material correlates of extinct social systems continues to be a major methodological problem for anthropological archaeologists" (Crabtree 1990:347). My hope is that the material presented here will help advance social inference generally, and will also make it a little easier to obtain dependable statements about status systems of the past. And learning all we can about former status systems is worth the effort. The better our understanding of equality and inequality of the past – in what contexts it took on its divergent forms, and what aspects of lifestyle have derived from the differing systems – the better we can understand the manifestations of hierarchy today. I realize this kind of claim is made often enough to pass from cliche to charter myth and beyond – to the kind of sentence we just skip over. But we could do with a better understanding of inequality as we seek to comprehend the sometimes surprising struggles around the world, and the even more surprising passivity of people whose aspirations are diminished and lives impoverished by unyielding hierarchies. Perhaps it can even help us understand ourselves.

2

Social theory and social life: models of society in the archaeological study of status

The intent of social archaeology is to understand a former way of life in the same terms we use to study modern society. I do not believe this is at odds with efforts to understand the past "on its own terms," but certainly it is different. Whether or not any current approach really tells us what the participants would have said about themselves, social archaeology does not even try. Yet this does not exclude us from saying something real and significant about life in the past, for in describing former societies in terms roughly comparable to a social anthropologist's understanding of living societies, it provides a basis for answering questions about the nature and history of social life. Its method is the application of social theory to the findings of excavation, which is a dangerous business, for if we are not careful we can easily "read into" the data what is not there. Hopefully, we know better than to expect "pure objectivity," but neither have I seen any compelling argument for the contrary assertion, that the use (imposition) of Western social theory (our models of society) inevitably negates the past, subsuming it as a self-serving extension of the present.

A model is a representation to help us visualize something we either cannot observe directly, or wish to see from a different angle. Many central concepts of anthropology – society, culture, status – are models in this sense. Thus, while real and important, "society" is not something we actually observe but a "theoretical" ordering (or sometimes explanation) of a set of empirical observations. Any model is more or less compelling depending on how well it makes sense both of what we have seen and what we hope to see. To bring genuine insight, models must represent, however abstractly, what actually goes on, "simplify complex observations whilst offering a largely accurate predictive framework structuring these observations – usefully separating 'noise' from information" (Clarke 1978:31). A good model can often meet these demands within properly bounded conditions, but we must be able to recognize the bounds, distinguishing problems the model helps address from those it frustrates. Archaeologists have sometimes used the type models of Service or Fried as though suitable for uncovering all we need to know about socio-cultural evolution, but it has long been clear that neither model can serve all kinds of archaeological investigation, and many have now rejected them, scorning the naivete of anyone "still" taking a typological or even evolutionary approach to prehistory. But as I will show, they *are* valid (if properly understood), they are useful (for certain purposes), and they are productive of insight into questions many of us find interesting.

The most fundamental connection between archaeology and social models derives from the fact that we cannot make even basic interpretations of archaeological data apart from analogy with living society. But while the interests of archaeology and social anthropology overlap, they are by no means identical (Renfrew 1984a:9), and we need not be bound by models developed for other purposes. Because social archaeology requires some model that makes reference to living society, but is not tied to any one in particular, archaeologists have made use of social models in widely differing ways, among them the following.

(1) A very common approach is to use archaeology as an extended data set for addressing questions in social anthropology. Archaeology as anthropology includes attempts to determine if an archaeological case is an instance of the social phenomenon described in the model (e.g. a case of gradualistic evolution), and use of archaeological material to test a model. Anthropologists "may propose sophisticated theories of social change," Bradley observes, "but they cannot test them in the field. This can only be achieved by historical methods, and since so few societies have written documents, this places a greater emphasis on the techniques of archaeology" (1984:3). Of course the difficulty of analyzing archaeological materials in terms similar to those used to study living society is not trivial; hence the need for the methodology of social inference.

(2) An alternative is to emphasize archaeological relevance, as is done with settlement pattern studies, for example, and those in which "complexity" is used as an independent variable. The primary advantage is that the models are easily operationalized for archaeological data; it is much easier to describe the settlement pattern of an archaeological case than to describe the nature of the status hierarchy. Yet if we wish to address questions that are not purely archaeological, we must eventually connect with social models, "translate" settlement patterns into a descriptive category relevant for living society.

(3) Social theory is also used, reflexively, to critique the field itself. Archaeology is a social practice, even an institution – something which influences how it is conducted and affects our view of the past. The use of social theory to understand the practice of archaeology is a striking feature of much post-processual archaeology, perhaps nowhere more prominent than in the sustained critique of Michael Shanks and Christopher Tilley in *Reconstructing Archaeology* (1987a), and *Social Theory and Archaeology* (1987b). Hodder has observed that *Reconstructing Archaeology* "issues in a new generation of archaeology – a new age of a philosophically informed and critically aware discipline" (Hodder 1987b:xv). This sounds like standard post-modern hyperbole included more for starkness than factuality, but these works have indeed begun to alter our view of how archaeology should be done (which is not the same as saying they are correct about human reason, the world around us, or archaeology). This use of social theory has not been customary in archaeology despite an ongoing introspection, and strikes some as a troublesome complication. But it *is* archaeology, for at every step this "reconstruction" has significant implications for our understanding of life in the past.

(4) Encompassing models of human nature are also important, if only because each of us holds fundamental assumptions about what it is to be human. We embrace these

ideas with conviction even when they remain implicit in our thinking, and they profoundly affect our work. Much the same might be said of another layer of modeling, abstract social theory. We may never "apply" it to a body of data, but it affects how we understand our material. These basic perspectives on humanity will even influence what social models we choose. While a model is putatively a way of ordering a set of empirical observations, we do not accept it unless it also satisfies our presuppositions about the way the world is.

As an example, many of us feel strongly about the tempo and mode of evolution, some holding to a view that expects change to be smooth and gradual, hardly perceptible to the participants, while others expect change more often to be a matter of rapid responses to crises, responses which (unlike in biological evolution) may be explicitly willed by the participants. Our view of this issue will affect which evolutionary models we consider most "reasonable." This choice is not so much a response to "the data" as an outgrowth of ideas on human nature and society, ideas which may well relate to our individual intellectual histories. I find it intriguing that in the mid 1970s archaeologists interested in socio-cultural evolution were moving toward gradualism (manifested in part by a strong reaction against social typologies) just as the punctuated-equilibrium model was catching on in biology. I am more inclined toward jumps, pauses, and qualitative distinctions, but this may be because I was a student of biology and biological anthropology at the time. In any case, it was not through the data of archaeology that I began to find gradualism and continua unappealing. Certainly we can find empirically based arguments for rapid, uneven, perhaps even discontinuous culture change,[1] but these are not yet conclusive. Other developments may have been gradual,[2] but in neither case is this kind of information fully determinative of our views. This does not mean we lack reasons, even *good* reasons, only that they are not empirically determined.

(5) Models can also be used in different ways depending on the problem, the most common archaeological use of social models being for descriptive, analytical or heuristic purposes. A model is descriptive if it helps shape a wide range of information into a useful picture. Most often used for classification, such models will define classes based on assumptions about which differences are important. This borders on analysis, but analytical models go much further. David Clarke defines analytical archaeology as "the continuous elucidation of the relationships which permeate archaeological data by means of disciplined procedures directed towards the precipitation of general theory" (1978:485). And some of this analysis will be conducted with the aid of social theory. Social models might help us look for relationships "of more than chance regularity" (p. 485), define our analytical units or help define the domains within which regularities might be found.

Social models are also important to archaeology for heuristic purposes, as aids to discovery, either as heuristics themselves or in developing heuristic methods. This is the primary use of the evolutionary typologies of Elman Service (1971), Morton Fried (1967), and Johnson and Earle (1987) in my approach to studying inequality. They are not used here for description, classification, or for analysis of social change, but to help us consider just what to look for when we try to find inequality. These models provide excellent descriptions of how a structural principle of ranking or of socio-economic stratification might play out in real life.

Social models in the archaeological study of inequality

Social theory most directly relevant to the archaeological study of inequality includes models that describe and classify the varied manifestations of inequality and models of social change. Shanks and Tilley observe that "[i]n a very real sense the study of long-term social change marks out an intellectual field in which archaeology and social theory do not just come together, with perhaps slightly different perspectives, but actually coalesce" (1987b:137). They also suggest that models of social change have mainly been evolutionary models, and have been "imported" to archaeology from other fields. For better or worse they are largely correct on both points.[3] To learn about the past, two distinct questions are at issue: whether ranking characterized the society, and whether our social theory of ranking says something true and important about human relations. But as important as the second question is, social inference proper is largely concerned with recognizing a social feature, applying a model, and much less so with the value of the model. I have chosen to use the models of status developed in three well-known typologies. These not only yield insight on social functioning but point to significant ways in which societies differ. Thus they are worth using in the study of former peoples regardless of what else we may wish to know about status relations in the past. But other models of society are being used to advantage in archaeology. And it is also the case that despite the great appeal the concept of evolution has for scholars whose subject is dominated by the time dimension, other kinds of social theory are also being used to order, explain, interpret or otherwise draw insight from archaeological data.

World systems theory (cf. Wallerstein 1974) for example, is valued as a means for understanding interaction and exchange among distinct societies, thereby balancing the emphasis neo-evolutionary models have (sometimes) placed on internal social or adaptational functions (Kohl 1989:218). It recognizes that interlocking economies and political empires are not always commensurate, and emphasizes the unequal relations that develop among participating (thus non-peer) societies (Kohl 1989:227; 222). Marxist approaches (cf. Spriggs, ed. 1984) which explicitly acknowledge their debt "to a theoretical perspective emphasizing the primary significance of the relations of production to the dynamics of social change" (Gilman 1989:63) are held to be valuable among other things for addressing "the questionable historical realism of certain aspects of the New Archaeology's ecological functionalism and the pretensions to objectivity inherent in the New Archaeology's scientism" (Gilman 1989:65). And among post-processual approaches Ian Hodder's interpretive archaeology (Hodder 1991a) is already exemplified in *The Domestication of Europe*, a remarkable study of changes accompanying the assimilation of agriculture in Europe, which stresses the interpretation of symbols, both as a means of learning about the past, and in recognition of the importance of meaning and symboling in the process of social change itself (Hodder 1990b).

A concern of this book is how we might demonstrate ranking in the past, a term I use broadly (following Berreman) to mean institutionalized status inequality, any hierarchy of statuses which are a part of social structure, and which "extend beyond age, sex, personal characteristics, and intrafamilial roles" (Berreman 1981:9).

Social models and social life

Just as we never see gravity, only planets in orbit and apples falling on physicists, no one has ever seen ranking. What we observe – even among living peoples – are activities that we interpret as manifestations of inequality. Some people are bowed to, carried on litters, bedecked with jewelry, and given an attentive ear regardless of their wisdom in the case. To say that ranking is present is to claim that it usefully models the social basis of this differential treatment. And to study inequality of past society, we face the additional step of inferring the actions themselves.

Archaeological inference proper largely concerns accuracy (e.g. that ranking is correctly identified) and less so whether our model is a meaningful way of characterizing observed behavior. (In what ways the concept "ranking" is meaningful, and how it might be useful as an approach to modeling society, are considered in the following chapter.) But we must be clear on *what* the model means, what circumstances of lifestyle it describes. One approach is to backtrack to everyday life[4] for an "operational description" useful for identification purposes. Evidence is left not by social structures but by specific things people have done, and to the extent that behavior is in part patterned by social rules, we can use our knowledge of past activities (inferred from archaeological data) to reconstruct those "rules" in terms of our social models.

A social feature like ranking can be expressed materially in any number of ways. It can be manifest in different activities and these activities can have varied material consequences. This is so because, as Hodder argues, material culture is meaningfully constituted and people are active agents, ensuring that behavior is not fully predictable (1991b:1). People have cultural attitudes about, and attribute meanings to, the material things they produce, use, and finally discard. We cannot reduce material culture, not any of it, to simple utilitarian fulfillment of environmentally determined needs.

> The relationship between material culture and human organization is partly social . . . But it is also dependent on a set of cultural attitudes which cannot be predicted from or reduced to an environment. The cultural relationships are not caused by anything else outside themselves. They just are. The task of archaeologists is to interpret this irreducible component of culture so that the society behind the material evidence can be "read."
> (Hodder 1991b:4)

Hodder is persuasive (to a point) in arguing that material culture is rarely a direct reflection of human behavior (1991b:2). One of his deepest objections to the New Archaeology is its yearning to become a generalizing science, which he considers impossible because "it is ideas, beliefs, and meanings which interpose themselves between people and things." Daniel Miller and Christopher Tilley concur.

> A consideration of ideology and power means that we are no longer able simply to 'read off' the nature of past societies from material evidence. Instead the archaeological record must be understood as actively mediated and manipulated as part of the social strategies of the individuals and groups that constitute a past society. Material culture can be used to express interests and ideas which may very well be contradictory. In order to understand ideology and power successfully a historical, particularlist and contextual approach to the evidence is fundamental.
> (Miller and Tilley 1984b:vii)

A contextual archaeologist might emphasize that while burial reflects society, it is not a *direct* reflection as through a universal one-to-one correlation between material configuration and social feature. The relationship is mediated by attitudes toward death which affect *how* society is reflected in burial. One cannot squeeze the meaning out of actions or artifacts expecting to find relations between material culture patterning and social organization which hold regardless of historical context. This is the main reason contextual archaeologists reject middle range theory, but in fact it only conflicts with certain approaches to middle-range theory, not those needed for the inference of social organization. Bridging arguments can be constructed in various ways (see below), but their value also depends on just *what* we want to know about the past. If we want to learn about the "interests and ideas" of individuals who lived in the past, then middle range theory (in its current state) is of little help. And of course, we *do* want to know this. To understand status relations fully, we must know the thinking behind the structure. Were "low ranking" people seen as underprivileged and downtrodden, dirty and lazy ("stinkards" as among the Natchez), or even not quite human? Cross-cultural bridging arguments are also less successful with detail than generalities. But while ignoring local context will mean a sketchier view of social relations, cross-cultural inferential methods like middle range theory are not ruled out.[5] For example, people simply would not erect a monumental tomb stocked with large gold statues, while scratching out little pits for everyone else, if there were no significant, hierarchical status differences. Here is something we can claim about the former society quite apart from other knowledge of the culture, ideology, or ecology. Admittedly it merely whets our appetite, but no amount of detail undermines the importance of knowing whether or not inequality was present.

Hodder also argues that theories of material culture and social change must incorporate the individual as an active agent, not a passive, reacting, culturally determined "factor" that can be eliminated from the equation. Material culture is made by someone, for the purpose of doing something, and is not a passive reflection of society (Hodder 1991b:6).

> The acts of individuals are not determined by a cultural code because the culture is itself constructed in those acts. Neither do the internal, intrinsic relationships of the code determine their meaning from the roles they play, their use, and in the daily patterns of existence. Each moment is created. Each act and each artifact exist only after their construction. They have to be produced, to be "brought off," and it could not have been otherwise.
> (Hodder 1985:4)

It is hard to disagree. The one who asks me to believe that my sense of willed and creative action is a delusion, demands a contradiction – willful acceptance of the proposition that I am incapable of willed behavior. Perhaps some who recognize their own creativity and volition think otherwise of the ancients and primitives under study, for it is common enough to forget that in archaeology, our subject has (at least from the later Pleistocene) much in common with ourselves. To avoid either incoherence (belief in a model of humanity that undercuts itself and so can never be both true and meaningful), or assuming that others are less human, we must accept Hodder's basic point. But once again, this does not mean accepting the picture of archaeology he draws from it. People do work largely from within their present social context, but this is not the same as being passively controlled by the rules of their social organization. The environment, too, may be less an overlord than we sometimes allow. Individuals, Hodder says, "find that they accomplish certain things by using and manipulating the cultural world in specific ways" (1985:4). This includes material culture, with significant consequences for the understanding of society that we derive from archaeological study.

> A direct implication of ascribing an active intelligence to past peoples, as opposed to a passive stimulus–response conception, is that the remains we recover are to be interpreted as creations by people in accordance with their representations of the natural and social world. This is not a determinant response but an active intervention; the social production of reality. This represents a radical shift in perspective in the direction of making the past *human*. It is a perspective that respects the agents that created what we find and grants them the same abilities and intentions that we would credit to each other as sentient social beings. It is also a recognition of the importance of taking into account the conceptions we hold of our own society which inevitably mediate our understanding of the past.
> (Miller and Tilley 1984a:2)

The patterns we see in material culture do not provide us with an image of a social system like the reflection of a mountain in a still lake, an image we can use to reconstruct the mountain "as it was" merely by knowing the correct methodological formula (turn right-side-up, reverse). Rather, material culture images society more like a photograph images a mountain. The photograph *is* a reflection of the mountain, but the mountain as the photographer wants it to be seen. Alternative emphases – on the cold, austere strength of rock and ice as the winter sun fades vs. the warmth of summer alpenglow above valleys already in shadow, say – can affect how we perceive mountains. For these authors, a configuration of material culture is a reflection of human *activity* which always includes purposeful manipulation for personal ends, ends which may one day require a person to stress the importance of traditional ways, and the next to strain against them. Such manipulation must be within a shared context, but working within the bounds of social rules and of culturally approved behavior (at least knowing how not to push too far too fast), is far different from the idea that our actions are constrained to passive determinism by fixed social rules. Hodder attributes the latter idea to processual archaeology.[6] He may be correct in some instances, but this view is not intrinsic to middle range theory. I agree that we cannot predict what a true human will do in any instance; not on the basis of the rules of social order, nor on any basis. But while this may be a fair portrayal of what some archaeologists attempt, most middle range theory is not prediction of what people will do, but inference of what they have done.

Consider what the loose connection among social features, behaviors, and material manifestations implies for the inference of rank. Ranking is a feature of social organization. While not material, it is real, at least if social theory makes sense, and our use of it is appropriate. It is real, also, in that it captures something important about how many people view their own world. But there are several reasons why its material expression will vary. First there are many ways of understanding social order that could all be called ranking. At one level there are as many conceptualizations of ranking, as many different rank systems, as there have been rank societies. At another level there are more, for ranking will be understood differently by those of different rank within one society, and how people *view* social relations influences both actions and the material consequences of those actions. Parker Pearson reminds us that "ideology is not the spiritual as opposed to material reality but is present in all material practice" (1984b:60), suggesting that what people mean by ranks, not just their existence, affects their material expression. "Material culture plays an active symbolic role in social relations. Interacting groups manipulate and negotiate, consciously and unconsciously, material symbols according to their strategies and intentions" (Shanks and Tilley 1987b:107).

We see this around us everyday – for example, people leasing automobiles they could not begin to afford, simply to appear wealthier. But if we know enough not to use the model of car that someone drives as a correlate of status, how do we approach the likely circumstance that people did much the same in the past? The first step is being aware of the possibility and recognizing that, especially in the arena of status and power, it is unlikely to be a trivial detail. But my second point is that it will not matter as much for the archaeological inference of social organization as this discussion might lead us to believe. Some families may use the symbolism of burial to make it seem as though they are of higher status than people would otherwise acknowledge, but these are still symbols of status, and we would still be correct to infer inequality. We would be misled only on the question of who held the highest statuses. This greater detail, if attainable at all, must come from an understanding of the context, but while contextual archaeology offers great promise, it does not negate the value of cross-culturally-based inferences. Indeed the inference of rank could provide a firm starting point, the outlines of the context, on which interpretations can be built.

In any case, it is clear that actions based on a principle of ranking will vary with social and historical context, as will material manifestations of this activity. To mention but one example from the many levels at which this works, Feinman notes that a leader might control access to exotic goods as a manifestation of a structural principle of inequality and leadership with behavioral and material implications. But these implications, exactly *how* it is expressed, can vary. If leaders redistributed the items "the deposition would not necessarily be limited to a single structure or household" (Feinman 1990:349). This point is of major import for developing specific methods for the archaeological inference of rank.

Material manifestations of socially significant actions

The archaeological record is a contemporary phenomenon consisting of the full pattern of presently extant material remains of past human activity. Archaeologists study contemporary data "generated by them in the act of observing the archaeological record" (Binford 1987:393). Our data, then, are neither past events nor artifacts and other phenomena presumed to relate to past events (the archaeological record) but contemporary observations on this record. This record is static but we use it to infer the living, "dynamic" past (Binford 1981:25). For Binford, "[t]he only meaningful statements we can make about the past are dynamic statements. The only statements we can make directly from the archaeological record are some form of descriptive statics. Getting to the past is then a process in which the archaeologist gives meaning to static phenomena in dynamic terms" (1983:23). Doing this, using observations on the archaeological record to draw conclusions about the functioning of a former society, depends on what Binford has termed middle range research or middle range theory. This label is the subject of some confusion; as Salmon (1982:170) notes, some have seen middle range theory as referring "to generalizations ... capable of fairly direct empirical testing," while others (Schiffer 1988:463) use it to denote an intermediate level of abstraction within a hierarchy of theory levels. These are understandable, but in Binford's (and my) use, middle range theory concerns the relation between actions and their material remains, and is the basis of archaeological inference. It is middle range theory, in contrast to general theory, which seeks the causes of human behavior without reference to this specifically archaeological problem.[7]

> What we are seeking through middle-range research are accurate means of identification, and good instruments for measuring specified properties of past cultural systems. We are seeking reliable cognitive devices; we are looking for "Rosetta stones" that permit the accurate conversion from observation on statics to statement about dynamics.
> (Binford 1981:25)

Isolating the agents that cause a certain pattern in the archaeological record requires a context in which both cause and effect can be observed, what Binford and

Sabloff call research in the dynamic mode, "actualistic or historical studies" (Binford 1983:408). Middle range theory overlaps with ethnoarchaeology, a primary means of obtaining this information (Watson, LeBlanc, and Redman 1984:264) and is a search for signature patterns, specific archaeological observations by which we may identify aspects of a former society. It is analogous to the identification of an animal from its tracks without seeing the animal itself. Whenever possible, a theory on what a track signifies is best tested by studies of living animals making tracks. Middle range theory is also tied up with notions of the archaeological record (considered in more detail below). Peter Kosso observes:

> Middle-range theories are used to make the information link between present and past, and to say of what the material remains are evidence. They do this by describing the formation of the archaeological record as it is today. This description will include general theories about how artifacts are used and subsequently deposited by burial, neglect, or intentional discard, and general theories about the alteration of deposited artifacts by both natural and cultural activities ... All of these claims are middle-range theories in that they contribute to the description of the causal lineage of the debris that is observed today.
> (Kosso 1991:622)

Historic and ethnographic studies help show if a connection is reliable, not just fortuitous correlation, but we must assume that this same relationship held in the past. This makes middle range theory more difficult than comparison with animal tracking suggests, but not impossible, as suggested by Hodder who believes that the "keys," the results of middle range theory, cannot be independent of cultural context.

> There can be no universal cultural relationship between statics and dynamics, because the historically contextual structuring principles intervene. Thus the notion that Middle Range Theory is distinctive because it involves independent theory which can be used to test other theories is false. The cultural processes which form the archaeological record are not independent of our general understanding of culture and society.
> (Hodder 1991b:116)

Hodder says that "contextual structuring principles intervene," but Kosso observes that "it is more accurate to regard the structural principles as part of the theories" (Kosso 1991:625). Recalling that the relevant "context" need not be a culture-historical moment, we can argue that middle range theory attempts to "[track] the flow of information from interesting past to observable present" (Kosso 1991:623) by clarifying the intervening structural principles. Some will be historically contextual principles unique for each case, and contextual archaeology brings into focus just how powerful these are in the lives of people and in material culture patterning. There is some potency, then, to another of Hodder's objections to "the cross-cultural, processual approach"; much detail is lost if this method alone is used (Hodder 1984:53). But none of this invalidates middle range theory. Since human behavior cannot be predicted just by knowing the rules of social organization, some kinds of general connections cannot be made.[8] Thus there is no inviolable connection between ranking and the practice of placing giant golden statues in some graves, but pots in others. But middle range theory can take other forms; on finding graves with divergent inclusions, we could instead ask, why? The most detailed answer would require knowledge of historical context but there can be no other basis for this pattern than individual status differentiation. This is a statement connecting social organization with the configuration of material culture, and one that *can* be made apart from a cultural context. Such arguments also have their limits, not least our need to make certain that there really are no other social bases for this material pattern. But this kind of argument is not subject to Hodder's objections, since it is an attempt, not to predict actions, but to infer social organization from actions known to have taken place. We are not saying there was something about the society that made people put gold statues in some graves when they might have used *Spondylus* shell arm bands, or nothing at all; we are simply observing that they did in fact do this. The inferential question is whether people would have done so had they lived under any other social organization than one of differential wealth or prestige status. It may not be possible to answer a question of this sort with complete certainty (and our confidence would decline drastically if we found tiny ceramic, rather than giant golden statues – admittedly a distinct possibility), but in principle arguments of this kind are, as Hodder (1985:7) notes, possible.

De Montmollin objects that "invariant" bridging arguments (1989a:5,13) are reductionistic, and so lead to oversimplification, triteness, and overemphasis on apparent similarities between cases.

> Opposed options for developing bridging arguments concerning ancient complex polities involve differing degrees of generalization. The more generalizing options seek to develop relatively invariant rules for relating political (or other) behavior to archaeological remains, either through cross-cultural analysis ... or through actualistic studies ... A more particularizing option, adopted here, is one which seeks to treat each case on its own merits, attempting to justify assumptions about the relation between political behavior and material culture by drawing on direct-historical materials to delimit the range of possibilities.
> (1989:5–6)

There is, first, nothing particularly "opposed" about these options. Who would spurn valid historical correlates just because they cannot be transferred to all other cases? And while we can conceive of bridging arguments that are reductionistic in this sense, it is not their natural trend. They must be *applied* in each real case, which, far from the mechanical process implied by the tag "invariant," requires judgment and imagination. Further, to say that two societies had ranking is not at all to claim they were identical, to reduce them to sameness. It *is* a claim that they have something important in common, something which also distinguishes them from societies without ranking. It is a recognition of real similarities, not an overemphasis on apparent similarities. Yes, it may sometimes be "trite" to use correlates of ranking; what would we learn by applying the mortuary correlates of chapters 4 and 5 to the Royal Cemetery of Ur that was not already clear? But the same cannot be said of Çatal Hüyük (chapter 8). Here a good but hardly overwhelming case for ranking has emerged by using these correlates.

For any bridging argument – whether generalizing, or uniquely relevant for one historical moment – to carry weight it must be invariant over its domain of applicability. De Montmollin uses historical materials to justify assumptions about the relationship between political behavior and material culture in the past. But even with a narrow domain of applicability, this still requires that we assume (or perhaps demonstrate) that the relationship between social feature and material expression is invariant over a certain portion of the Maya space–time occupation, a domain that includes at least the historically known time and place, and the archaeological sites investigated. With the possible exception of immoderate proposals concerning "universals of human behavior," generalizing correlates are no more reductionist than this. There is no need to argue that wherever there is inequality people will be the same as everywhere else where there is inequality and will always heap a few graves with mounds of gold. The invariance works the other way; if a few graves are stuffed with gold and the rest are not – a simple empirical observation – I want to say this means, invariably means – whether for the Maya, the Chaldeans, or anyone else – that there was inequality among those people.

Of course, most real examples will be more ambiguous. Rarely will the absence of a specific material configuration adequately demonstrate the absence of the activities associated with a social feature. And there may be more than one social basis for a material configuration. In the review of archaeological correlates, much attention will be given to isolating alternative social explanations for a material configuration and revising correlates, better to distinguish among them. We cannot be certain all options have been considered, since logic can supply no more than the negation of the original hypothesis (Salmon 1982:55). There is no getting around imaginative use of substantive archaeological knowledge, and it follows that assessment of correlates can never be final, since it depends on our having thought of all possible alternatives. If a loose connection is found, we may be able to tighten it by revising the correlate, perhaps with a more precise specification of the material configuration used as evidence of activities, or of the social organization behind them.

Ethnographically-based models and data in archaeology

Early one morning I was leafing through an issue of *Archaeology* magazine with my two-year-old daughter, and as we turned to a color photo of what I naively took to be an elaborate chariot she declared, with enthusiasm worthy of Leonard Wooley, "Look at that stroller!" Mute stones are in fact mute, and we need some way of relating them to living society. But our challenge is using the familiar to help us understand the unfamiliar, without so domesticating it as to miss the genuinely other.

Social archaeology takes advantage of both social models and ethnographic data, two uses of anthropological materials that have much in common, since models of society are, like ethnographic examples, used as analogies to help understand an archaeologically known society. Nevertheless, archaeology has been ambivalent to analogy. Indeed, from a study of what archaeologists have said on the subject, Alison Wylie detects "an increasingly acute concern that analogy seems to be both indispensable to interpretation and always potentially misleading" (1985:81). Murray and Walker suggest further that this problem of analogy "is likely to remain ... resistent to permanent or universal solution" (1988:248–249). It is important to review this ambivalence, even if we cannot resolve it, because it is hard to imagine attempting archaeological inference of social organization without significant, often sustained analogy both with the social life of living peoples and with models of society derived from the study of living society.

There can be no interpretation of archaeological materials apart from analogy with living society; as Albert Spaulding puts it, the past can only be understood through the present (1968:37). Early interpreters of archaeological remains often drew on their knowledge of peoples of the Bible, classical antiquity, and any number of legends, but it soon became clear that if an analogy must be made, some societies make better models than others. There are times and places for which descriptions found in the Bible and other early writings *are* appropriate models, but prehistorians generally "have viewed their subject matter through ethnographic spectacles: they have seen prehistoric man as primitive" (Orme 1981:2). Neither have Biblical and Classical archaeologists ignored ethnography (e.g. Finkelstein 1988). Yet present societies, however primitive, are not identical to those of the past. Their use as analogies can be defended not as infallible, but as better guides than either *a priori* speculation or modern industrial societies (Clark 1957:172, Orme 1981:14), something long recognized by scholars in varied fields (e.g. Wilson 1898:1). It is from here that more explicit uses of ethnography diverge.

Orme's (1981:21–25) five categories offer a good summary of the many ways of using ethnographic data in archaeological interpretation. In *Piecemeal Parallels* a one-to-one correlation is made between a feature of a living society and archaeological data. You choose a feature similar enough to feel confident about attributing its function to the archaeological feature (p. 21). Studies in *ethnohistory* "combine the information available in the earliest ethnographic reports from a region with the results of archaeological fieldwork in the same area" (p. 22). While dependent upon the availability of good records, this can be most productive since the link is often close. Sharer and Hearne note, for example, how closely the burials found in the Cocle area of Panama illustrate the Spanish historical accounts of ceremonies accorded the *quevi* or high chiefs (1988:56–57), this despite the accounts being from about 700 years later. *Ethnoarchaeology* is the study of a living society from an archaeologist's point of view, "an attempt ... to establish the link between behaviour and its material results" by studying a living community (Orme 1981:22–23). This often involves actual fieldwork (Kramer 1979a:4). The *ethnographic background and models* category includes a range of approaches, among them ethnographic studies designed to develop predictive models on how societies differ under varied conditions; and studies of a practice in a number of societies as background for those interested in this practice. *Comparative studies and syntheses* also vary, but start with anthropology rather than an archaeological problem, and emphasize use of theory developed in social anthropology, not just ethnographic data (Orme 1981:24). We are concerned most often with how archaeologists can use ethnography better to understand the past, but collaboration for mutual benefit is also possible. "Ethnology is valuable to archaeology chiefly because the ethnographer can observe and record phenomena that are lost in the archaeological record. Archaeology is valuable to ethnology largely because of the temporal depth of archaeological data" (Maclachlan and Keegan 1990:1012). In their study of Taino kinship (1989), Keegan and Maclachlan found this integrated "archaeo-ethnography" productive of insight for both fields, providing archaeological answers to ethnological questions and ethnological answers to archaeological questions (Maclachlan and Keegan 1990:1012).

Use of analogy has had to endure extensive criticism, much of which is justified. But not all discussions recognize this great range of methods. Piecemeal parallels, choosing an example from here or there which looks good, is subject to the most criticism, and may be the reason some have rejected analogy altogether (Orme 1981:ix). But structured comparative studies (using more than one example and exercising care in their choice) make a good alternative, since most potential problems with analogy concern one or the other of these issues. It is sometimes held that the only effective counter to a random choice of examples is to draw analogies with cultures historically related to the archaeological culture. It may indeed be most rewarding to search for suitable analogies in settings as similar as possible (Kramer 1979b, Watson 1979b:277), but these are rare and in any case the possibility of culture change means that "the degree to which modern people are analogous must be as much an object of our inquiry as the behavior we wish to observe" (Hole 1979:197). This also counters the stipulation that comparisons be drawn with societies as similar to the archaeological data as possible (Harris 1968:156). Only sometimes is this either possible or necessary; "comparative studies are unlikely to be bound by any such restrictions, and indeed may progress as much via contrasts as resemblances" (Orme 1981:25). Societies similar in some ways are not necessarily similar in all, and there may in the past have been social features not known from any living society (Kramer 1979a:3, Gould 1978:249, Binford 1968:268, Orme 1981:18, Freeman 1968:262), or vice versa (Hole and Heizer 1973:312). Since it cannot be known beforehand how much alike they are, Gould advocates a contrastive method. Ethnography is used as a baseline model of social order from which predictions are made about material culture patterns that should occur in prehistoric sites.

> If as will probably happen in most cases, the actual patterns of occurrence found by the archaeologist do not conform to the predictions, then it should be possible to specify in a controlled manner just what the points of difference are from the "base-line" model. These differences ... then must be explained by positing alterations in the model to account for them. (Gould 1978b:252)

These cautions concern matters of relevance, "underlying 'principles of connection' that structure source and subject and that assure ... the existence of specific further similarities between them" (Wylie 1985:94–95). Analogies incorporating considerations of relevance are usually relational analogies in which analogs are compared not just for the presence or absence of each individual property they may hold in common, but for the relations that hold among the properties they share. Arguments used in social inference are usually of this kind and can readily incorporate considerations of relevance, making unnecessary a general assessment of the similarity between the source of the analogy and the archaeological society. In particular, we are seeking connections between social organization and material culture. For example if we find variation in size and elaboration among domestic structures at a site, we may infer ranking. Ethnographic analogy can strengthen this assessment and refine the domain of its validity through a study of the connection between status systems and domestic architecture. Finding among the Shilluk differences in both status and domestic architecture is support for the inference regardless of whether the Shilluk are similar overall to the archaeological people. That question is irrelevant because the analogy concerns the relationship between ranking and housing, not that between the Shilluk and prehistory.

Relational comparisons are strongest when we can demonstrate that the same *causal* connections relating features in the source society were also in operation in the past society (Wylie 1985:95). Since it will be difficult to demonstrate causal connections within an archaeological data set on its own, what we could really use are connections among features that can be shown to be universal. If we could demonstrate that major differences among dwellings are *always* connected with ranking – that is, they never occur apart from ranking – then finding similar residential variation in our archaeological data demonstrates ranking as well. Ethnographic analogies are used precisely to strengthen such conclusions (as well as to help us discover more examples of this kind of relationship). Of course considerations of relevance are unlikely to be this strong; it is difficult to demonstrate causal connections even in ethnography. Mostly what we find are reasonably consistent correlations which we are more justified in attributing to our archaeological example if found predictably over a wide range of ethnographic examples. But this is not proof that a configuration of social order and a pattern of material culture *must* go together. An analogy can be strengthened – rendered more useful in supporting a proposed archaeological inference – in several ways.

> The standard criteria for evaluating what I have described as formal analogies are ... number and extent of similarities between source and subject, number and diversity of sources cited in the premises in which known and inferred similarities co-occur as postulated for the subject, and, finally expansiveness of the conclusions relative to the premises.
> (Wylie 1985:98).

This last point concerns whether the conclusion is true for more, or more diverse cases than it needs to be to cover the archaeological example. Nevertheless, something can be used for analogy if it has only one thing in common with the archaeological example, as long as the consequences of that trait are clear and known. In this way an analogy can be made without assuming the archaeological society was like some known society.

It is difficult to design an ethnographic "test" of an archaeological correlate; even a well-designed test will not be a true experiment and will not eliminate every alternative. Ethnographic analogy can suggest alternatives we may not have considered, can show whether a postulated correlation occurs in real societies, and with what regularity. But we cannot be sure that a correlation is truly universal until we search all relevant examples and find no contradictions, and even then we cannot be certain none existed which could contradict it. Because of the inevitable theoretical limits, and equally onerous practical concerns, it is important not to put too much trust in an ethnographic test. Any number of correlations may be found in a few real examples which are not so much reliably connected traits as things that happen to co-occur in that sample. Yet even just a few examples can help corroborate a theoretically reasonable correlation. And, if examples are chosen to allow for likely alternatives to come up, yet they do not, the use of ethnography goes beyond mere illumination of a theoretical point, and approaches the level of a test. Further, attention to the nature of a connection between social organization and pattern of material culture may provide clues to the field of applicability of a correlate. For example, I will argue that there is a relationship between energy expenditure (on domestic architecture, or mortuary practices, say) and status. A study of living peoples can help our use of this correlation by illustrating the typical magnitude of energy differences that we can consider to be evidence of status distinctions.

Activities and the archaeological record

The next gap to be bridged in the inferential process is that between material manifestations of activities and the archaeological record of them. Our vision of what archaeology can accomplish (its goals) and of how to go about it (methods and theory), depends, of course, on how we conceive our subject matter and the character of its data. On this question, roughly that of the archaeological record, there is currently a profound divergence of opinion. Probably the most fundamental question concerns how the dynamics of a living society are recorded in the present configuration of static remains.

> Is it more like a fossil record or an historical record? ... it is like fossils,
> because it comprises the enduring physical effects of past physical objects,
> events, and residues; it is also similar in some of its formation processes. But
> [it] ... is also like historical evidence because it has been produced by
> human activity, and much of it has been distributed spatially through
> behavior that was regulated by convention.
> (Patrik 1985:34)

Which model we emphasize will affect our attitude toward social archaeology, particularly the problem of confirmation. Processual or New Archaeologists tend to see the archaeological record as a kind of fossil record, what Patrik calls the Physical Model. It is formed by processes that are law-determined, and past activities are recorded as living organisms are recorded in a fossil record (Patrik 1985:3–39). It is not that these are simple or straightforward processes – the work of Michael Schiffer (1976) has surely put that idea to rest – but that they are regular and (in theory) predictable; they are law-like. The main alternative is the Textual Model. While not necessarily excluding causal laws in accounting for the present configuration of material remains, the textual model assumes the influence of three additional factors.

(1) It attributes a special sign or symbol function to archaeological evidence, over and above any causal connection between this evidence and what it is evidence of. (2) It postulates culturally specific sets of behavioral rules as well as the more flexible behavioral strategies of individuals, by which these signs were created, ordered, used, and deposited; these rules are not, strictly speaking, causal laws, primarily because they are not invariable in time and space. (3) It attributes a "non-passive" power to material signs: it emphasizes the creativity of (some of) the individuals who produced or used these material signs within social action, and the active transformation of social structures through human use of such signs.
(Patrik 1985:37)

The Physical Model offers greater optimism about inferring the past by postulating a physical recording connection, not just a causal connection between the archaeological record and past dynamics. This tighter fit between cause and effect is, Patrik believes (1985:45), what Binford is seeking through theory that isolates properties of the archaeological record with unambiguous and uniformly relevant referents in past dynamics. If such a connection can be found we have a means of deducing a cause from an effect. However, recognition of creative, willed, and symbolic activity suggests at the least that there are limits to this kind of recording connection. The textual model appears to account for real and important aspects of the archaeological recording process ignored by the fossil model. Hodder's approach (1985; 1991b) is more like Patrick's Textual Model, and in his rejection of the Physical Model, he also rejects middle range theory which he assumes depends on it. But while it is unwise to *assume* a recording connection, and while some (perhaps many) recording connections in use are not in fact universally valid, we are still able to develop correlates which, within a specific domain, can approximate the same result.

The structure of such an argument, one that acknowledges human volition and cultural unpredictability, but which does not forsake the possibility of reliable recording connections, will be similar in outline to arguments based on the physical model, except in how the proposed recording connection is justified. If there is a universally valid objection to the physical model, it is that many proposed recording connections between social features and archaeological patterns are either not valid, or can only be trusted within more carefully specified domains. Consider the following simplified example:

> If monumental construction is found in the archaeological record, the
> society was hierarchical.
>
> Monumental construction has been found, therefore the society was
> hierarchical.

Although this argument is logically valid, it is obvious that it will only yield correct
inferences if the conditional statement is true. The conditional statement serves the
same purpose as a recording connection, but is in a form which does not assume the
predictability of human behavior. As an archaeological correlate of inequality, this
argument does not assume that the social condition "hierarchy" will always lead to a
specifiable configuration of archaeological data, "monumental construction," but
instead proposes that monumental construction, when it exists, is always evidence of
hierarchy.

Of course, we cannot simply "assume" such things, we must demonstrate them,
and this is the reason we must give careful attention to developing and evaluating
archaeological correlates of social organization. I do think this recording connection,
this conditional statement, is true, but among other concerns, we must understand
what is meant by "monumental," a concept not easily operationalized to provide
unambiguous conclusions about any particular structure (see chapter 7). It is, I
believe, possible to describe universally reliable recording connections, cross-
culturally valid middle range theory, without assuming the Physical Model of the
archaeological record, but this requires careful attention to human agency when
specifying the domain within which the connection is universally reliable. Because of
the unpredictability of human action, conditional statements in an argument of this
form will often be much narrower in scope than those we would like, because
demonstration of the conditional statement means showing:

(A) that the archaeological configuration (presence of monumental construction) is a
    possible result of the social condition (social hierarchy)
    AND (not or),

(B) that no other social condition could have been the cause of the archaeological
    configuration.

Part A can be demonstrated with just one ethnographic example, and failing that,
with a reasoned case for how it could be possible. Part B is clearly the sticking point.
It means showing that no other condition we can think of could cause the
consequence, no other condition known to ethnography has caused it, and finally,
that we have thought of all possibilities. We can never do this last part, and inevitably
our arguments will fall short of proof. This is important, and I suppose that,
technically speaking, it amounts to an admission that the physical model of the
archaeological record is not true, and that perfect physical recording connections are
not ultimately possible. But the problem is not unique to the approach I have
outlined. It is not possible to structure our arguments so as to escape the burden of
eliminating all other possibilities. We must always avoid assuming an invariant
recording connection, yet come as close as possible to demonstrating one by careful
specification of both cause and effect, and by eliminating alternate possibilities. It is

not possible to use the logical structure of our argument to get around what is essentially a matter of empirical fact.

But that is not all. While not part of the inferential process itself, we must also keep in mind that the configuration of materials used by a people can be rendered yet more confusing through both the depositional process and the distorting influence of post-depositional transformation processes. One of the unique strengths of mortuary data comes from the fact that it involves purposeful deposition. Statements about spatial relationships and associations of features are much easier to develop when we can depend on the structures, artifacts, and human remains having been placed that way on purpose. Probably the most obvious, but also most far ranging, depositional and post-depositional problem (for any archaeological material, burials included) is loss of information. Consider gift exchange at mortuary ceremonies. Most material gifts passed around will eventually enter a deposit, but not in a context having much to do with the exchange ceremony (except quite indirectly). And even when an activity results in a material deposit, there is nearly always substantial loss through incomplete preservation. This basic fact of life has several consequences for social inference. First, the more a correlate depends on a complete sample the less often we can use it at all, and the greater the chance of results being unreliable. This is obvious enough, and I know of no correlate which intentionally depends on a complete sample. But any need for a representative sample faces similar problems since deposition and preservation do not always work "randomly" (or even predictably). Another consequence is that material evidence for a feature may be absent from an archaeological deposit, even if it was both a feature of the former society and one with material correlates. Yet if evidence *is* found, we can infer that feature even though: (a) there may be no particular reason known as to why the people should have expressed their social rule in that way, and (b) there was a chance of the evidence not being preserved. Often this may be all we need to know, but for some problems data loss is of more direct concern. In particular, to compare one society to another as to presence (or degree) of a feature, we must know whether the differences found archaeologically were due to a distorting factor or to real differences between the societies.

Implications for the design of archaeological correlates of social hierarchy

Each step in the inference of social organization outlined above represents a gap between a functioning social order and our knowledge of it from the few remaining material traces. When evaluating correlates my approach will be to isolate problems in making the connections, and suggest means of avoiding them. It is not always possible to construct a correlate carefully enough (e.g. stipulating the exact nature of the evidence required) to eliminate alternate social conditions as plausible causes. But the weakness of individual bridging arguments can be countered through overall method; specifically, taking advantage of the significance of patterns, and combining and cross-checking lines of inference.

Human activity may not be fully predictable, but neither is it always or even commonly capricious. Furthermore, archaeological data used to infer social features do not generally consist of the residue of one isolated event. Looking at *patterns* of events can aid the inferential process by suggesting that there is some reason for our finds other than independent, potentially whimful actions. The range of possible eccentricity behind any isolated event is (somewhat) masked by socially acceptable behavior when a pattern is found. The repetitiveness suggests also a consistency in the cause of events. The range of potential causes is thus reduced.

Much can also be gained by combining and cross-checking lines of inference rather than viewing each as an independent argument that must stand on its own. A conclusion using several lines of analysis can often profit from somewhat tenuous individual correlations. Alternative social explanations will often be possible for each configuration of material culture, but any overall conclusion must be drawn from the more limited set of explanations compatible with all the evidence. In this way, each line of inference is used to set limits on, or choose among the possible conclusions from each other line. Referring to work by Tschopik (and quoting his 1950 article) on an Andean ceramic tradition, Hodder offers this interesting example.

> Tschopik has been able to trace continuity in Andean Aymara ceramics of the Puno region over at least five centuries up to the present day. Methods of manufacture have not changed and many vessel shapes and some design motifs have remained the same ... 'If the data furnished by the Aymara ceramic tradition *taken alone and by itself* were our only evidence of change (which of course is not the case), the Inca era in the Puno region would have passed virtually unrecorded, and Spanish contact would have appeared to have been slight and fleeting. By and large, Aymara ceramics have been modified to a far less extent than other, and more basic aspects of Aymara culture.
> (Hodder 1978a:4–5)

The value of comparing independent inferences to narrow the range of possible conclusions is nicely illustrated in Renfrew's work on the Neolithic tombs in Europe. When thinking of monuments like tombs located in mounds, we tend to picture complex societies. Renfrew describes two islands of Scotland, on each of which are found a number of mounds. He also found, however, that the population was rather low. On the basis of the tombs themselves a wide range of suggestions about the society may be possible, but not all of them can be reconciled with the population figures.

> These estimates of population are useful in setting some limits on the kind of social organization involved. If the population of individual territories was as low as 25 or 50 persons, we cannot possibly think in terms of groups with a very large number of ranks or statuses or of territorial chiefs.
> (1973a:137)

Any valid description of the society must be drawn from the overlap between these two ranges, and additional lines of evidence could well add further insight into the society responsible for these mounds. Binford thinks of this ambiguity that arises when different lines of reasoning could lead to incompatible conclusions as an opportunity for the past to object. If intellectual systems, like social systems, are to be open, this openness "must be provided by our methods and procedures. We must ensure that the past 'gets a say,' that it can object and guide our growth toward understanding" (Binford 1986:472). Use of multiple lines of evidence (especially those that at first seem incompatible) may be the best way of choosing among alternatives, but it also has a purely practical value. If we have just one test for a social feature and the data are unavailable, we are held captive to ignorance.

3

Inequality and social life: a working model

"To an anthropologist," said Andre Beteille, "... the idea of natural inequality is inherently ambiguous, if not a contradiction in terms" (1981:59–60). Certainly there are great differences among people, many of which have both "natural" and "socially constructed" dimensions, but these are not elements of inequality "unless they are selected, marked out, and evaluated by processes that are cultural and not natural" (Beteille 1981:60). "Equality" and "inequality" are ideas, and as fundamental notions of how the world is ordered, have important implications for how we relate to each other. Ideas about who is "better" than whom and in what ways, deeply influence practice.

Inequality as an instituted process

There are many ways in which people have defined themselves as unequal, and out of the major dimensions of inequality, Gerald Berreman has developed a "typology for a comparative study of social inequality" (1981:4; Table 1.4). This is an excellent starting point for considering what it is we intend to look for in the archaeological study of rank.[1] The human condition is characterized by differentiation. *Inequality* "refers to the social evaluation of whatever differences are regarded as relevant in a given society or situation" (Berreman 1981:8), while *social inequality* is generally a combination of inequality with dominance, "the behavioral expression of those differences" (p8). Social inequality has been recognized as a moral phenomenon in that people evaluate each other, and a structural phenomenon in that social differentiation exists in society. Social inequality is also

> 1. a behavioral phenomenon, in the sense that people *act* on their evaluations; 2. an interactional phenomenon in that these actions occur largely in the context of interpersonal relations; 3. a material phenomenon in that their actions entail differential access to goods, services, and opportunities; and 4. an existential phenomenon in that people experience their statuses and respond to them cognitively and affectively. In short, inequality is a major part of people's lives.
> (Berreman 1981:4)

The most basic division is between unranked and ranked organizations. Unranked organization is roughly what Fried calls egalitarian, and while there will always be systematic, unequal distribution of status, in unranked organizations these differences are largely within families, and based on familial roles which in turn are based almost exclusively on age, gender, and personal characteristics (Berreman 1981:8). The fact of systematic status differences in unranked societies makes the term "egalitarian" distinctly misleading. It also adds ambiguity to the concept of ranking. In ranked organizations "inequality is institutionalized into a hierarchy of statuses – superior and inferior positions of prestige and dominance – that extend beyond age, sex, personal characteristics, and intrafamilial roles" (Berreman 1981:9). If status is based on age, everyone who lives long enough will get a turn. It is also easy to see how individual personal distinctions differ from a structure of achieved ranking. But it is not clear how gender-based status differences relate to this definition. Although specifically excluded from the definition of ranking, gender-based status differences bear much of the character of different ranks (unlike age and personal distinctions). That is, they are superior and inferior positions of prestige and dominance that extend beyond age, personal characteristics, and intrafamilial roles. Certainly this is a complicated question (how, for example, do we decide what differences, if any, are essentially intrafamilial roles with limited prestige implications, and what are hierarchical status distinctions), but if there is or ever was a social situation in which there were major gender-based status differences but no other system of hierarchy, this would still constitute, in an important sense, a ranked social order. In suggesting this, I am not saying that all status differences are really ranking, for situations in which the elderly accrued higher prestige and authority, and individual personal differences in respect, would not themselves constitute ranking in the same way. I believe that most of the methods I review (see Chapters 4 through 7) for the archaeological inference of ranking would recognize any substantial gender-based distinctions of prestige and authority as easily as the distinctions which more directly fit Berreman's definition of ranking (as long as we are careful not to eliminate them by definition). This I take as evidence for their similarity. Nevertheless, whether or not we should consider these distinctions more like ranking in kind than, say, simpler kinds of gender-based role differentiation, age-based prestige, or esteem based on personal characteristics, is in part a definitional and in part an empirical question, and remains a matter of debate.

All further distinctions in Berreman's typology of social inequality are within ranked organization, the most important being "kin/role" ranking versus stratification – what Service calls a "watershed" (1975:3), what Fried singles out as the core of a new social type (1967), and what Berreman views as "the greatest distinctiveness to be found . . . in types of social organization" (1981:10). In a kin/role ranked system, a person's rank depends on position in the kinship system or on particular roles. The roles may themselves be kin-based, or they may be activity-based – perhaps religious or military. But under stratification (the mode of ranking experienced by most people in the world today)

> *all* members of society are ranked relative to one another according to
> certain shared, non-kin characteristics defined by the society as important
> and used to allocate access to the basic resources that sustain life in the
> society . . . In such systems, people are differentiated by class, status, and

> power, and the three tend to be highly intercorrelated ... Categories of
> people form layers; hence the term *strata*. From stratum to stratum, there is
> differential ... access to the means of subsistence.
> (Berreman 1981:10)

Compared to kin/role ranking (what might also be called non-stratified ranking or
simply ranking), stratification has profound implications for other aspects of social
life.

> *authority* is exercised on the basis of the territorial unit ... rather than over
> the kin group; *prestige* results primarily from accumulation rather than
> generosity or redistribution; *power* results from control over productive
> resources and consequently control over persons. As a result, there is
> exploitation of categories of people – systematic exploitation of one category
> by and for the benefit of another through application of economic sanctions,
> threats, and physical force.
> (Berreman 1981:10–12)

Berreman then develops an insightful typology of stratified systems, and although
my goal is simply to distinguish ranking from non-ranking, and stratification from
non-stratified (kin/role) ranking, these variations do offer further understanding of
what stratification implies. The primary types of stratification are those with *status
strata*, "based on culturally specific criteria of differential honor, prestige, and
privilege," and those with *class strata* which have their basis in economic
relationships (p. 13). Membership is determined quite differently; for status strata it
is essentially race, caste, or ethnic group, while economic criteria differentiate class
strata. Of course, the specific criteria and rationalizations people use will vary
considerably, and this is in large measure the basis for Berreman's finer distinctions
among stratified systems. Interestingly, these otherwise very different systems
converge in terms of the effect on people's lives (which would make them difficult to
distinguish archaeologically):

> the consequences (or implications) of ranking in status strata according to
> criteria of honor and privilege include prominently and importantly
> economic differentials; the consequences ... of ranking in class strata
> include prominently and importantly honor and privilege differentials.
> (Berreman 1981:13)

Within each of these ranking structures are other mechanisms of distinction which
affect the character of life, among them ascribed and achieved criteria, and
differentiation based on age and sex. Ascribed rank is that based on birth, and in kin/
role ranking this is simply one's place in the kinship system versus one's role (e.g.
priest) or a status based on industry, ability or circumstance. In stratified systems,
one's position may also depend on birth, but not necessarily as a position within a
kinship system. Berreman observes that all birth-ascribed stratification systems
"seem to include a claim that the social distinctions are reflected in biological (i.e.,

'racial') differences revealed in physical make-up or appearance" (1981:14). Because these criteria may be unreliable (often enough they are not even real) cultural features (dress, language, occupation) are used as markers of differentiation. In the social-class form of stratification, class membership may be based on "achieved characteristics," including source and amount of income, education, and cultural features comprising lifestyle. Berreman prefers, though, to distinguish between *intrinsic* and *extrinsic* criteria because it may not be accurate to say non-ascriptive characteristics are really achieved.

Age, sex, and stigmatization are common bases for role differentiation, and (often in combination) for various socially defined categories, so they are also "potential bases for inequality" (Berreman 1981:19). Debate continues concerning whether females universally suffer exploitation and oppression. Berreman cites studies which indicate that role complementarity between the sexes (which *is* universal, however variable in detail) rarely if ever includes exploitation in unranked or kin- and role-ranked societies. This no doubt depends on how we conceive exploitation, but gender- and age-based social categories (e.g. unmarried women; grandfathers) are characteristically the basis for institutionalized inequality among stratified societies, societies in which inequality and exploitation are central to many social relations quite apart from age and gender. Further, age and sex are actual rather than putative physical differences, and while as categories they differ from social strata (and, as suggested earlier, from each other) in important respects, "the experiential consequences of sex and age identities seem to be closely allied to those of the most rigid forms of stratification ... race and caste" (p. 21), which also use intrinsic criteria.

Distinctions based on gender tend to be of a degree that parallels the level of ranking or stratification in *magnitude*, while often cross-cutting this structure in how a person's position and role is defined; situations where status differences between genders and among age groups are great without ranking and (particularly) stratification are unlikely. And while men and women will be ranked or classed, they will *also* be differentiated by criteria applied only to gender, such that, for example, women of the higher strata will not necessarily or even likely partake in the channels of power and prestige open to men of the same strata. It may not be easy to sort out what kind of differentiation is represented by archaeological indicators – rank, class, gender, or age hierarchies – which seriously limits our understanding of what it would be like to be an actual person in those circumstances.

Certainly there is much room for the maturation of middle range theory, but my emphasis will be on the simpler and more basic question of recognizing whether or not there was institutionalized hierarchy. I do not propose to cover all forms of structural inequality, or all aspects of *any* one form. Features of a status system that give "local flavor," that contribute to what it would mean to be Tikopian rather than Tahitian, are (in detail, and almost by definition) unique to a society, and it is possible, as contextual and interpretive archaeologists suggest, that much of this can never be uncovered through cross-culturally applicable methodology. Certainly there are important characteristics that now escape our attention. But whatever the ultimate limits of archaeological inference, reliable means of distinguishing ranked from unranked organization, stratified from ranked, and achieved from ascribed, will certainly improve our understanding of the past.

Models and the significance of inequality for real life

The social models of Service, Fried, and Johnson and Earle draw attention to real and significant variation in ranking. I will make use of these models by asking how the defining principles of inequality for each of the type models affect everyday life, and will then use these to argue that differing structural principles of rank (particularly achieved versus ascribed, and basic ranking versus stratification) have important implications for actual living. Determining how principles of inequality affect lifestyle also helps us decide what to look for archaeologically, and is important both for constructing and for evaluating archaeological correlates of hierarchy.

Theoretical perspectives: the types in context

Typological models are grand theories of sociocultural evolution and at the same time models of variability in social organization, and each is organized around a general theme, with groupings based on aspects of society thought to make a difference. Service (1971:173) distinguishes types based on fundamental mechanisms of sociocultural integration: familistic bonds of kinship (bands); pan-tribal sodalities (tribes); specialization, redistribution and centralization of authority (chiefdoms); and bureaucracy using legal force (the state). Fried's main concern is with developing inequality (from none to ranking to stratification) and mechanisms for maintaining these distinctions, while Johnson and Earle (1987) stress the growing influence of a political economy at the expense of an autonomous subsistence economy, and the mechanisms to maintain and run it.

The typologies also differ in their basic structure as models. While Fried's model is dominated by logical coherence, Service's seems more like a few concrete ethnographic examples generalized into types. Although organized by clear defining features, his types are described almost as real functioning societies. Many criticisms of typological models have been voiced in recent years (see Wason, n.d. for a review), but most concern their plausibility as overall characterizations of known social variation or as models of social evolution. But one concern that is important even for our purposes is that not all major variables that make up a "type" always co-occur. Archaeologists have responded in two somewhat different ways: by rejecting the idea of types altogether, or by modifying the types. The chiefdom concept in particular has had more staying power than critics would lead us to expect, but current definitions have grown distinctly less specific. In their recent typology Johnson and Earle (1987) offer broader descriptions of social forms than in the older models of Service and Fried, and also move toward what we might call a nested hierarchy of classification. That is, they identify three major levels of integration, and within each distinguish a range of variants. They distinguish their most encompassing set of forms primarily by the number of people integrated into one society, hence the family-level group, local group, and regional polity. These they call "levels of socioeconomic integration" (Johnson and Earle 1987:19) for in this model, the economy is considered central to the social structures and cultural rules that allow stable relations among larger numbers of people (p. 11). A more centralized economy means central control of a greater part of the economy, further intrusions into what, in a less hierarchical society, is a more self-sufficient household-level subsistence economy. With more of the economy centralized, more of it a "political economy," will come a tendency toward economic expansion.

Models of unranked society

In the previous chapter I noted that scholarly opinion remains at least as divided as ever on the question of whether human society has always been hierarchical or whether institutionalized hierarchy arose at some time in prehistory out of a more egalitarian primal condition. Indeed, even the question of modern social variation, particularly the social organization of modern foraging peoples, is more open to discussion than in the recent past. And while the two basic positions concerning the early history of human society still follow roughly the divisions established in the eighteenth century (and earlier), this debate is far from just a tired rehashing of the same material. With the serious use of new analytical perspectives (particularly gender, race, and post-Kuhnian epistemologies) and efforts to take advantage of primatology, sociobiology, and other fields, discussions have become more exciting and, in a limited way, quite productive.

But the question remains far from being resolved. Thus, to take just one example, while on the one hand dominance and leadership among non-human primates is given as evidence that we were hierarchical before we were even human, others respond that not all primates are as hierarchical as the savanna baboon, and in any case moving from these observations to human social order is unjustified biological reductionism (Coontz and Henderson 1986). I do not propose to enter into this debate here (much less try to resolve it), but I would offer two observations. The first is that there is room in these discussions for a stronger voice from archaeology, and it is my hope that the methodological program proposed in this book will help us to make a more decisive contribution. But secondly, the fact that it is *not* clear whether or to what extent early human societies were egalitarian has important implications for this methodology itself. Specifically, we must take either possibility seriously, and so consider not just models of hierarchy, but models proposed as descriptions of un- or minimally-ranked societies. And so, while the main point of this chapter is to review some ways of modelling inegalitarian societies, I begin by setting these in context with brief summaries of several models of unranked society.

Morton Fried groups non-hierarchical societies together under the type "egalitarian society." This label is more striking and elegant than "non-ranking societies" and avoids suggesting they lack something they should have. But it would rarely, if ever, be an accurate description if taken too strictly. For Fried it is a political statement, not a broad and literal summary of status relations. For Fried, then, an egalitarian society is one "in which there are as many positions of prestige in any given age–sex grade as there are persons capable of filling them" (1967:33). No one experiences restricted access to needed raw materials (p. 58). This relates to lax territorial boundaries and is consistent also with having limited private or group property. Reciprocity is the main form of exchange, and apart from sexual division of labor, all adults are expected to fulfill nearly all roles. Status based on sex and age will differ in light of this division of labor, but is unlikely to be hierarchical among people whose society is without other kinds of social hierarchy (Berreman 1981:19). Defining leadership as the setting of a course of action followed by others, Fried says no known society has completely lacked leadership (p. 82). But in egalitarian society it is transient, moving from person to person with context. Authority is "the ability to channel the behavior of others in the absence of threat or use of sanctions" while power "is the ability to channel the behavior of others by threat or use of sanction" (p. 13). Given this view, leadership in egalitarian society rests heavily on authority. Lee observes that patterns of leadership can be found among the !Kung San, people unencumbered by formal institutions for the purpose, and who are egalitarian in Fried's sense (Lee 1981:89). A leader has no formal authority but can be discerned from the use of his (or less often, her) personal name to identify a group (e.g. "Bon!a's camp at !Kangwa"), and from behavior at group discussions, during which they "may speak out more than others, may be deferred to by others, and one gets the feeling that their opinions hold a bit more weight" (Lee 1981:90).

Fried's egalitarian society covers a lot of territory, and his point is to emphasize that what these societies all have in common – a lack of ranking or stratification – is central to their character. But it is not surprising that other classifications subdivide this group, particularly since, as observed earlier, significant status distinctions are possible. In Service's typology the "band" and "tribe" cover the unranked forms of social organization and thus together correlate roughly with Fried's egalitarian society. Service's main concern is the patrilocal band, a society comprised of several related nuclear families with from thirty to over one hundred persons, characterized by reciprocal group exogamy and virilocal residence (1971:54). The exogamous, named, semi-local group (the band) is not the entire society. This consists of at least two bands, while all cultural functions are organized by and take place within no more than a few associated bands (1971:98). There is no specialization or division of labor other than by sex or beyond the nuclear family (p. 57). Bands lack separate government, political, and legal systems above the authority of family heads or ephemeral leaders. Statuses, too are primarily kin-based, a fact greatly influencing the character of the band (Service 1971:98).

A tribe, as Service describes it, is something of a large collection of bands, the new mechanism of social integration being the ties holding the band-like parts together (1971:100). As self-sufficient residential units (usually lineages) these parts are near duplicates of one another and for the most part not interdependent. They would tend toward disunity if it were not for additional means of integration (1971:131–132) and even so, tribes are rather fragile compared to bands or chiefdoms (p. 103). The new mechanism of integration is the pan-tribal sodality which for Service is simply a non-residential group. Clans may be most common but others include secret societies, age grades, and special-purpose groups like curing or warfare societies (p. 102). Tribes are egalitarian and lack institutionalized leadership. Residence groups are largely self-sufficient economically and in terms of defense. Wrongs to individuals tend to be punished by the group, and external polity is largely military (1971:104). Determination of common descent may be important, but people are not concerned with genealogical descent, and no one line predominates (1971:112).

In Johnson and Earle's model the distinction between un-ranked and ranked organization is not as clear. They make a point of using examples to illustrate the complexity of interrelations among social features and their model makes fuller use of variation among non- or minimally hierarchical societies. The "family group," one of their three major socioeconomic levels, is characterized by the ability of individual families to retain access to land, labor, and capital technology, the primary factors of production (1987:92). Those without and with domestication differ, but in each case, while there may be leadership of a sort (e.g. Shoshone rabbit bosses), "the authority of skill or experience does not confer superior status in any formal or permanent way" (1987:93). In their model it is the "erosion" of a family's "unrestrained access" to the factors needed for subsistence production which "underlies the formation of more complex social institutions" (Johnson and Earle 1987:92). The next level is "the local group," several families joined together around a "common interest" like food storage or defense (1987:20), and forming a ritually integrated political group. A village of some 100–200 people, subdivided into hamlet-size clans or lineages is a common settlement pattern. There are important intercommunity relationships, but "[r]esources are held exclusively by kin groups, and territorial defense is common" (1987:20). Within this "level" they distinguish the "acephalous local group" from the "big-man collectivity." The latter is characterized by larger communities (300–500 people) with multiple clan or lineage segments, local groups represented by a strong, charismatic leader. Important for maintaining within-group cohesion, external alliances, trade, and other relations, the big man "represents his group in the major ceremonies that coordinate and formalize intergroup relationships" (p. 20). But the big man's influence over his following is based on "personal initiative" and "if his support group deserts him for a competitor, little may be left of the reputation he has tried to build for himself, and his local group, or of the alliances he has contracted" (pp. 20–21).

The local group level encompasses both non-ranking and ranking societies. Northwest Coast Indians are included in the big man collectivity and the next level, the regional polity, begins with the chiefdom. Johnson and Earle largely succeed in avoiding the assumption that a clear line exists. They observe that among the Tareumiut (coastal North Slope Eskimo), an example of their acephalous local group, there is a kind of leader (the *umealiq* or "boat owner") whose role strikes me as distinctly more regular and influential than !Kung San leaders. This man will organize labor, and has a larger ice cellar which is available in time of need, but otherwise is used to host feasts (Johnson and Earle 1987:136–137). Some manifestations, at least, of the big-man collectivity are characterized by a ranking of statuses, and thus along with Fried's rank society type and the simpler chiefdoms, are appropriate models to begin the discussion of ranking and social life.

Models of non-stratified ranking

Known societies with institutionalized status inequality but without stratification are numerous and diverse, varying in the nature of ranking, those aspects of the character of society influenced by ranking, and of course in other often unique ways as well. The three most prominent models used to describe them are the big-man society, ranked society, and chiefdom. Real variation strains any attempt at modeling, but this is most clearly a problem when the models are used as classificatory "types" meant to encompass all real societies. And certainly, like any model, they simplify. The fact that they inevitably treat some variables as fine details, as variation within a basic pattern, could be problematic for some purposes. I further caution that these models were not developed as part of the same overall system, so they can be expected to have an ambiguous relationship to each other as well as to the corpus of known social variation.

In mentioning these caveats, I am of course making reference to the extensive critique of the social typologies from which these models derive. Such critiques are often overdrawn and sometimes simply illogical (Wason, n.d.), yet there can be no question that grand typological classificatory schemes are of limited use to archaeology. They are, nonetheless, valuable for raising questions about sociocultural evolution. In addition – and this is how I use them in the archaeological study of status – they help clarify some fundamental principles of inequality. Even more important, they suggest how these principles are "played out" in social life, which is useful for recognizing inequality from archaeological data. And finally, for our purposes the concerns mentioned above are actually advantages. When the models are used to address real examples, or when put side-by-side with each other, they illustrate real and important variation in ranking structures.

The big-man collectivity: achieved but irregular ranking

The big-man society is characterized not by pervasive ranking, but by leaders and others. Leaders attain that position through their own actions, even if, as among the Central Enga of New Guinea, the big man is a clan leader, and kinship is important (Johnson and Earle 1987:177–183). A corporate kin group may, for example, be a primary source of support to a potential leader in his climb, but no one is a big man because of genealogy, and such a leader can be replaced by someone more successful at securing a following. In addition, each group will likely go through times when no big man is acknowledged; it is not a true office that exists apart from the one who fills it at the moment. As Johnson and Earle put it, in a chiefdom, leadership positions "constitute *offices* with explicit attached rights and obligations. Chiefs thus 'come to power' that is vested in an office, rather than building up power, as Big Men do, by amassing a personal following" (1987:220). Of course this distinction is not absolute. When a big man does rise to power, it is to a culturally accepted status with certain rights and responsibilities, much as if a permanent office, whereas true officeholders, for their part, will use varied means to make the most of their position.

Given this method of recruiting to high rank, ranking will tend not to be pervasive, and will be closely tied to leadership. Also, since people become leaders by getting results (e.g. group prestige, security, and wealth), big-man societies are not faced with incompetent leaders who cannot be replaced, nor with high-status individuals who do not serve leadership functions. Finally, and perhaps most significantly, there is a pervasive ethos of competition within, and often between groups. When big men compete as peers the stakes include the prestige, wealth, or even physical well-being of their respective social groups, not just the leader's own status. Often the clan or lineage segments that a big man heads are part of a wider society, but since big men represent the most encompassing level of leadership, the label big-man collectivity used by Johnson and Earle (1987:171) seems appropriate.

The rank society: permanent status positions, achieved or ascribed

Ranking refers to statuses with different levels of prestige, arranged in a hierarchy; "A rank society is one in which positions of valued status are somehow limited so that not all those of sufficient talent to occupy such statuses actually achieve them" (Fried 1967:109). Statuses are distinguished and made more highly desired by association with rights and duties which are valued in themselves. They may also be accorded greater prestige. But while the big-man society fits (and appears to have been on Fried's mind at times), the "typical" rank society assumes hierarchy and leadership will be regular.

The rank-society model might be most important for its recognition of the distinction between ranking and stratification, and for acknowledging the importance of non-hereditary ranking (the chiefdom model commonly emphasizes hereditary ranking). Fried describes, for example, the hosting of large-scale distributions "on the way to achieving the status of redistributor" (1967:118). Otherwise rank society largely overlaps the simpler chiefdom. Redistribution is central to, and similar in each model. It is considered the major process of economic integration, and taken together with feasting, distribution, and associated prior arrangements, constitutes "a major portion of the ties binding discrete villages into a wider ... social system" (1967:179). The big-man society with achieved but impermanent leadership, and the chiefdom, with real offices but hereditary ranking, both underplay the society with genuine ranking and true offices, but with ranks and positions filled by character and achievement. The Cherokee of the Southeastern United States seem a good example.[2] Leadership positions were achieved – both high status as a warrior and membership in the council of elders – and good, if indirect evidence points to a lack of hereditary ranking in general. Other peoples of the Southeast, similar in many ways, had inherited ranks, and the Cherokee may have also. But still others, also similar to the Cherokee, did not (Swanton 1946:651–

652;662), nor can it be said that those with hereditary ranks were physically nearest the Cherokee. Swanton suggests that "Cherokee chiefs seem for the most part to have been self-made men like those of the Choctaw" (1946:653), but notes that there is little mention of these matters in the primary sources (Royce 1887:134–144). Significantly these sources offer no direct claim that hereditary ranking was lacking, but in his classic monograph "Priests and Warriors: Social Structures for Cherokee Politics in the 18th Century" (1962), Gearing is able to model Cherokee society, accounting for all major social relations on the basis of principles other than hereditary rank. Also, there is no positive evidence for hereditary rank among the Cherokee.[3]

This is important because the distinction between achieved and ascribed ranking is both real and significant. Feinman and Neitzel (1984:61–62) say one should view social differentiation not as a set of traits (like hereditary status) that are present or absent, but as a continuum. Based on the variables they studied (and how they looked at them) they found wide variation in the degree of ascription versus achievement among known societies. While clearly an important observation, this is no reason for saying distinctions between achieved and hereditary ranking are meaningless; a continuous range of variation (even if not just an artifact of our measuring technique, or extrapolation from a few intermediates), in no way precludes major qualitative differences. This would be like saying that if we cannot define how many hairs make a beard, and since men have different numbers of hairs (therefore obviously forming a continuum), the distinction between a clean-shaven and a bearded chin is misleading. These two presumably distinct face types ignore real variation and are therefore descriptions which must be avoided.[4]

Also, despite clearly intermediate forms, an amorphous mix may not be so much the norm as Feinman and Neitzel imply. First, they do not describe relative rank so much as succession to specific office. Among the Hawaiians, there were precise, entirely hereditary rules for who should be the high chief: the one male who could trace his ancestry through first-born males all the way to the founding ancestor. But it happened that no such person existed by the 1700s AD, and the system was not unambiguous about second best. That personal ability sometimes influenced the choice can be related to the likelihood of several individuals having equally legitimate ancestral claims. Thus achievement (or Berreman's "extrinsic factors") may affect choice of officeholders even if rank was ascriptive both in principle and in general. This raises an important question: what would qualify as a "pure" type in the first place? This is not easily answered in the abstract, but I suggest one reason Feinman and Neitzel's sample seems to consist mainly of societies intermediate between ascriptive and achieved ranking is their rather extreme definitions of the pure types. In particular, they mix together practice with structure in making this decision. Thus they note that sometimes leadership is based largely on achievement but tends to follow family lines. Yet even if this trend is significant it is not structural, not a rule for how leadership is determined. A person could well inherit physical ability or receive a distinctive upbringing, and it is not in the least surprising that a child of a leader would seem more able. This differs in both structure and ideology from ascribed leadership; a child of a leader may in fact become the new leader, but the position was not inherited.

This does remind us that achievement and ascription are idealized concepts not easily applied to real examples. Yet the distinction remains significant in several ways. First, there is greater likelihood of ascribed ranking applying to everyone, whereas it is more likely that achieved statuses will be leadership positions only. Among the Natchez a man could, by achievement in warfare, raise his status a notch, achieve a status unrelated to a leadership role. But this is simply a small degree of mobility within an essentially hereditary system. What Service says about chiefdoms is not true of societies with achieved ranking like the pre-state Cherokee: "The most distinctive characteristic of chiefdoms as compared to tribes and bands is ... the pervasive inequality of persons and groups in the society" (1971:145). Another major implication concerns the nature of leadership positions. Chiefs and other hereditary leaders in rank societies are said to have wide-ranging, paternalistic authority. They have broad leadership roles because they are seen as inherently better people, who thus should be followed in everything. Achieved leadership roles will tend to be more specific, for they are based on demonstrated abilities. Of the Cherokee Service observes:

> High status as a warrior was, of course, of the achieved kind ... To be a leader in the council of elders was also an achieved status, but Gearing argues reasonably that a rather different kind of basic personality type is required in the two statuses, and that age differences and ceremonies do not have the power to alter personal characteristics sufficiently to guarantee success in both.
> (Service 1975:142)

In contrast, chiefs are often descended from gods, or are themselves in some measure divine, which affects both their position and the functioning of society. It is unlikely that those who achieve positions of leadership will be viewed this way. *How* one becomes a leader does affect what that position means in real life.

The chiefdom and hereditary ranking

Kalervo Oberg (1955) may have been the first to use the concept of a "chiefdom" society in a classification system, an idea taken up and broadened by Steward and Faron (1959). Elman Service continued the trend; in *Primitive Social Organization* (1962 [1971]) he sought to make it "a stage in general cultural evolution" (1971:133). This, along with his extensive description of the chiefdom as a "type" mark his contribution as a major turning point in our use of the chiefdom as a model of society. The concept of a chiefdom society has become very important, but Service's definition no longer answers its original purposes. It was meant to cover all ranked but non-state societies. It was also an evolutionary stage, meant to bridge the gap between non-ranking bands and tribes, and the repressive state. Current approaches work from Service as a "baseline" but have moved in two divergent and probably irreconcilable directions – each a valid use of the concept, each addressing critical questions, but different enough to require that we define the word at each use.

One approach is to define the chiefdom more broadly. This allows those concerned with overall typologies to continue thinking of it as *the* "intermediate" society, the cover term if you will, for societies with ranking (any kind of structural inequality) but which are not states. Thus at a recent seminar devoted to the subject it was "rather loosely defined as a polity that organizes centrally a regional population in the thousands" (Earle 1991a:1). Earle goes on to observe that while "[s]ome degree of heritable social ranking and economic stratification is characteristically associated," (p. 1) others at the seminar held different views. In an article on pre-Hispanic chiefdom trajectories, Drennan says of these sequences that

> all involve the development of societies that are larger and more complex than autonomous, egalitarian villages, yet not so large or complex as the societies of the Mesoamerican Classic and Postclassic or of the central Andean Middle and Late Horizons. I mean to imply nothing more than this when I say that I will deal with sequences of chiefdom development. (Drennan 1991:264)

Feinman goes another step by defining the chiefdom as "a sociopolitical form" not a class or type, saying that "chiefly formations should be associated with a supra-household decision-making structure or relatively permanent positions of leadership, but not with the marked internal differentiation of such structures" (1991:230). This approach of focusing in on one (or a few) critical dimensions is a useful way of approaching a large data set, and can be applied to other dimensions like status inequality (to choose a random example).

The other main direction chiefdom research has taken involves viewing the chiefdom itself much as Service described it. The definition used by Johnson and Earle (1987) has much in common with Service's, including an emphasis on both scale and economic factors, the latter usefully refined and modified (Johnson and Earle 1987:207–209). So does that of Gibson and Geselowitz (1988:24–26) who, perhaps because of materials available for the later prehistory of Europe, outline the kinship basis for status with more interest and care than is usual among archaeologists. What is sacrificed in this approach is any chance to use the chiefdom to encompass the great variation among ranking societies in terms of complexity, economic forms (e.g. mode of financing), structure, and specific history (Earle 1989:84). Not everyone, though, considers this a loss.

The bases for rank distinctions

Kinship is central to the ranking of statuses in many chiefdoms and rank societies, in that people are accorded differential prestige, rights, and obligations – are arranged hierarchically – on the basis of their place in a kinship system. The kin system is the mechanism, but also needed is an ideology justifying the appropriateness and meaning of rank distinctions. Irving Goldman refers to this as aristocracy or "rule by the best"(1970:4). Status differentiation is based on the belief that people really are different; "[w]hat has given aristocracy its command has not been expediency, but a deep and elementary notion of distinctions in human worth" (1970:4). One implication is that leadership roles of statuses will tend to be broad, "highly generalized" (Johnson and Earle 1987:207). One of high status is thought better endowed for authority generally, sometimes conceived in terms analogous to genetic heredity – some individuals enter the world with a greater share of the humanness transmitted from the ancestors (who may themselves be "quasi-deific"). Chieftainship may well be "sacred and imbued with a sacred power (*nemed* – Irish, *mana* – Polynesia)" (Gibson and Geselowitz 1988:24–25). Invariably it seems – although perhaps in theory it could be otherwise – it is the kinship system which transmits these differences in worth.

One structural principle that facilitates a rank system based on ascription is a descent system requiring demonstration of membership, generally a specific, non-mythological genealogy (Fried 1967:116) useful for calculating rank. A genealogical descent principle is commonly accompanied by an arrangement of people into clans and/or lineages. This corporate nature (Radcliffe-Brown 1950:41) of the grouping is the most important function of a descent system (Fortes 1953:163, Fortes and Evans-Pritchard 1940:6). Concerning kinship in chiefdoms or rank society, it is customary to refer to a 1955 article by Paul Kirchhoff, "The Principles of Clanship in Human Society." The unilineal exogamous clan might be found among highly stratified societies like the Maya (Flannery and Coe 1968:278–280), but for Kirchhoff, the configuration he calls the conical clan is more open to "economic and social differentiation" (1955:265). In addition to membership based on a common ancestor, how closely one is related to this ancestor is also important. Descent is often counted through either male or female lines (p. 267) and boundaries are not fixed but "shade off" from the core. The term conical clan is descriptive and widely used, but the structure seems rather a special form of lineage (cf. Goldman's status lineage [1970]; and Firth's ramage [1957:198]). And while this model has been taken as basic to chiefdoms, Knight observes that clan organization of Eastern North American groups (as inferred from ethnohistoric records) differed in important ways including "the ranking of persons versus the ranking of social categories, rules of descent versus rules of filiation, endogamy versus exogamy, and corporateness versus noncorporateness of the kin group" (Knight 1990:3).

Ranking is rarely based on just one or two specific criteria. Thus "Polynesia takes account of primogeniture, of senior descent lines, of sex line, of genealogical depth, and, in the overall, of genealogical distinction (that is, the history of the line). Each individual criterion . . . establishes sharp divisions, but the combination of these four factors reopens ambiguity" (Goldman 1970:9). This flexibility also allows an ascriptive system to adjust to discrepancies in personal ability, although it may also inspire contention. As Drennan insists, regardless of the *idea* that the position of chief is inherited, among chiefdoms of pre-Hispanic Mesoamerica, Central, and South America, "considerable politicking was clearly necessary for a young man to take possession of his birthright" (1991:280). Likewise, Goldman has found examples of Polynesian chiefs replaced for incompetency.

This "variable mix" of hereditary and non-hereditary bases for status (or at least leadership) profoundly affects the character of a society, as Kirch recounts for the Marquesas Islands of eastern Polynesia. Marquesan society differed from most other Polynesian chiefdoms in that "certain achieved statuses (priests and warriors) had wrested substantial control of both ritual and production from the hereditary chiefs" (Kirch 1991:121). There were hereditary chiefs who "at least in theory, were the genealogically senior and thus sacred (*tapu*) leaders of the ... ramified descent group" (p. 125). These chiefs "were certainly important forces in the community," and the focus of substantial resource and labor expenditure, but protohistoric Marquesan society was fluid and dynamic, and appeals to legitimacy did not have the importance typical of Polynesia (Kirch 1991:126). One result was an active competition among hereditary chiefs and non-hereditary ritual and war leaders that "differed markedly from the 'rigid' hierarchy of the Hawaiian ruling chiefs, whose control of chiefdom ritual was uncontested" (p. 144). The implications for how people used their energy and creativity are significant. Kirch observes that the *tohua* monuments of the Marquesas are similar to the *heiau* of Hawaii "in size and labor investments (although not in function)" yet were built by populations roughly one-tenth of those commanded by Hawaiian chiefs. Cannibalism was also much more pervasive; "the emphasis on both monumental construction and cannibalism in the Marquesas reflects the involuted cycle of competition that dominated the late historic period" (Kirch 1991:145).[5]

Status, power and leadership

It may be that differences in status always imply unequal access to power; certainly they imply differential authority and influence, which are sometimes subsumed under "power."[6] But in chiefdoms this is quite explicit, for chiefs are leaders who hold offices and exercise centralized direction (Service 1975:16, 71–72; 1971:145, 147). Feinman (following Wright) says "chiefly formations should be associated with a supra-household decision-making structure or relatively permanent positions of leadership, but not with marked internal differentiation of such structures" (1991:230, Creamer and Haas 1985:740). For Service an incipient chiefdom marks a change from someone acting as central coordinator to the function becoming an office; it is "the office of chief that makes a chiefdom" (1971:140).

The right to be a leader – to exercise authority or power – will be based in one sense on heredity and the legitimizing belief system which holds this to be "only natural." To otherwise bolster their legitimacy, chiefs may seek ways of "securely connecting themselves to the past" (Earle 1991a:6) perhaps by drawing attention to their genealogy (e.g. with elaborate ceremonies in honor of important ancestors), or by associating themselves with the "symbolic capital" of earlier periods, as by re-using ancient monuments (cf. Bradley 1991:53), thus connecting current political organization with a venerable past. Other important sources of power include control over the economy and over war. There is disagreement on the nature of chiefly economic control with some holding that leadership is always based on economic control, however dressed up in formal legitimizing ideology. But whether or not it is the *source* of power, chiefs will *exercise* economic control.

Chiefs often have a functionally generalized leadership role. Earle (1978:169) observes for Polynesia that the chief, as senior member of the dominant lineage is looked to as a "paternalistic" leader with a "very broad and largely unspecified" role. Certainly the range of affairs in which the chief provides leadership varies but in general, hereditary chiefs offer direction whenever something needs to be done. Yet the chief is also one who lacks absolute authority. It might be said, at least of the simple chiefdoms, that chiefs will be listened to, especially if what they say appears reasonable, but if commands are not obeyed, there is little to compel compliance; chiefdoms lack true government to back up decisions by legal force (Service 1971:150). Of course, there are other ways of getting action. The authority of those of high rank is real, for they are considered people who *should* be listened to, and neither are they altogether without power. Even if they do not have exclusive sanctions unavailable to others, this position of authority makes their use of sanctions more effective. When arbitration is needed to settle a dispute this will often involve the person of highest rank. Chiefly proclamations will likely be carried out, especially if public opinion is favorable and the chief made his points with skill. Disobedience would mean inaction or, in arbitration, keep the dispute alive, and no doubt incur the displeasure of the chief, but lacking forceful alternatives, in a sense here it ends.

Ranking and economic life

Redistributive exchange is commonly a central feature of chiefdom models (e.g. Service 1971:134), and discussions of the subject usually refer to the work of Karl Polanyi.[7] George Dalton, one of the foremost interpreters of his thought, defines redistribution as "obligatory payments to central political or religious authority, which uses the receipts for its own maintenance, to provide community services and as an emergency stock in case of individual community disaster" (1968: xiv). Polanyi used the concept in analyses of specific economic systems (1960, 1966), but it was in his classic article, "The Economy as an Instituted Process," that he gave clearest expression to his mechanisms of economic distribution.

> Reciprocity denotes movements between correlative points of symmetrical groupings; redistribution designates appropriational movements toward a center and out of it again; exchange refers here to vice versa movements taking place as between "hands" under a market system. Reciprocity, then, assumes for a background symmetrically arranged groupings; redistribution is dependent upon the presence of some measure of centricity in the group; exchange in order to produce integration requires a system of price-making markets.
> (1957:149)

Redistribution can vary in importance to the economy and can be related to any institutional centricity; indeed several levels of redistribution may be present at once.

It is not always recognized what a range of activities can be so characterized (Polanyi 1957:153, 1960:308) and economic systems have been given this label simply because of the concentration and dispersal of goods. Earle's four-part typology is a useful step toward careful definition. "Mobilization" is the type "basic to ranked and stratified societies," and involves recruitment of goods and services for the benefit of a group not identical with those contributing (1977:215). "Householding" and "share out" differ mainly in the size of the group. Mobilization involves intercommunity production and a public economy, while share out is allocation of goods produced among domestic units within a community, and householding is the pooling of goods produced through the division of labor within the domestic unit (1977:215). "Leveling mechanisms" include any system countering wealth concentration. Earle includes here the potlatch, a custom also qualifying as mobilization.

In non-stratified societies, ranks are not based on or even necessarily accompanied by major wealth differences. Chiefs often gain prestige and power, and carry out their duties most properly by giving away rather than consuming (Sahlins 1960:397–398). In Oceania, accumulation and redistribution "stimulates production, disseminates goods through the community, supports tribal activity, and bolsters the power of the central agent" (1960:407). Flannery and Coe envision the redistributive system joining an entire region and involving specialized products and localized resources (1968:274). One implication of redistribution being of specialized products rather than basic subsistence, is an economy with two distinguishable parts, the subsistence and prestige (Sahlins 1960:398) or subsistence and political economies (Earle 1978:168). Among the Hawaiians, redistribution does not unite specialized environments or subsistence producers (Earle 1977:225, 1978:162), but involves items meant for use by the chief in personal maintenance and for carrying out chiefly duties. However much these activities benefit the people, they also support the chief's position, so in Hawaii the redistributive economy is intimately connected with political activity and largely separate from subsistence. It is part of a political economy.

On the basis of Earle's analysis, Peebles and Kus argue that "there are a number of problems in using the concept of redistribution as either a one dimensional measurement of economic activity or as a necessary hallmark of chiefdoms" (1977:423). Assuming they mean that redistribution varies significantly among societies this is both true and important, but to use this as a reason for saying the concept should be "abandoned as an indicator of chiefdoms" (p. 421) would follow only if Hawaii (or at least some known chiefdom) did not have redistribution. Earle's findings help us see how differing responsibilities and privileges associated with rank affect the economy. Yet by generalizing his conclusions to all chiefdoms – Hawaii was characterized by social stratification – Earle misses the chance to recognize variation in ranking with important consequences for lifestyle.

It is clear that redistribution does not often integrate a region of specialist producers (increasing production efficiency) or of different environments (regularizing the food supply in an unpredictable environment). As one example of the unimportance of risk management in redistributive activity, Steponaitis relates ecological studies of the Moundville area (Alabama) which indicate that "the risk of large-scale crop failure – the kind that might require chiefly intervention – was virtually nil" (1991:213). Presumably some other purpose for redistribution must be sought besides this managerial, functional benefit. The usual alternative is to see redistribution as benefiting chiefs in their role as leaders.

Other aspects of economy related to non-stratified ranking and central coordination include wealth, specialization, trade and group labor. In unranked societies a few individuals may amass more personal goods than others, but social pressure will work against accumulation. Differentiation in quality of possessions is also possible, and through varied ability a few people anywhere may possess higher quality utensils or perhaps a sturdier, more neatly finished dwelling. But again such differences will not be great without extensive ranking. Allowing for the rare artistic genius, countered by the odd incontrovertible slob, we might find a smooth but narrow range of quality in material goods. More prominent variation in material possessions is likely in the big-man, chiefdom, and rank societies, but it would be misleading to expect those of high rank to be wealthier. Ethnographic reports refer to chiefs owning the lands and resources of the society, but they are typically also responsible for ensuring that others have access. Thus the "[s]o called private fishing grounds and other vital resources [of the Tolowa-Tutuni (Oregon Coast)] were freely used within the village. Food was rarely if ever sold and was freely dispensed" (Sahlins 1960:402). Yet, those of high rank do have rights through redistributive collections. Drucker's (1939:240) reference to the chief's role as "custodian" does much to clarify the rights and duties of ownership, for while chiefs gain much in material resources, their use is largely proscribed. They will not be wealthy or wasters of group resources, although they may have a very different life style, one *we* would associate with wealth. Concerning this privileged position, "rights" are also duties. Chiefs may indeed exercise some degree of economic power through this system, but "without control over production and procurement of major subsistence resources, a chief lacks a true economic power base and the means of establishing an independent physical power base (a specialized police force or standing army)" (Creamer and Haas 1985:740). Of course some chiefs do possess this control over subsistence resources, but this is stratification.

Variation due to sumptuary rules is more characteristic than real wealth differences. People of one rank may be permitted to wear clothing and display ornamentation others cannot wear or possess, perhaps insignia or crests, easily recognized badges of rank. Great variation in material culture may well accompany a status hierarchy even in the absence of personal wealth differences. A chief will not simply (not even necessarily) have more possessions but will have at least some different ones.

Part-time craft specialization is characteristic of chiefdom economics in most models (Service 1971; Sanders and Price 1968:43), and this also includes some specialization of chiefly activity. Ranking will also affect group activities in that high-ranking individuals will initiate and lead group projects. Chiefdoms vary in the extent to which the chief will give orders or instead have the task of convincing people to help, but chiefs importantly can recruit a labor force far more inclusive than the extended family (Peebles and Kus 1977:423, Earle 1978:7). A leader as "persuader" will have more influence on personal acquaintances, setting a limit (if rather vague) to the size of work groups compared to those directed by a leader who can use forceful sanctions. In complex chiefdoms the group can be extended by a paramount convincing local chiefs who, in turn, have their own followings.

Group labor projects relate to the redistributive system in that both materials and labor may be required contributions. The projects themselves may comprise a major value of redistribution, and include feasts, ceremonies, and public works such as irrigation systems, terracing, temples, and pyramids. Basic subsistence efforts may also be undertaken cooperatively. Northwest coastal peoples built elaborate weirs with large nets, and did the actual fishing as a group. In some island groups canoes were "owned" by the chief. Construction of canoes was a group project, as were the expeditions that used them. The nature of leadership has a major influence on what projects are undertaken. It is easier to convince people to contribute to something they see as worthwhile and honorable, but if a leader can use force to convince people, this threat would mask the opinion of the workers, so that choice of projects undertaken would be more dependent on the will of the leader.

Rank and religion
In many chiefdoms there are part-time (or full-time [Flannery and Coe 1968:274]) specialized religious leaders who fill an office. This role and that of economic and political leadership may be held by the same person. To the extent that ceremonies are valued for spiritual or physical well being, people grow dependent on the priest, adding greatly to the influence and authority of this status. Those of high rank bring little power or authority to the priestly role; what they have in any field may well come from ritual status (Fried 1960:467; 1967:141). Peebles and Kus note the particular importance of this for Hawaii where the paramount may lack a direct kin relation to local populations. Ritual control "integrate[s] the paramount chief into the day-to-day subsistence activities by making the commoner ritually dependent on the chief for supplication of the major deities" (1977:426). The ritual function may thus bring much-needed legitimacy to a leadership position.

The belief content of religions cannot be generalized in the same way as structural features, but Service notes that religions in chiefdoms have in common the inclusion of ancestors among supernatural beings, often in rank genealogical order (1971:162). Just how widespread this feature is may be questioned but certainly a people's understanding of the supernatural world and of the earthly social order will be interrelated. As observed earlier, beliefs about transmittance of abilities, powers, and general worth are often the basis of the ranking system. These are religious beliefs. The surprisingly common opinion in the popular imagination and the social sciences that religions follow the social order – perhaps they are "invented" as some kind of after-the-fact justification for the way things are – may actually be true sometimes. But it is in no sense empirically based and it is at least as plausible that the social order is adjusted to religious beliefs about how things are or ought to be. Nevertheless, either way, they are bound to be related, and a study of religious beliefs could potentially provide insight into the social order.

Ranking and external relations

It is unlikely that people often lived in isolation within a clearly bounded social unit that is also coextensive with our analytical unit. Indeed, several archaeological correlates reviewed later will show, unfortunately, just how complicated it can be to sort out boundaries of polities and decide what is an "external" relation. This may be as much due to the complex nature of relations as to archaeological constraints.

> The societies in which political entities are enmeshed typically extend beyond local borders. "Outside" developments regularly influence those "inside," and the locus of political authority and decision-making shifts over time and by issue. Accordingly, the boundary between "internal" and "external" blurs almost to the vanishing point.
> (Ferguson 1991:170–171)

But this is not how most people perceive their social world, and when political and social divisions are not the same, they each correlate with important us-versus-them distinctions. Probably the most important external relations are trade, warfare, and intercommunity feasts and ceremonies. Fried states that in rank society conflict is common and intense enough to alter demography (1967:113; 178) but is not highly organized or at least does not receive the effort and attention lavished on ceremonies. But while chiefdoms (Service 1971:141) as well as rank societies are rather warlike, "the degree to which intergroup relations are settled by violence varies considerably" (Fried 1967:181). Comparing Polynesia and the Northwest coast, Fried also suggests that the amount of warfare (and we might add intensity and organization) correlates with the significance of ranking. Because these external relations will be among roughly similar social groups, much, if not all of what Service and Fried describe falls into what Renfrew and others have called "peer-polity interaction."

> Peer polity interaction designates the full range of interchanges taking place (including imitation and emulation, competition, warfare, and the exchange of material goods and of information) between autonomous (i.e. self-governing and in that sense politically independent) socio-political units which are situated beside or close to each other within a single geographic region, or in some cases more widely.
> (Renfrew 1986:1)

Steponaitis observes: "Local success in chiefly politics may depend, in no small measure, on access to external knowledge, commodities, and alliances, all of which can be greatly affected by events outside the region of interest" (1991:194). He advocates studying local developments in relation to what was going on throughout a region.

We can also imagine great variation in the extent to which chiefly status *at home* is influenced by the conduct of external relations, or by the ability to associate themselves with what Earle terms an international style "used to set the ruling elites as a people apart" (1991a:7). Esoteric knowledge and elite goods symbolic of their travels brought the chiefs of pre-Columbian Panama "power (and material wealth) as chiefly teachers and priestly prognosticators and curers in their own right" (Helms 1979:141). This may be related to status rivalry *within* each chiefdom, the "serious competition for power" despite the largely hereditary succession to elite positions offered in some accounts (Helms 1979:23–24). That is, the importance of external relations, as well as their character, may vary depending on the basis and stability of succession to rank and office at home.

It is probable that external relations are always at some level competitive, even when also cooperative in that all parties benefit, and are aware of the benefits. We would be hard pressed to isolate *mutual* benefits of warfare proper, but most other external relations – from feasting to exchange and emulation – combine competition and rivalry with cooperation and mutual benefit in varied proportions. Renfrew, for instance, speaks of "competitive emulation" which may involve displays of wealth or costly gestures, and notes that they assume (or create) some correspondence. "The magnitude of these gestures has to be measured along some scale, and the gestures are thus similar in kind. If status is achieved, for instance, by erecting a particular kind of monument, the neighboring polity will most readily acquire greater status by doing bigger and better" (Renfrew 1986:8). Competitive emulation may help account for the otherwise perhaps surprising scale of some monuments. Whether or not related to competitive emulation, luxury goods will often show similarities over large areas, similarities which may "cross-cut wide regions and politically autonomous societies where the material culture of the non-elite majority varies noticeably by locale" (Kipp and Schortman 1989:373). The effort expended on production and acquisition of elite items can be extraordinary, and exchange of such items is common. Control of this exchange is increasingly seen as important for elites in obtaining or maintaining their status (Kipp and Schortman 1989:373), perhaps because of how this "wealth" can be used to influence people, for example to "attract and control local labor" (Earle 1991a:7), or to enhance – perhaps even generate – status distinctions.

Warfare is another common form of external relations (Carneiro 1981; Drennan 1991; Earle 1991a), and while far from unique to chiefdoms, the nature of status and political organization can affect the character of war, including scale, purpose, and outcome. One consequence of an area being unified within one chiefdom (however originally accomplished) is that warfare among people within that region will (largely) cease. Using skeletal analysis, Steponaitis observes that in Mississippi "intercommunity violence peaked in the centuries just prior to the emergence of political centralization" (1991:208).

Obviously this does not mean warfare ended. The small-scale raiding or ambushing, to kill or capture a few people, common in areas without political centralization, would cease (or be redefined as criminal behavior and repressed) as chiefs exercised control, but this might well be replaced with larger-scale conflict involving hundreds of fighters in pitched battle. This warfare is conducted for political ends "such as the enforcement of tribute demands or the elimination of threats to chiefly power" (Steponaitis 1991:207). It is closer to true warfare, more devastating, more demanding of energy (defensive works, training, weapons manufacture), and often a basis for diverting the allocation of prestige and favor, the limited and precious "honor" that could have been bestowed for other reasons. But in the smaller-scale chiefdoms it was *not* often about territorial conquest. Drennan concludes for the pre-Hispanic sequences he studied that warfare here

> was undoubtedly not about control of land ... but about status rivalry, as the cumulative effect of Spanish conquest period accounts of Intermediate Area chiefdoms makes clear. Warfare was not so much between corporate groups of people as between chiefs and their henchmen. It had to do with establishing pecking orders between chiefs and, at least as much as any other factor, with succession at the death of a chief.
> (1991:279–280)

Much of this characterizes simple chiefdoms generally – and the idea of warfare not being between people so much as their chiefs is disturbingly familiar to the world of states great and small. Warfare for territorial conquest – or to increase a tribute base – is certainly found in non-state societies (Earle 1991b), and thus, by some definitions, chiefdoms. I expect, though, that warfare of this kind relates more to stratified ranking.

Models of social stratification

The main defining feature of social stratification is differential access to essential resources, and a likely way of restricting access is through control of capital resources required for production. Thus, taking staple foods as an example of a basic resource, differential access can be based on some individuals having rights to agricultural land, fishing spots and the like, such that the rest of the people, who also need this land to grow their food, must depend on those in control. In the chiefdom model, the leader will characteristically be an overseer of the society's major resources, with responsibility for their proper allocation. Everyone has rights to a share and it is the chief's duty to see that they receive their due. The idea of a chief owning the land is quite different:

> the possession of land, no matter how traditional or paternalistic the relationship between owner and cultivator, must create political power of an entirely different dimension than that exercised by those who are essentially stewards of large, corporate, kin-based landholdings.
> (Sanders and Webster 1988:528)

Chiefly stewardship has been called ownership, and in practice some gradation from stewardship to ownership is likely, since chiefs may have any number of specific rights and responsibilities. "Intermediate" forms may be common enough, confusing attempts to make a definitive distinction in any given case, but this is nonetheless a fundamental qualitative distinction which has had immense – and still growing – implications for life in this world.

Morton Fried has contributed much to the concept of stratification, and even used it as the defining feature of a type: "A stratified society is one in which members of the same sex and equivalent age status do not have equal access to the basic resources that sustain life" (Fried 1967:186). What these basic resources are will vary with differing "environment, technological equipment, and what may be called the historically determined perception of the exploitable environment" (p. 186). Basic resources cannot simply be listed, but they will be largely capital rather than consumer goods. Stockpiling of tools or food has only transitory advantage at best, and may in fact decrease mobility or be seen as antisocial. This would not qualify as stratification. Land (or parcels with special characteristics) may be a common "basic resource." One means of impairing access "is total exclusion by virtue of assigning all available usufructs to specific individuals or groups, the latter being composed of members fewer than the total population" (Fried 1967:188). Among peoples with non-stratified ranking, resources are held by a kin group. Everyone (or each adult male, or the senior member of each household) is a part of one or another resource-holding group and thus has access to resources. It is not technically direct, for the chief's permission must be had, but it is "functionally direct," since the chief's task in distribution is providing for everyone in the group. Among those who make up a stratified society not all are members of a resource-holding group. Those "outside" are left with few choices; go without (impossible since these are basic resources), leave (in which case they would no longer be part of the society and everyone left would be in a resource-holding group) or get what they need through someone with direct access. This has important consequences for livelihood: "Given stratification, but holding other things constant, assuming equal energy inputs, a person enjoying unimpeded access to basic resources will end up with a larger final product under his control than one who lacks such access" (Fried 1967:189).

Stratification, Fried argues, is unstable without mechanisms for its maintenance, and the most important ramifications of this change constitute his defining features of the state. Under a stratified system people experience differentiation (in standard of living, security, even life expectancy) far beyond distinctions in egalitarian or rank society. This requires unprecedented means of justification and enforcement, as Berreman passionately observes.

> Cross-cultural data make clear that no rationale is too tortured, self-serving, or hypocritical to be put forward to justify systems of stratification; no mechanism too bald or brutal to be employed to enforce them … People of deprived strata or groups are rarely (if ever) so credulous as to accept their deprivation without resentment; elites are rarely so perceptive as to recognize the depth (or even the presence) of that resentment.
> (Berreman 1981:13)

This is significant for the character of stratified versus unstratified societies. In particular, we can expect much greater internal strain and conflict, and the state, says Fried, develops as a mechanism to maintain stratification in the face of these interpersonal tensions (1967:230). It is a system for maintaining social order in societies which are larger than can be functionally kin based and where the social order includes stratification. The specific means by which the primary functions of the state (maintenance of social order and of social stratification) are carried out, Fried calls secondary functions (1960:476). These are population control, taxation, disposal of trouble cases, and maintenance of sovereignty.

Not everyone, however, has seen the state society as so intimately tied to the rise and defense of social stratification. Because Service (1971, 1975) does not expect social stratification to be a characteristic of all states, in his model, stratification cannot have so formative a role in the origins and character of the state. His own definition is meant to distinguish it from the chiefdom. Central leadership (1975:xii–xiii), government (hierarchical offices of leadership), fixed political boundaries, and civil law (1975:90) are all important to the character of states, but these, he argues, are also found in the chiefdom. Eliminating also features he does not believe characteristic of all states – urbanism and stratification (1975:xiii; 8), we are left with monopoly of force as the one distinctive feature of states. "We must declare that the power of force in addition to the power of authority is the essential ingredient of 'stateness'" (Service 1975:15). Many definitions of the state have been (and continue to be) offered and, not surprisingly, Johnson and Earle suggest another alternative. For them, "[i]ntegration on a massive regional or interregional scale is a defining characteristic of states" (1987:269–270). But concerning the question at hand, they agree with Fried that with the state "stratification appears to be inevitable."

The distinctiveness of stratified social life

Whether or not stratification is a central feature of states (even, perhaps, a major reason for their being) this mode of inequality has profound implications for the character of society. The eighteenth-century Hawaiians experienced a system of stratification. Their society would be a chiefdom by most definitions (as well as a stratified society in Fried's terms), yet in important ways it was really quite unchiefdomlike. Because of this anomalous relation to the models, Hawaii is an excellent example for helping us use the models to illumine the functioning of society.

Social stratification may be described as differential access to essential resources, a division among people that might involve restricted rights to the means of producing essential resources, like land and fishing spots. This is precisely what we find for Hawaii.

> The *ahupua'a* were organized into large political units, each of which was under the control of a ruling chief, usually a male, who "owned" the land and its produce. He or his representative allocated the use of the land to the

commoners, who supported themselves and the chiefs from its production.
An overseer, usually a low-ranking chief, represented the interests of the
ruling chief within each *ahupua'a*.
(Tuggle 1979:178)

Sahlins (1958:17–18) observes that among pre-contact Hawaiians there was little
differentiation in how people ate. Yet the mechanism of differential access to the
means of producing food was present, and not without effect. The ordering of land
use involved several levels of chiefly managers, each responsible to those on the next
higher level (1958:14, also Earle 1978:15). What characterizes stratification are the
specific rights and obligations for each level. Members of each rank level were given
the right to manage by the next higher level, a right not automatic either with
membership in the social group or with rank. The right to manage and rights of
commoners to use their land were conditional on meeting certain obligations and
while rare in practice, the land tenure of commoners could be revoked (Sahlins
1958:15).[8] Earle (1978:13) quotes Malo as saying that everything commoners
produced technically belonged to the chief, who had the power to expel them from
the land and take their possessions. Commoners could be dispossessed from their
personal plots for failure to contribute to the cultivation of land meant for chiefly
support (Earle 1978:15). It is significant that the conditions for land use involved
service obligations of direct personal benefit to chiefs. In making these demands,
chiefs were exercising real ownership rights, not simply stewardship. Land was not
the only essential resource manifesting this principle of differential access; Sahlins
(1958:15) notes that commoners who did not contribute labor to the maintenance of
irrigation dams and ditches could be relieved of water or land rights. There was, in
short, a mechanism whereby some people depended on others for access to critical
resources. Although Hawaiians did not experience major differences in diet, the
amount and type of work required of people did vary; in life style if not nutrition the
difference between direct or indirect access to land and water was no mere
technicality. Also, significant differences in wealth developed even among commoners, as a direct result of the land tenure system (Davenport 1969:5).
Hawaiian society was characterized by "a proliferation of specialists" most of
whom were directly involved in the ruling operations of chiefs (Earle 1987:68).

First and perhaps most prominently the ruling paramount chief and other
chiefs were surrounded by retainers who provided special goods and
services to support a sumptuous lifestyle ... Second were those specialists
involved in information processing and administration ... Third were the
land managers, who were responsible for guaranteeing the smooth operation
of the subsistence economy so as to generate the necessary staple surplus
used in finance ... Fourth were the military specialists, chiefs trained in the
art of war and responsible for combat in battles ... Fifth were the religious
specialists who conducted annual and special ceremonies related to warfare
and legitimization.
(Earle 1987:68)

There is reason, I believe, for distinguishing stratified ranking from non-stratified. Hawaii differs from many chiefdoms, in several ways which are closely related to stratification: social classes, significant wealth differences, full-time specialization (including leadership), chiefs not necessarily lineage heads, unbalanced redistribution or a tribute system in the form of required labor for support of the elite, and finally, substantial military activity which also affected succession to the higher statuses – a degree of actual achievement despite ideological ascription. There is reason, I believe, for distinguishing stratified ranking from non-stratified. A society newly stratified (or which otherwise displays only minor stratification) may seem little different from one with only basic ranking. Yet the underlying order differs. To appreciate the significance of this we must consider to what extent stratification differs qualitatively from non-stratified ranking; what effects it has on the character of society. Price holds that a clear distinction may not exist in reality, that the concepts define poles of a continuum rather than qualitatively distinct mechanisms.

> the critical observation is that while the two contrast definitionally . . . they appear operationally as a continuum, as quantitative scaled changes rather than a presence/absence dualism. The economic underpinning of the definitions, moreover, suggests development rather than contrast.
> (1978:167)[9]

Demonstration of a developmental continuum would not, however, deny qualitative differences. Viewing differences among rank systems as a continuum is just a different perspective, one stressing the importance of intermediate or transitional forms. Further, Price does not successfully demonstrate this continuum on which the argument rests.

> to the extent that the ranked society is based on a redistributive economy, and that the ranked nodes direct this economy, it is difficult to avoid some implication of differential access at least to those aspects of the economy which derive from the redistributive network.
> (1978:167)

This continuum depends on a flawed view of redistribution. The amount of actual differential access to critical resources you can justifiably postulate will in most cases be far less than she suspects. I question first the assumption that simply by running a redistributive system, agents had true differential access to the goods circulated.

> it seems inescapable that the nodal position seems to have some sort of differential access to – or first crack at – any goods, however significant or insignificant quantitatively in terms of the local ecosystem, procured through redistribution.
> (Price 1978:167)

As steward of the resources, the chief does not have free reign on their use. They are not for the redistributor's personal benefit and in terms of rules of organization, chiefs do not have more direct access to those resources than anyone else. As for non-legitimate access, it is true that a redistributor will have physically at hand a good deal of material and may take some off the top. But we cannot assume this will be done, anymore than we can assume all accountants fix the books. In any case, it is hardly a structural principle of differential access. The second problem concerns the types of resources, and proportion of the economy involved in the redistributive system. A substantial portion of the goods will be sumptuary items which, of course, are not among those resources essential to survival.[10] Basic resources will be included, notably foods, but rarely would so much of the total go through the redistributive system as to allow the redistributor differential access to that resource. Indeed, Price notes the low volumes "in that this economic sector controls relatively little of the total energy harnessed" (1978:167). But differential access to a small portion of a critical resource is not a small degree (low on a continuum) of differential access, since if enough remains outside your control, what you do control is not critical. It is not essential to anyone's survival, and however valuable it may be in the construction and maintenance of the social hierarchy, it does not make that hierarchy stratified. Ranking and redistribution can exist without stratification.

Price's other argument for this continuum is that a definition based on sharp difference in principle should be paralleled by some clear presence–absence criteria of recognition. She mentions one, site stratification, said to be "the material isomorph of all nonegalitarian society" (1978:168). From big man to state, site stratification changes in scale but "any break in the continuum is ultimately arbitrary." Thus for Price, so is any break in the development from ranking to stratification. But it is not true that all non-egalitarian societies are characterized by more than one site, never mind their being stratified (e.g. Greek city states [Renfrew 1986:11]). Further, no support is given for the claim that any break is arbitrary. There are several ways to measure site stratification, and just because Price chose one of continuous variation does not mean site stratification is in itself inherently a continuum. But even if we were to grant this, the approach itself is suspect, for she has mentioned only one feature of non-egalitarian societies and it is one she assumes from the beginning to be characteristic of them all. Naturally, if she were correct in this assumption, it would not serve as a presence–absence criterion for distinguishing *among* them.

Feinman and Neitzel (1984) also argue, on the basis of a presumed continuum, that the distinction between simple ranking and stratification is not meaningful. Their argument, like so many of this type, is flawed by the erroneous assumption that a range of variation, and qualitative distinctions within that range, are mutually exclusive. They offer different evidence, but like Price fail to demonstrate the existence of a continuum, even apart from the limits to what it would mean if they had. They studied a large number of societies, and one type of information sought for each was the number of ways high status was marked, or more specifically how leaders are marked, as they tend to conflate these categories.

> In our sample of cases, leaders are distinguished by one to as many as eight attributes marking their higher position ... Although all these attributes involve costs, some are more expensive than others. Based on these costs, we

suggest that high status does entail at least minimal economic consequences that are present in each case but to a variable degree. The continuous rather than step-like frequency distribution of the total number of status markers per case suggests that no clear societal modes can be identified within our sample of prestate sedentary societies. Contrary to Fried (1967), no clear distinction can be seen in our cases between *ranked* and *stratified* societies. (Feinman and Neitzel 1984:57)

There are several problems with this. First (as with Price's arguments) just because they have used a measure which suggests continuous variation does not mean all meaningful measures would do the same. Even their own measure can be seen differently; why not consider each number of attributes, 1–8, as steps? Even more importantly, the observation is not relevant to Fried's distinction, for they use a very different definition of stratification. Feinman and Neitzel say any differential access to wealth, resources, and social position will constitute social stratification, as long as those benefits are inherited (1984:57). Elsewhere (p. 62) they make it clear that their concern is with "social distinctions with economic implications" and that their continuum is in the amount of economic difference. Fried (I should hope) would not deny the possibility of material differences associated with unstratified ranks. But social stratification is differential access to essential or basic resources; something rather different from their vague "economic implications." Indeed the difference between definitions is so great, it is not even clear that any of their examples is stratified in Fried's sense. If so, this remains an important analysis of variation among societies with non-stratified ranking, but does not address the question of whether there is a qualitative difference between this ranking and stratification as used here.[11]

The question of definition is also the main reason Johnson and Earle can speak of all chiefdoms as stratified societies.[12] Chiefdoms are "based on unequal access to the means of production" (1987:209). If you define stratification this way, then it makes good sense to say chiefdoms are stratified. But while a chief might control the production of valuables, and while chiefly control of production could take the form of organizing work parties and conducting essential agricultural rites, neither is differential access to basic resources. These are important economic roles, roles which chiefs could use for their own ends, but with Fried I hold that differential access to basic resources (such as means of subsistence) provides a different base from which to work, one that ultimately uses economics as the leverage for affecting what people do in all aspects of life even if contrary to their will or beliefs. Stratification is not sufficient to make an oriental despot in Wittfogel's sense (1957) but it is a genuine step in that direction compared to non-stratified ranking.

There is no reason for saying the distinction between ranking and stratification, so clear in theory, is not also a reality. But it remains to demonstrate how it is significant for the working of the society. I here describe several ways stratification may affect day-to-day living. Viewing social stratification not as an abstract mechanism, but from how it works out in real activity will clarify the magnitude, qualitativeness and importance of the distinction between ranking and stratification. It is also an important step toward archaeological recognition.

The effect of social stratification on the working society

Both Gilman and Earle see leaders in ranking societies as more oriented toward self-aggrandizement than functional service. Earle (1978:168) distinguishes the subsistence economy from the political, the latter being that controlled by chiefs. While the goal of the subsistence economy is to meet the needs of each household (a minimizing strategy) the political economy has the maximizing strategy of producing the greatest possible income to further political aspirations. Studying irrigation, redistribution, and warfare among contact-period Hawaiians, Earle concluded that the usual functionalist explanation could not have been the purpose; redistribution did not emphasize exchange of food from areas of specialized production; with sufficient room, warfare could not have been due to population pressure; and the small irrigation systems did not require so complex a managerial system. The goal of leaders is increased production, and Earle suggests that this was instead an investment, a mechanism for expansion or intensification of the political economy on which their livelihood was based: irrigation by intensifying local production, and warfare by expanding the chiefdom, increasing the aggregate resources that could be channeled to the political economy (Earle 1978:195).

Earle sees this political economy as a feature of Polynesia in general. But while chiefly prestige and influence are often – perhaps always – affected by economic success, in much of Polynesia the political economy has less influence on a chief's position and life style because of very different rights to the materials involved. Among the Hawaiians, leaders gain more personal benefit from running the system than is usual in Polynesia, and this can be related to stratification versus non-stratified ranking. With greater personal benefit, leaders will run the system with more emphasis on expansion, hence aggrandizement of their political position in terms of both personal disposable wealth and extent of leadership.

Johnson and Earle contrast the simple chiefdom with the complex chiefdom and the state in these terms.

> As political control incorporates greater numbers of local groups, it necessarily becomes increasingly impersonal. For the simple chiefdom kinship continues to provide the language of property relations, debt and credit, and labor allocation. Rank is still justified on grounds of genealogical closeness to a common ancestor. And even warfare is fought "for the group," to displace other groups so that one's own group may enjoy access to their territories.
> (Johnson and Earle 1987:307)

> By contrast, the economic functions of the complex chiefdom and the state center more on the use of staple finance (i.e. taxation in kind) to underwrite public works. The highest elites are now far removed from local populations, and the fiction of kinship links between elites and commoners

is rarely maintained. Elites fight wars to gain control of new regions and their wealth.
(Johnson and Earle 1987:307–308)

Gilman (1981:3) also holds that institutions under elite management may be avenues to elite self-aggrandizement and not beneficial to the bulk of the population. For example he points to the lack of evidence for managerial benefits of elite activity throughout Bronze Age Europe: "In later prehistoric Europe, virtually the only evidence for social complexity is the wealth of the elites themselves" (1981:3). This makes it hard to justify a functionalist explanation for the development of stratification. Gilman's argument seems to work well for social stratification, but he does not always distinguish this from simpler ranking. His emphasis on a non-functionalist explanation as *opposed* to a functionalist one may also be valid for stratification. Yet, there seem to be societies which differ from this model in that the chief is very much an "altruistic redistributive agent" (Renfrew 1982:6).

I suggest that this difference between functionalist operation and self-aggrandizing marks that between ranking and social stratification. It is only with stratification that the elite can "get away" with extensive personal use of the society's resources.[13] We can think of inegalitarian society as having both a household and a public economy. Under non-stratified ranking, leaders control the public part, directing group projects and aspects of the economy involving specialization. Indeed, this public economy would not likely exist (significantly or regularly) without central coordination. But Hawaii differs significantly. Here leaders also control the basic household economy – through the very mechanisms that define stratification among Hawaiians: chiefly *ownership* of land and water rights, and the requirement of commoners to produce the basic economic needs of the elite. Under stratification central economic control extends to the day-to-day subsistence economy. There may be other ways of doing it, but control over the household economy is one form of differential access to basic needs. Ramifications for life style (tribute becomes taxation), and for leadership (leaders operate with conflicting goals and an agenda that can be fully articulated without reference to the welfare of others) are significant.

One feature of that agenda may be warfare for conquest. The idea that chiefdoms expand by conquest does not fit well with other aspects of the model, for if a chief is the leader of the people in a conquered area, it is only because he has conquered them. The authority claim is not based on natural rights, implicit (and unforced) acknowledgement that he is best suited, nor on genuine kinship ties, but simply on the ability to enforce his rule. Of course the conquering chief may attempt to claim legitimacy, where possible, in terms of kinship status. Among the Hawaiians, not all such claims were entirely vacuous either. But from the perspective of those conquered, leadership is fundamentally based on force. The leadership status claimed will be of the achieved kind. This will make reciprocal obligations (often important to chieftainship) harder to establish, since people will not likely see them as legitimate. To what extent could we really expect redistributive "donations" to be given willingly? And chiefs for their part will not be as inclined to carry out their duties for the welfare of the people or view themselves as stewards of communal resources. If that part of a chiefdom obtained by conquest is substantial, it is unlikely that the chief will have a status and leadership position much like that in a simple chiefdom.

Models and the archaeological recognition of inequality

Renfrew notes that while recognition of ranking in the archaeological record is not easy and has not been well thought out, the problem goes deeper than archaeological method.

> The root of the matter may in fact be in the absence of any very clear
> definition of exactly what is meant by ranking in the ethnographic present,
> even before its archaeological correlates are sought in material culture.
> (Renfrew 1982:2)

While I have not produced that definition, several aspects of ranking and its varied manifestations have become clearer. If the evidence in any given case allows us to go no further than to infer ranking itself – some hierarchical, but otherwise unspecifiable pattern of differentiation – this is certainly better than lacking that information about a former society. But it is also obvious that whenever (and however) possible, we will always want to know more than this about the former status system. I submit that among those aspects of status worth studying are the questions of whether or not ranking was hereditary and whether or not social stratification was present.

The distinction between achieved and hereditary rank may have its most obvious effect on the degree to which ranking pervades the society rather than being primarily related to leadership positions (the latter more likely for achieved status). It should also affect how ranks determine social behavior. Since ascribed ranking is associated with an ideology of differences in human worth, authority will be more wide ranging than that of a leader who moved into or constructed a position primarily through practical considerations of ability. The distinctiveness of a stratified system might be seen in such variables as differential wealth and standard of living; the nature of central economic control; and the indications of leadership goals, manifest in public works emphases, tendency for self-aggrandizement among leaders (and others of high status), and the extent to which the leadership agenda is aimed at real benefits for the people – or not.

4

Mortuary data as evidence of ranking, Part I

Whatever else it may accomplish, the central and immediate goal of burial is the proper "laying to rest" or disposal of the body of a former member of the society. But there have been widely varying ideas on what exactly constitutes "proper" treatment, actual practice being influenced by beliefs concerning death, and any of the ways a person had been of significance to others. Another obvious yet important observation is that of variation within the practice of one society. Differential treatment among contemporaries means not all mortuary traits can be fully explained apart from significant differences among people.

It has often been observed in both ethnographies and synthetic works that treatment in death is closely related to social position in life (Keswani 1989); mortuary practice is heavily influenced by social organization. It is also influenced by ideology, particularly the meaning and significance of death both for the one who died and for those who are left. It is not clear to what extent each of these factors influences burial custom, but probably very little of actual practice is affected by one and not the other. Further, many aspects of burial practice will be overtly symbolic, over and above the sense in which all products of human activity embody meaning. Using this to learn about the society, for example to understand religious beliefs, or the place of status within a world view, may require unlocking the meaning of mortuary symbolism, a difficult if potentially rewarding study. Binford (1971:16) observes that a symbol is by nature an arbitrary assignment of meaning to form. This may be true in a technical sense, but it does not mean the interpretation of symbolism is simply speculation, for symbols are unlikely to be arbitrary *in relation to each other*. Despite the arbitrary relation of written symbols to speech, it is possible to decipher unknown scripts. And while few other symbols are part of so systematized a context – there may be no such thing as a grammar of mortuary representations – we may still be able to decipher meanings of individual symbols through their context. Indeed, in the case of material culture, the connection between a concept and its representation may not be as arbitrary as in language. Hodder observes that "a material culture 'word,' such as a photograph or sculpture of a human being is not an arbitrary representation of that which is signified: thus, in contrast to the majority of words, many material culture signs are iconic" (1991b:176–177). If reliable interpretation of mortuary symbolism is more difficult than deciphering a language (the context being simpler and less systematic) this iconic nature of the symbols adds some hope. Thus placing weapons in the grave of a warrior is not at all arbitrary as a way of symbolically representing prowess in battle, and Humphreys notes that certain symbols recur regularly in mortuary contexts, the contrast of dryness and water, or moving and still water being especially common (1981:10). However, the same symbol may mean different things within this general association with death (Chapman and Randsborg 1981:8). Among historical-period Arikara burials, O'Shea found that rank could be indicated in alternative ways. In cases checked against independent records, chiefly rank was variously marked by central location among burials, an arrow-maker's kit and varied other artifacts or by various artifacts plus a stone pipe (1984:271).

Recent studies using mortuary data to infer social organization have largely ignored ideology and oddly enough, despite the influence of beliefs about death on practice, and the overtly symbolic nature of much mortuary ritual, ignoring "meaning" in this sense nevertheless seems to work. As Pearson *et al.* point out concerning O'Shea's findings, "despite the changes in symbolic expression ... the relative position of the individual is still recognizable" (1989:4). We cannot expect anything like a full understanding of the burial program, but there is reason to believe valid inferences about social organization are possible from mortuary practice (particularly fairly general statements about status) without understanding the specific ideological context (Jacobsen and Cullen 1981:79–80).

This of course, has not gone unquestioned. Comparing modern British mortuary practice with that of the Victorians, Parker Pearson concludes that ideology is a significant influence (1982:101). For modern England he found little correlation between expenditure on mortuary ritual and status (measured by wealth): "today only royalty and major national heroes and some ethnic minorities receive expensive ceremonies in death" (p. 109). Things were quite different for the Victorians; elaborate ceremonies and monuments were common, and scale strongly correlated with social position. Modern Britain remains hierarchical but the relation of burial practice to social position has changed, largely as a consequence of changed *beliefs* about what burial is for (Parker Pearson 1982:99,112). This demonstrable influence of ideology makes it clear that the status system is not directly mirrored in burial practice. Still, it does not undermine modern mortuary analysis, for this study reflects a very different kind of ideological influence than we would normally expect in archaeological studies. Britain is more pluralistic than groups likely to be encountered by the archaeologist, and this varied ethnic and religious background means the coexistence of different belief sets concerning death and its ritual. Such beliefs will always affect ritual, but when held in common their effect will be more uniform. Variation in practice among members of a less pluralistic society would more likely follow from status differences than from differing views of death, or different ideas on what burial is. But Parker Pearson's study does show that ideology cannot be as easily ignored when studying variation between societies (or one society over time) as when drawing inferences from variation within one society.

When using mortuary data simply to infer status inequality (as distinct from trying to learn as much as possible about ancient mortuary ritual, beliefs about death, human nature, and so on) it is probable that the greatest chance of being misled is in underestimating the degree and complexity of the status hierarchy. Trinkaus makes the interesting observation that among peoples with distinctly hierarchical social organization, actual mortuary remains may not fully express these distinctions because of eschatological concepts opposing the social order of the living to that of the dead (1984:675). For adherents of many religions (including Christianity, Islam, Buddhism, and Zoroastrianism),

> death (or the end of the cycle of births) is a promotion into a more egalitarian society. Written documents emphasize this new-found equality, and the material remains of corpse disposal symbolize it. Grave goods are discouraged or prohibited, physical burial is simple, or cremation or exposure may be enjoined.
> (Trinkaus 1984:675)

This is not to question the main point that social persona will be expressed in mortuary ritual. The expression of rank and extensive material wealth in life is shifted from the burial proper to mortuary ritual through "much nonmaterial symbolism and lavish nonpermanent display (feasting, elaborate hearses, flowers, the presence of significant persons, etc.)" (Trinkaus 1984:675). To the extent this is true, it may be a shift of status display to those aspects of ritual further removed from treatment of the dead and more tied up with the living society. Either way, in the absence of reliable information concerning beliefs, we would not recognize how hierarchical the society really was, and this because of the effect of ideology on burial practice.

But returning to burial practices in Britain, Trinkaus's analysis may serve as much to underscore as resolve Parker Pearson's observation concerning changing burial practices, for whatever we might say about those who indulged in lavish display, a view of the world influenced by Christianity probably had at least as much influence on Victorian as on modern Britain. It may be that not all differences in mortuary practice are the result of changing ideas on death. Changes in social organization may have been important as well, for while the status systems are complex in both periods, the specifics have changed, particularly the place of nobility in the functioning of the society. The hierarchical structure has changed little in outline, but the *significance* of ascribed social position to the lives of people has changed greatly – for the most part becoming less affective in politics, economics, and, overall, in any one person's life style. The lavish Victorian expression of status may have been a reaction to these changes; on the part of some a last-ditch effort to reaffirm the old order, for others an attempt to leverage new-found wealth into acknowledged high status.

If we can assume that beliefs concerning death are held in common, it follows that most variation in mortuary treatment *within a social group* relates to differences among people as to their "place" in society. This can be expressed as the composite of someone's statuses, the social persona (Tainter 1977:331–332). But this is more complicated than it seems, for it is only generally true, and in any case, there are many variables which contribute to a person's status, any of which can be marked in mortuary practice. To clarify how a status is translated into burial features, Peebles distinguishes status in life from status in death, which combines past statuses with circumstances surrounding death, and the activities of mourners (1971:69). The idea of a terminal status is valuable since circumstances of death can greatly change how one is viewed by others (and treated at death), as when someone dies a hero (Humphreys 1981:9).

The next question concerns what aspects of status are likely to be expressed in mortuary ritual. Based on a survey of the ethnographic literature, Binford (1971:14) compiled this list.

> The following were offered by many ... as the basic components of the social personality symbolized through differential burial treatments: (1) age, (2) sex, (3) relative social status within a given social unit, and (4) social affiliation in terms of multiple membership in the society itself. In addition it was frequently noted that peculiar circumstances surrounding the death ... may be perceived ... as altering, in a substantial manner, the obligations of the survivors to acknowledge the social personality of the deceased.

These may be taken as the main features of social organization about which burial customs provide clues. But they will not be simple clues, for these variables are interrelated both in the functioning of the society, and in being expressed in the same body of evidence. For a configuration of burial variation to represent ranking means it is not entirely due, say, to age-based status, or unranked social affiliation. Further, in an archaeological sample changes over time would be yet another superimposed source of variation. Very few burials will be exactly contemporaneous unless some unfortunate circumstance befell the community. But while this limits how finely time distinctions may be divided, it need not be just a source of confusion. Change over time may itself provide clues to the social system and its evolution.

Only a small fraction of all mortuary activity – that directly related to corpse disposal – is recorded archaeologically in a way that is now recognizable (Bartel 1982:54). Ethnographic accounts often bear this out forcefully.[1] The Tikopia, for example, hold gift exchanges, with volume depending on the status of the deceased. Elaborate feasts are also common, but none of this enters the archaeological record associated with specific burials. This tendency for burial to comprise but a small fraction of the total mortuary effort, appears to be true for those practicing elaborate burial (as among the Natchez and Tahitians) as well as those where burial even for the highest statuses is relatively simple (as among the Tikopia). Nevertheless archaeological data will be more useful than this would lead us to suppose, for each ritual phase appears to convey similar social information.

> That there is a large amount of redundancy along the entire mortuary sequential chain is shown in an analysis of mortuary practice of 27 ethnographic societies ... When the mortuary sequence was divided into its component parts and then multivariately analyzed cross-culturally, the component dealing with burial shifted in importance directly with other variables within the chain vis-à-vis age, sex, status, and social affiliation of the deceased.
> (Bartel 1982:55)

Table 4.1. *Recognizable dimensions of variability in mortuary practice*

1. Treatment of the body
   a. degree of skeletal articulation
   b. disposition of the burial
   c. number of individuals per burial
   d. mutilations and anatomical modifications
2. Preparation of disposal facility
   a. form of the facility
   b. orientation of the facility and the body within the facility
   c. location relative to the community
   d. location within the disposal area itself
   e. form of disposal area
3. Burial context within grave
   a. arrangement of bones within the grave and relation to furniture and facility
   b. form of the grave
   c. quantity of inclusions
4. Biological dimensions
   a. age
   b. sex
   c. disease states and circumstances of death
   d. nutritional evidence
   e. genetic relationships

There is no denying that much valuable information is lost, but this finding is of great importance, telling us that there is more justification for social inference from burials than one might expect on the basis of its being so small a portion of the total.

Even this small part of mortuary ritual is itself a complex of activities. Binford summarized the process of corpse disposal into treatment of the body itself, preparation of the facility in which it is placed, and contribution to the furniture placed with it (1971:21). For each he lists several subvariables. Goldstein adds usefully to this by including spatial variables, and her list (1981:59) is reproduced here (Table 4.1).

Using ethnographically known societies, Binford correlated his list of social variables frequently recorded in mortuary practice (see above) with his version of this list (1971:22), the result being an outline of the associations between social feature and mortuary variable that one might try looking for. In his sample for instance, whenever someone was buried with a different quantity of grave goods this correlated with social position and no other aspect of social persona. On the other hand, he found that while form of grave goods is used to mark social position, it even more commonly distinguished between the sexes.

In the following sections (and in chapter 5) I review a series of archaeological correlates of ranking which attempt to relate these mortuary variables to social organization.

Osteology, paleopathology, and demography

As "givens," biological features are not part of mortuary ritual but they may affect the choice of burial treatment; sex and age are particularly important, and the social meanings both of gender and lifecycle are among the features of social persona most commonly distinguished in mortuary practice. Because sex and age as such are innate, they can (with good preservation) be determined apart from any assumption about social context. This allows us to "break into the circle" and begin distinguishing variations in burial treatment which mark gender and age from those which mark other social features, and begin considering the social implications of gender and age. These data can also help determine if the burial sample is representative of the population, an assumption which must be met for some correlates. This is important since "non-egalitarian status cemeteries are often selective in the segments of the population represented" (Saxe 1971:41). In her study of the burials at Koster, Buikstra (1981:130) found how drastically this could alter interpretation.

Many applications of human osteology and paleopathology to archaeologically relevant problems are fairly new. Cohen sees the development of this field as among the "most important trends in archaeology in the 1980s," and looks forward to the resolution of some important controversies in prehistory "because opposing theories explicitly or implicitly offer conflicting predictions about changes in human health and nutrition" (1989:117). Among these are certain questions concerning the nature and effects of status inequality. Current osteological approaches and their relevance to the inference of status may be summarized as follows.

Diet and nutritional status

Techniques for reconstructing prehistoric diet from skeletal material include the study of tooth wear patterns (at both the macro- and micro-levels), proportions of trace elements (including strontium, magnesium, zinc, and copper), and proportions of elemental isotopes (particularly of carbon, nitrogen, and strontium) (Cohen 1989:118). It is also possible to assess the "nutritional status" of individuals, including specific dietary deficiencies or undernutrition generally, through skeletal measurements, size of cortical area, bone density, and patterns of delayed growth in children (p. 118). Because most of these approaches are fairly new or developing rapidly, we have only just begun to exploit them for social inference. The basic goal is most often to isolate dietary differences among contemporaries which indicate differential access to materials and critical resources (Plog and Upham 1983:204). Unfortunately, this remains difficult even when we have good evidence of past diet and nutrition as such. A few examples will illustrate some of the potential of diet and nutrition studies.

Adult stature and general health are affected by living conditions which in turn may be affected by status. Children given a better diet will often grow taller (than they would have, or than others), the improved diet allowing them to come closer, loosely speaking, to their genetic potential. This assumes (reasonably in many cases) that most people receive less than adequate nutrition. If the burial population shows marked differences in these features, major status differences may be indicated. Attempts have been made to extend this as a basis for distinguishing achieved from ascribed ranking, but in itself this correlate often remains ambiguous. Height may have been a preference in the choice of high status individuals, thereby representing a system of achieved status, or it may be attributed to differential access to food during childhood, suggesting hereditary status – and also social stratification. Braun (1979:71) and Brown (1981:36) have argued for the inference of achieved and ascribed status (respectively) from the same Klunk-Gibson mortuary data set. Other factors aside, either argument is plausible, but if we can show (independently) that status was hereditary, a skeletal record showing high-status individuals to be consistently more healthy and robust would also be evidence for stratification. Tahiti serves as an example of the latter. It was frequently remarked by early European observers that chiefs (*ariki*) were larger than most, and some extremely corpulent – a difference sufficient to inspire the suggestion that they were of a different race (Oliver 1974:787–789). Chiefly status was hereditary, and children of chiefs were given more and better foods from early on (Oliver 1974:223, 258, 273–274). Major size differences were not characteristic of (at least not noted for) other hereditary ranking societies reviewed, not even Hawaii. This situation among Tahitians may be due not just to special foods associated with status, but to the belief that chiefs should be large.

Another line of inference uses physical data to distinguish dietary differences within a population. Although still being worked out, this has developed considerably in the last decade, and is based on the trace element content of skeletons; "if one knows the trace element content of different types of food [found to be relatively constant] then there is the possibility of using the content of bone to examine dietary changes and periods of nutritional stress" (Chapman and Randsborg 1981:23). But while there have been some striking achievements (unambiguous means of tracing the use of domestic maize, and detection of marine foods) there remain serious stumbling blocks to developing paleodietary technique. For example, the "isotopic signature" of bone collagen – the tissue studied – is not after all a direct reflection of the proportion of foods in one's diet (Sillen *et al.* 1989:506). Yet this is potentially resolvable and does not affect all studies, so it is not unreasonable to remain optimistic about this "independent" source of information on diet.

Differential diet is one indicator of resource distribution *within the society*, not general cultural adaptation. But while evidence that some people ate, for example, substantially more meat than others is important, there are several possible causes. A priestly group or a sect may have a diet excluding meat, as might an under class. This kind of alternative can be eliminated by considering the proportions of the population in each diet type and with which aspects of mortuary ritual the variations correlate.

Hastorf found, using stable carbon and nitrogen isotope values that following incorporation of the Sausa into the Inca empire, significant differentiation developed between men and women in the consumption of meat and maize (probably in the form of the fermented maize beverage *chicha*). This alerts us to increasing gender differentiation with significant impact on life style. Men were becoming more involved in the "wider" economy through participation in state work parties, during which times they were provided a different diet than usual (1991:148–152). The method, then, did uncover significant changes in social relations, differences which were based on changing political structure.

"Dental health" is another potential source of information about diet and status. In a study of sociocultural variables affecting dental health among pygmy hunter-gatherers and Bantu horticulturalists of Zaire and the Central African Republic, Walker and Hewlett (1990) confirmed the common assumption that a high-carbohydrate diet is correlated with cavity rate, and that while dental health does correlate with diet, minor differences in the techniques of food preparation (e.g. frequency of utensil cleaning) can affect tooth loss. Of particular interest, pygmy leaders had much better dental health than others. As with other dietary effects (e.g. stature), it is not clear to what extent good dentition is a cause or effect of being a leader, since those with well-preserved dentition may have a better chance of becoming leaders.[2] However, leaders do consume a diet of more meat and less carbohydrate than others as a consequence of their wide-range of social contacts and the many gifts they receive (Walker and Hewlett 1990:395). Ironically this striking result of the survey may actually be reason for caution in drawing interpretations from dietary and health variables.

> Even though pygmys are famous for the lack of importance they place on social distinctions, we, nevertheless, found a large difference between the dental health of pygmy "leaders" and "nonleaders." This finding has implications for archaeologists who study the relationship between social stratification and health in prehistoric societies. Significant status-related health differences apparently exist in societies that deemphasize the significance of status distinctions.
> (Walker and Hewlett 1990:396)

Of course, it may also raise questions about just how those societies traditionally classified as hierarchical or complex differ from those viewed as egalitarian or simple, and serves as a reminder that people do not necessarily view each other as "equal" even in the absence of invidious social rules. The real and consequential differences in prestige among the pygmys are due to recognition of differences in personal ability and personality in the absence of structural status inequality.

Infection, stress, and trauma

Although infection, stress, and trauma are often related experiences (and commonly related to nutrition as well) they can be distinguished using skeletal material. Certain diseases (leprosy, tuberculosis, and such treponemal infections as yaws and syphilis) can be identified from diagnostic traces left on skeletons, and it is also possible "to identify and quantify the occurrence of low-grade or chronic infection or inflammation in the skeleton even when the specific pathogenic agent cannot be identified" (Cohen 1989:119). Various trauma events (including fractures and skeletal dislocations) can also be recognized (Cohen 1989:119), and the nature of the event can often be inferred to some degree (as well as whether or not it was the cause of death), providing clues to lifestyle or environmental conditions. If a population is analyzed in terms of frequency and distribution of trauma we may find clues to the importance of warfare or major differences among people as to participation in dangerous activity.

Also promising for status inference is the ability to isolate childhood "episodes of growth-disrupting or growth-retarding biological stress" (Cohen 1989:119). Dental enamel hypoplasia – deficient enamel thickness due to a disruption in its otherwise regular ring-like secretion – may provide clues to stress in early life, and its long-term consequences for survivors of stressful periods (Goodman and Armelagos 1988:936). A consequence of "systemic disruption," stress due for example to undernutrition or infection, hypoplasias can be distinguished from enamel defects due to hereditary or localized trauma. Indeed individual stress incidents can be isolated, and each pinpointed within a six-month span between ages three-and-a-half and seven years. Among adults buried at Dickson Mounds during the Late Woodland, Mississippian Acculturated Late Woodland, and Middle Mississippian, those who had not experienced a detectable stress period lived longer on average than those who had survived a hypoplasia-stress period, who in turn lived longer than survivors of two such stress periods. The variation was greatest during the Middle Mississippian, when mean age at death of those without a stress period was 37.5 years, 7.3 years and 15.7 years longer than those who survived one, and two or more, stresses (Goodman and Armelagos 1988:940). Goodman and Armelagos suggest three possible processes for the association: (a) differential lifelong biological susceptibility to the adverse effects of physiological disruption; (b) permanent damage from the early stresses, leaving these people less able to respond to subsequent stresses; and (c) "differential lifelong patterns of behaviorally and culturally based exposure to stressors" (Goodman and Armelagos 1988:941–942). While none of the three could be ruled out, it is interesting that the most marked difference between stressed and non-stressed groups was found in the Middle Mississippian, probably also the period of greatest status differentiation. The authors conclude "that lifelong differences in social status, and therefore differential cultural buffering from stress may be important" (1988:942).

Workload experience

Techniques have been developed which allow us to "assess the nature and severity of the workload in which an individual has engaged" (Cohen 1989:119). Periods of high physical demand especially, but heavy workload generally, are "recorded" in the skeleton through muscular development and the nature of arthritic changes in joints (p. 119). Patterned differences in workload and stress would mark task specialization.

There are limits to what we can conclude from this alone, but it could contribute to determining if simple ranking or stratification was present, as well as offer insight into the rights and responsibilities associated with statuses.

More traditional approaches of the physical anthropologist may also be of use in the study of status differentiation – alone, or combined with these measures. Wilkinson and Norelli (1981) propose using a range of measurements of skeletal material to determine the extent of endogamy. In a chiefdom with ranked lineages (or clans) for instance, one might well choose a marriage partner from another lineage, but if real social classes occur, these are more likely to be endogamous. In time, those of one class may become genetically distinct from the other classes (or, they may have started out that way), and resulting phenotypic differences might be recognizable from skeletal data (1981:745). If the burial population divides into biologically distinguishable populations and if these in turn can be correlated with mortuary markers of status, there is reason to believe the social order included endogamous classes. However, there are other possible reasons for biological variation, so the lack of clear groupings argues for the lack of endogamous groups more strongly than distinctions evidence the practice of endogamy.

Energy expenditure and rank

Joseph Tainter, who has done much to further the energy expenditure hypothesis (see also Braun 1979:65, Jacobsen and Cullen 1981:38, Peebles and Kus 1977:431), describes it as follows:

> In any system of hierarchical ranking, increased relative ranking of status positions will positively covary with increased numbers of persons recognizing duty–status relationships with individuals holding such status positions. [This] entitles the deceased to a larger amount of corporate involvement in the act of interment, and to a larger degree of disruption of normal community activities for the mortuary ritual.
> (Tainter 1977:332)

This greater involvement can mean greater expenditure of effort, which may in turn be reflected in a larger tomb, more grave associations, and the like. The energy expenditure argument for inferring rank from mortuary data may be the single most important advance to emerge from the extensive interest in the subject during the 1970s. Yet there are significant and not always recognized limits to the potential detail of conclusions. The expenditure of energy is by no means the only way of honoring rank, and people may see other aspects of their response to death as more important. Further, the value people bestow upon an object is not based solely on how much energy went into its making, but may be affected by frequency of natural occurrence, utilitarian value, a history of cultural associations, or subtle personal preference. This does not deny the basic trend, but does limit the precision with which we can correlate energy expenditure and rank.

Tainter's ethnographic test may help in further establishing the validity of this line of inference.

> This proposition linking labor expenditure in mortuary ritual to the rank of
> the deceased has been tested on a large ethnographic sample (103 cases). In
> this sample, there was not a single case that contradicted the labor
> expenditure argument ... Such strong results suggest that the analysis of
> labor expenditure is essential for identifying patterns of rank grading in
> mortuary data.
> (Tainter 1977:332)

Although an impressive outcome, this test says nothing about the correlate being
essential; as will be shown, it is neither the only nor always the most informative use
of burial data to infer ranking. Such strongly positive results do support the validity
of the correlation tested, but it is important to consider what exactly the test
demonstrates. Some examples (pp. 126–127) indicate only a very general correlation.
For Hawaii, Tainter demonstrates the correlation of energy-expenditure differences
among burials with status, but only by way of contrasting individuals very near the
extremes of status variation (as he clearly notes [1978:127]): community outcasts and
chiefs. In other examples, the relationship is demonstrated for less divergent
statuses; even minor rank differences might be marked by recognizable energy
differences. The precision with which small energy differences dependably evidence
rank differences probably cannot be determined by ethnography, for accounts often
contrast the highest status with at most one basic alternative. Thus deeply impressed
observers described Natchez chiefly burial in minute detail, yet apparently no early
observer ever penned a record of an ordinary burial (Swanton 1911:138). What these
descriptions do indicate is that high-status *burials*, not just mortuary rites, involve
greater effort and community disruption.[3] Although the correlation of energy
expenditure and rank is essentially an outsider's measure of the results of complex
duty–status obligations, the relationship may be explicitly recognized, even
regulated. Pearson *et al.* (1989:37) relate that records of the reign of the Japanese
Emperor Kotuku (begun ca 645 AD) include regulations on tomb construction
outlining five grades from princes whose tombs should be five fathoms high, built by
1000 laborers in seven days, down to those of Dairei to Shochi rank who should have
tombs without mounds and completed by fifty laborers in one day.

One difficulty with the energy expenditure approach is that the reasoning
necessary for its use with archaeological data is just the reverse of how I have
described the connection between social organization and material culture.

> Reversing this reasoning, when sets of mortuary data cluster into distinctive
> levels of energy expenditure, this occurrence will signify distinctive levels of
> social involvement in the mortuary act, and will reflexively indicate
> distinctive grades or levels of ranking.
> (Tainter 1978:125)

Since the validation of a proposition does not validate its reverse with the same
certainty (we fall easily into the fallacy of affirming the consequent), this does not
follow from the previous discussion, and the ethnographic cases do not test it
directly. There is no doubt that this correlate expresses the most likely connection,

but other factors than grades of ranking might influence the relative energy expended on death ritual. Someone may have been more widely known and liked. This is a status difference, although not a structural one, and could well affect the effort put into a burial. Perhaps an individual of high status died during a busy season and people only spared the time and energy absolutely required of them. Or again, suppose sons and daughters have the prime duty status relations. If so, a person with many offspring would receive elaborate treatment, regardless of any other aspect of status. Any such possibility could cause unevenness in the theoretically smooth picture of rank grading, as measured by energy put into burial. It is most unlikely that this would affect the overall trend, but it does limit the fineness of rank distinctions we can make based on energy differences. Tainter's emphasis on *levels* of energy expenditure must not be ignored.

> Ultimately, the goal of studying labor expenditure is to quantify the amount
> of human energy expended in mortuary behavior. [This] ... must await
> physiological studies documenting the quantities of energy human beings
> expend on the activities that comprise a mortuary ritual.
> (Tainter 1978:332)

But the problem remains of comparing energy values for varied materials and processes. These are not easily correlated (Brown 1981:29), making the overall measure less objective in practice. Without those physiological studies – which while theoretically possible, I suppose, are surely a long way off – measures of energy expenditure are *comparative measures* (platform A is larger than B) not *specific measures* (platform A took one billion calories). To say measures from different samples or variables (size of mound, amount of gold) are comparable, can be like saying length measurements are comparable, without considering that one might be in inches, another in meters. This is not a flaw in the correlate itself, but an important technical consideration for its application.

Mortuary ritual for one of high status will involve more people, but this does not necessarily mean more of them will work on grave digging, and so leave an archaeologically observable mark of their numbers, a bigger grave. Perhaps some will give gifts, contribute to or attend a feast, or line the streets as the body is paraded through on an impromptu holiday (disruption of normal activity). The correlate assumes that expenditure of energy, like symbolism, is redundant, but total expenditure is cumulative, so even when more energy is lavished on a mortuary event, it cannot be assumed that the part leaving material remains will receive expenditure proportional to the overall energy differentiation by status. Thus the magnitude of variation among burials may not give a dependable picture of the magnitude of status hierarchy. But this is merely another caution against fine-grained conclusions; it is unlikely that the order of energy expenditure in any one part of mortuary ritual will be the reverse of the overall order.

A major strength of the measure is its ability to use a range of evidence, making it useful in widely varied archaeological situations (Brown 1981:29, Goldstein 1981:56). Combining lines of evidence to establish energy expenditure levels can strengthen a conclusion, but multidimensionality is not inherent to the method. In actual use, for example, Tainter bases rank levels largely on one measure of energy expended; burial platform size (and in one case, workmanship). Yet it *can* be multidimensional and can benefit from whatever data are at hand. This is no small advantage.

It is not clear how much detail can be inferred from energy variation among burials. The finer the distinctions, the less certain one can be that they mark structural social features. Certainly it is possible for those performing a burial to make striking use of small energy differences to mark rank differences, but my concern is with reliable inferences. I believe Tainter and Cordy have, in analyzing Hawaiian mortuary remains, exceeded the detail for which this method is demonstrably valid. Their definitions of "levels" are clear but some, especially in the second group (1977:101–102,106), seem rather minimal considering how much all the burials have in common.

> Level 1: Individuals accorded the construction of a wall to demarcate their place of interment. Level 2: Individuals buried in or associated with a canoe or canoe parts. Level 3: Disarticulated bundles of bones. Level 4: Individuals buried in an articulated state with no associated stone walls or canoe parts.
> (Tainter and Cordy 1977:106)

None of these distinctions is great enough to imply the participation of more individuals. Even the stone wall would not require either more people or the services of specialists.[4] There may also be a problem with the order of levels. Since the caves were used repeatedly (p. 106), disarticulated bundles of bones (Level 3) may not have been secondary burials, but the earlier or least important burials, pushed aside in a heap to make room for others. If Levels 3 and 4 represent real rank differences at all, they are as likely to be in the reverse order from that suggested. To say the degree of detail in these distinctions is not justified by the method is itself a subjective judgement, and it is certainly not the same as saying their analysis is wrong or without value. Detecting such distinctions is useful if we recognize that this correlate does not really demonstrate them. Armed with a set of distinctions, other archaeological correlates (or as here, ethnographic data) can be used to test them.

Another limitation is that this measure gives little insight into the nature of and basis for ranking. Tainter uses the term rank broadly; for Hawaii (1978:127) it is clear that outcast and chief are different orders of things. Various status-affecting factors are joined together in an overall rank level set, in what Goldstein calls "classification without context." Concerning a different example of the problem, she states:

> Burials are classified by internal differentiation, but the *context* of the classes is not taken into account. What does each group or status type mean? How do the groups relate to each other? What are the functions of each group, and what are the functional relationships between groups? While many of these questions may not be easily or reliably answered, current mortuary

analysis does not even approach or attempt to *ask* these questions. Can we
really say ... that a culture in which we have determined seven social
groupings is more complex than one in which we find six groupings?
(Goldstein 1981:56)

In short, no – not if groupings are based on energy. This correlate is not concerned
with the context or social basis of ranking, but this means only that it is incomplete
(Tainter 1977:332), something true of any single correlate (and, as contextual
archaeology makes clear, something true of middle range theory in general). Energy
expenditure is a good generalized starting place, helping to narrow the range of
societal forms our burial data could represent, and offering a rough idea of the degree
of social complexity.

Inferences based on general principles of the society

While the archaeological study of inequality generally depends on patterned
variation *within* a burial set, mortuary practice also differs from one society to
another. There is more reason to attribute these differences between societies to
beliefs concerning death, making social inference more difficult. Yet, the study of
variation between societies may not only be useful for inferring inequality, it may
even disclose something of what status means to a people. I wish particularly to
consider what we might learn from the general level of emphasis on mortuary
practice, asking why some people make so much more of burial than others. This path
has not yet led to reliable specific results, but I believe these ideas offer great
potential.

Some people have a more elaborate mortuary program than others. Brown relates
this to resource availability and the widening of authority which "entails an increase
in the field of allegiance that leads to greater effort and wealth being applied to the
funeral and the burial" (1981:28). When ritual is elaborate, this is likely to be a
reason, but it is not a sufficient cause, for interest in mortuary ritual is not always
proportional to the breadth of authority, or to the size or prosperity of the society.
Among twentieth-century Americans, rich though we are in comparative terms,
there is little tendency toward elaborate burials. If there are major status differences,
they will certainly be marked somehow, but not necessarily through elaborate
mortuary ritual, which helps refine the question: why would some people go to such
lengths to express status in mortuary practice while others do not?

Several explanations of the importance of mortuary ritual are based on the
significance of ancestors. Sanders relates the change in mortuary ritual at
Kaminaljuyu to religious ideology. There was here a heavy focus on a funeral cult
"with the implications that the ancestral spirits or chiefs themselves were their main
objects of worship rather than high gods" (1974:110). In the following periods,
funeral ritual is further elaborated, and included some very grand burials. But this
was followed by a de-emphasis of the funerary cult and a shift to a different kind of
religious system. These changes likely signal social changes, perhaps a growth in the
importance of ritual followed by a decrease in concern for commemorating ancestors,

or a period of instability followed by a more stable status system, as through the consolidation of power. Sanders sees the second period of change as the move from chiefdom to state – in other words, both of the above social changes. Alternate possibilities to a general rule include declining prosperity or increasing mortality (from famine or plague), making it harder to put great effort into each high-status burial (see Firth 1970:388 and 1959:88 for an example of the latter). These alternatives could easily be detected, however, and it is likely that the changing emphasis on mortuary ritual at Kaminaljuyu signals major changes in either religious ideology or the status system, or both.

Contrasting the Berewan and the Kenyah of Borneo, Huntington and Metcalf (1979) suggest the kind of status systems associated with elaborate mortuary ritual. The Berewan have important ranked statuses, with both ranking and associated leadership roles largely achieved in the classic big-man style. Berewan mortuary ritual consists of either a simple ceremony or the complex *nulang* which traditionally involves secondary burial, feasting, and construction of an elaborate mausoleum (Metcalf 1981:573). The choice does not denote qualitatively different pre-defined ranks, but reflects ability to mobilize resources. Only those of high status command the support for the *nulang* ceremony and mausoleum, and since ritual choice does not affect afterlife, the difference is based on complex considerations of prestige. Another point, helpful in clarifying motives, is that a person of high rank will host a *nulang* for another person's burial, and will receive much of the tangible benefit.

Rank among the Kenyah is more clearly ascribed, and they do not practice anything like this elaborate mortuary ritual. In particular, they do not build mausoleums, the most visible and lasting part of Berewan practice. The observation that these two social features covary is the key to this analysis. Rites marking a lifecycle phase vary in importance for societies with different rank systems. Among the Berewan, status is not clear until one has had a chance to achieve, hence the stress on ceremonies at later stages of life. For the Kenyah, status is largely determined at birth and ceremonies which publicly demonstrate a person's rank very early are prominent (e.g. name-giving ceremonies [Huntington and Metcalf 1979:139–140]). Among the Berewan there is also a greater need for visible permanent markers of prestige, not just for different markers.

> The Berewan have no naming ceremonies comparable to the Kenyah ones. They do appreciate the status implications of grand weddings. But when all the rice wine has been drunk, and the guests have shakily made their way home, what is there to keep a wedding in mind, to preserve it against the envious denigrations of rivals? The Berewan require something more concrete and it is mortuary rites that provide it. Mausoleums are always built on the riverbank so that passersby can admire them and wonder at the power of their architects.
> (Huntington and Metcalf 1979:140)

It may be that people whose status is achieved will emphasize mortuary ritual, especially the visible and lasting aspects, more so than when status is significantly ascribed. Rank might be displayed in other ways too, but burials have the advantage of taking place at a time when one's rank is clear. Among the Berewan one's status is not obvious each time one's name is heard (as among the Kenyah) but it is just as important that others be aware of it. One who hosts a great ceremony and builds a mausoleum for a relative is indeed a person of note – both for doing this and for being a relative of one so buried. When status is not inherent, it must be advertised clearly. Visible monuments and major ceremonies serve this purpose well, and may at the same time advertise – even help to establish – the status of the hosts. But before accepting this conclusion even as a general tendency, several other studies must be considered which help clarify the relationship.

Randsborg (1981, 1982) found a relationship among burials, runestones, and leadership during the Viking Age of Denmark (ca AD 800–1000) and offers an interpretation which is the more convincing as it explains the relative change in each feature for several time periods. Consider the time of the rise of the state in Denmark. Naturally, this was a season of major social change, the most pertinent being absorption of formerly semi-autonomous areas by an expanding central control. From the perspective of the conquered areas, local leadership was replaced by another hierarchy. While the rank of Danish kings was defined largely by heredity, conquering kings would not enjoy the same legitimacy as ousted local leaders, and we might expect the new hierarchy to exhibit some of the character of achieved leadership. From the discussion so far, we might expect burial practice to become elaborated in areas where normal succession was broken. However, the record reveals little change from the previous 400 years; apart from specific exceptions, burials were not very elaborate (Randsborg 1981:112).

But I think we are still on the right track, for burials were not the only enduring markers. Runestones bearing memorials and inscriptions were also common (Randsborg 1981:106). Most follow a formula "X raised this stone after Y"; thus King Harold had one raised for his parents, honoring them, as well as making it clear that he is their heir. Other rights are also marked in this way. Connecting runestones with the need to mark succession visibly makes sense because the period of their use corresponds with a time of social change, particularly the disruption of local successions.

> The traditional societies of the early and late Iron Age did not erect runestones over the dead, although the alphabet already existed in AD 200. Seemingly the rules of inheritance of position and property rested firmly within the precepts of the local communities and no monument was needed to underline the rights of the local potentates. The social transformation of the Viking Age included not only conflicts and the dissolution of traditional societies, but also the coming of new types of settlements and more personal types of rights. All of this would call for a special means of communicating the takeover of, for example, a village by a new social group. The moment this family was firmly established, the situation was brought back to normal and no further monument was needed.
> (Randsborg 1981:108)

This is evident in material from the ninth through the eleventh centuries. The chronology of runestones compared with their distribution reveals a patterned association with areas of great social instability. These were primarily the "conflict zones" of the developing polity which changed location over time. The Viking Age confirms that memorials to the dead are deemed important when status cannot be taken for granted, but at the same time questions the simple association between emphasis on mortuary ritual and achieved status. Status was ascribed among the Vikings (often the major claim made on runestones) but in common with the Berewan it was a claim that could not stand without reinforcement, at least in areas where they attained their position by conquest. As Parker Pearson observes: "Social advertisement in death ritual may be expressly overt where changing relations of domination result in status re-ordering and consolidation of new social positions" (1982:112).

These "changing relations of domination" may take other forms than conquest. From a study of mounded tomb development in China, Northern Korea, and Japan in the third to seventh centuries AD, Okaguchi found a roughly similar pattern in all three areas. Following an era of elaboration in which mounds became much larger, more complex, and far more numerous, use of mounded tombs declined dramatically. This coincided with political consolidation (Okaguchi 1986:136, 145–146), a point also observed by Pearson *et al.* for the Old Silla Kingdom of Korea (1989:38). The expansion of mound building was related to mounds becoming more widely affordable. For Japan, at least, it is known that many of the smaller mounds belonged to people with minor local administrative roles and who "gained the privilege of mound burial by virtue of their association with [the Yamato central] government" (Okaguchi 1986:145). This may have involved an expansion of the number of those who were of high status by virtue of being administrators – or, perhaps, an elevation in the status of existing officials. It may be that as lower ranks imitated elite practice, competitive pressures drove the trend toward more lavish practice (a process Bradley [1990:39] outlines for another context). The growth of administrators and elaborate display are both facets of instability in the status system. In Japan a dramatic decline in the practice during the seventh century can be related to political consolidation – and possibly an actual prohibition (the Taika Burial Law [Okaguchi 1986:146]), but theoretically such a trend could mean instead that competition had moved to another arena rather than actually diminishing. In some cases it may not be competition so much as establishing a "socially-visible hierarchy" which, as Rupp points out, requires more support than does its subsequent maintenance (1988:132–133).

Finally, this relationship can be expressed in changing symbolism, not just grandness of display. In areas of the Near East, symbolic artifacts which seek to link copper production to religion and the sacred are concentrated in burials from around 1200 BC, a time of crisis for Late Bronze Age palace-centered organizations and of possible political subjugation by the Hittites. Those items were not being cast and preserved during the prosperous period of about 1700–1200 when the copper industry was important (Zaccagnini 1990:495–496). Perhaps their inclusion in burials was meant to reinforce the connection of elite individuals to the industry precisely when, after 400 years of a real connection, it was now being seriously called into question.

Together, these ideas improve our insight into the social situation of each configuration. If a rank system is changing or if it is stable but of a sort where one's rank must be achieved or proven to others, there will be a greater need for visible demonstration. This may take any of a number of forms, but one likely course is toward elaborate funerary display. As Huntington and Metcalf note, something permanently visible might be particularly useful.

Alternative factors affecting overall emphasis

I have argued for a relation between the emphasis placed on mortuary ritual, and the type of status being recognized. Alternatively, differences in the degree of mortuary elaboration may relate to the extent rather than character of status distinctions. Elaboration may result from some individuals having statuses very much higher than the rest, as McGuire (1983) argues for the changing burial patterns among Egyptian Pharoahs. When the most elaborate burials are not nearly so grand, it seems legitimate to conclude that the range of ranked status variation was not as great. There is also an operational problem; to be useful this correlate must be more carefully defined in terms of what constitutes a degree of elaboration sufficient to claim achieved or unstable ranking as opposed to stable, culturally-accepted ascription. Among the Plains Indian societies studied by O'Shea (1981) there were small differences in degree of mortuary elaboration. But no burial could be described as very elaborate, and the differences tend to go against this basic correlate. Among the Arikara, for whom rank was largely achieved, burial practice was less elaborate than among either the Pawnee or Omaha, both much more hereditary in ranking. Small differences at least, do not always correlate with these ideas on status determination. Perhaps the elaboration must be above a certain degree for the relationship to work. In any case, it is reasonable to anticipate some difficulty in operationalizing this correlate. These problems make it difficult to use overall elaboration as a criterion by itself for reliable inference of the nature of ranking in a society. Yet in conjunction with other features of the mortuary program, I believe it can be put to good use even in its present state. The following propositions summarize the social features influencing how much effort people think it appropriate to expend upon burials.

1. If the ranking system had a strong hereditary basis and mortuary ritual was not greatly elaborated:
   a. Probably the ranking system is well established and stable. Also, both the basis for determining rank, and the privileges and duties claimed, are widely accepted as appropriate for that rank.
   b. One will also find that either rank differences are not very great or are strongly based in religion rather than wealth or the ability to use force.
2. If the rank system had a strong hereditary basis, and mortuary ritual was very elaborate:
   a. If the elaboration related mostly to religious matters (e.g. burial in a temple mound) or consisted of status markers, it is possible that the elaboration is in

good part related to the statuses being very important in a system which had a great range of status variation.

   b. If elaboration is the sort to warrant calling the burials "wealthy" or has a military element, it is likely that, while hereditary rank may be the ideal, another factor is involved, possibly: 1. hereditary claims are ambiguous; 2. stratification is present, or some other privilege is claimed by those of high rank but is not widely accepted as a privilege of rank; 3. actual leadership was partly based on conquest or holding a right to force, requiring an emphasis on other factors (heredity) as legitimizing claims to authority. Other factors are possible, nor are those listed incompatible with each other. For example, in (1) a reason for hereditary claims being ambiguous might be conquest (3) as was the case in the development of the Viking state.

3. If ranking appears to have little hereditary basis, and mortuary ritual is not greatly elaborated:
   a. Actual rank differences may not be great and/or
   b. High status is achieved by some means other than ability to mobilize economic resources – and may not have that ability as one of its privileges.

4. If ranking does not seem to have a hereditary basis, and mortuary practices are elaborate:
   This would probably indicate status rivalry where people are competing for highest status, and funeral display is an important arena for competitive display.

5. If it is not clear from other evidence whether rank is hereditary, and mortuary practice is not elaborate:
   a. If some individuals are nonetheless marked off as having important statuses, as by separation, association with symbols of rank or with evidence of important society-wide religious practices, it is probable that there was a component of hereditary, stable, ranked status of the sort widely acceptable as cultural givens.
   b. If these factors are not evident, either ranking was not significant, or ranking was significant (achieved or hereditary) but burial display was not thought appropriate.

6. If it is not clear from other evidence whether rank was hereditary and mortuary practice is very elaborate:
   a. If the elaboration is such that one can describe the burials as "rich" and/or (but especially and) there are indications that high rank has a military element, it is likely that rank is strongly based on achievement. The system is based on achievement or is in a state of flux, either in terms of how rank is determined or of the privileges and duties which go along with it.
   b. Elaboration mainly related to symbols of rank or religion is more ambiguous: It may indicate a need to reinforce one's claim to rank, or it may be the result of honoring a stable but highly respected rank.

These propositions may be a step toward archaeological correlates of inequality which distinguish achievement from ascription, but at present they are some way from being operationalized for use as correlates, a problem which is not unexpected considering the idea began as an attempt to isolate relative "tendencies." These propositions are long, complex, full of qualifiers, and generally not as productive as I had hoped for this line of inference. More thought must be given to sorting out the social factors influencing a people's approach to mortuary activity in general.

Yet (to end on a somewhat more positive note) these ideas are much closer to usefulness as correlates when applied to the same people as their social organization changes over time. It may be possible to trace changes in other aspects of rank (e.g. whether a military element to status grows in importance) along with a change toward greater (or lesser) elaboration of mortuary ritual. At the same time problems of operationalization are much reduced because rather than having to generalize about what is truly "elaborate" it is quite reasonable to assume that an increase in elaboration is the significant point, quite apart from an absolute "level" of emphasis on mortuary expression of social values.

5

Mortuary data as evidence of ranking, Part 2

Undoubtedly many particulars of personal status are embodied in any set of burial remains. It is likely also that many seemingly trifling details have been manipulated to carry important meaning. It may be inevitable that much of what a burial would have communicated to culturally-aware contemporaries will be lost on the rest of us, yet it is also true that much can be learned from a study of how individual burials differ. Any attribute which can be varied – size of tomb, position of the body, number of large golden statues – can be used to mark differences in status, and so can be a source of information on a former status system. In the following sections six dimensions of mortuary variability are examined for potential cross-cultural correlation with status.

Variation in tomb form

From an ethnographic study of what mortuary variables people use to mark dimensions of the person, Binford (1971:21) found that differentiation in grave form might indicate at one time or another condition of death, age, social affiliation, and social position. Among those peoples he studied, tomb form was never used to mark either location of death or sex, and was used most often to mark status, broadly confirming the relationship of size and elaborateness (or energy expenditure) with personal status. I also found (in a small additional sample) that different grave types do not always mark either statuses or social groups. Corpse disposal among the Arawak could mean burning a building housing the body, burial in a grave, or burial in a cave (Rouse 1948). Among the Nootka, bodies might be placed in trees, caves, or on the ground covered with rocks (Sapir 1921; Koppert 1930:106). Yet in neither case is the choice based on rank, despite the fact that both societies were hierarchical, and burials differed in both location and type of facility.

Yet there will often be ways of eliminating alternative explanations. For example, the portion of the population buried in each grave type may reinforce an inference of rank, indicate conspicuous gender inequality, or mark important non-ranked social groups. If about half the population was interred in each of two types, this would not likely represent limited positions of prestige (ranks) but the practice of marking sex or perhaps descent groups in a moiety system, alternatives easily distinguished if sufficient skeletal material is preserved. The different tomb forms might also reveal something about inequality between the sexes or descent groups while correlation of grave type with other variables would offer further insight. Finding that grave type largely covaries with quantity of inclusions may highlight qualitative variation when clear discontinuities are not apparent in number of inclusions, or it might clarify the nature of statuses distinguished by grave type.

Yet the particular ways in which burial facilities differ sometimes make it clear that they distinguish among ranks. Burials might, for example, be associated with elaborate, even monumental construction. Steward and Faron (1959) note that among peoples of the North Columbian Lowlands, some facilities included deep stone-lined shafts reached by stone stairways, while in districts of contact-period Hawaii, chiefs were placed in mausoleums (Tuggle 1979:180). In both cases mounds were also part of chiefly graves, a not uncommon elaboration of high-status burial.[1]

Naturally, learning that a mound was used for burial purposes does not itself demonstrate inequality. Important questions include whether it was built to final form all at once, and how many burials it contains. On Tonga chiefs were buried in large faced mounds, but those of lower status were also buried in what eventually became mounds, structures comprised of many layers and many burials (Davidson 1979:102). Layering may be ambiguous, but related features could aid interpretation, including number of burials (assuming they were not sacrifices), grave associations, and comparative lack of distinctive features, like facings. Some burial mounds served also as temples in which case it is probable that not all the construction effort was expended in honor of the one interred. At one extreme a burial might be a sacrifice in honor of the temple's dedication, while at the other, inclusions and positioning could suggest the structure was built "around" or "for the purpose of housing" the burial. But while a sacrificial victim might not be a high-ranking member of society, the practice of sacrifice, like that of building the temple itself, may nevertheless (see chapter 7) indicate great social differentiation.

If the most elaborate burials known are those associated with religious structures, we can infer that high status and leadership were closely tied to the religious system. Indeed it has been argued that those given elaborate burial in religious structures bore the high-status and specialist role of "priest." This term may be too specific in describing how leaders are connected with religion – they may be gods or their descendants rather than human mediators – but leaders in many societies have been of great religious import and have been buried in or near temples, as among the Hawaiians (Tuggle 1979:180), Tikopia (Firth 1970), Tongans (Davidson 1979:102), Tahitians (Oliver 1974:101, 507–509, 960), and Natchez (Swanton 1911). Among the Shilluk, shrines are built over a burial to aid worship of a departed *reth* (Howell and Thomson 1946:23–24), and among the Easter Islanders, chiefs were buried in religious structures, although so were many others (Metraux 1940:116). It is clear that the person thus treated bore a high status shared with few others – ranking was present. The importance of the religious dimension of the status (whether personal sacredness or ritual leadership) is also clear.

Among the Nootka (Koppert 1930:106, Drucker 1951:147–149) and Tlingit (Emmons 1916:13, Jones 1914:119), chiefly burial lacked religious association, but compared to the examples above, the status of Nootkan and Tlingit chiefs also had much less of a religious basis. Thus they also support the correlation, although of course, it would not be safe to conclude in general that when high-status burials lack religious associations, religion was unimportant to the status. Burials associated with temples, and additional elaborate burials lacking religious association, would argue for a distinction between priest and leader, or at least between priests and others of high rank.

The use of collective burial

Recent mortuary research has emphasized individual burial, and not all of its developing theory can be applied directly to collective burial. Yet the distinction itself raises interesting questions. What might collective burial say about a society as opposed to one for which individual inhumation was the norm? And what might documented sequences showing a change over time from collective to individual burial indicate about the developing social organization?

For purposes of status inference, communal burials are most distinct in that they do not represent the physical remains of one mortuary ritual, but the cumulative remains of several (Chapman 1981:398). Although these events are not easily untangled, a tomb's internal organization may reveal some correlation of inclusions with individuals, while relative positioning may suggest differentiation. Unfortunately, there are plausible alternative explanations for a number of configurations. If older burials were pushed aside, any association with artifacts would be unreliable, and if valuable objects from earlier periods have been removed (Keswani 1989:52), an individual apparently enjoying a prominent place in the tomb may simply be the most recently interred.

We must also distinguish communal from special-circumstance multiple burials. Knapp (1988:140–141), for example, associates three Middle Cypriot mass burials with warfare. He does not elaborate, but signs of physical violence, military equipment, chaotic placement, and indications that all were interred at the same time (e.g. no evidence of re-opening) come to mind as plausible ways of distinguishing a mass grave from a communal tomb. Tombs housing collective burials may also be of a different basic structure due to the need for re-opening, and may incorporate a chamber that is not filled in while the tomb remains in use. Multiple burial in which sacrificial victims accompany an honored individual is a not uncommon practice in the ethnographic record of hierarchical societies.[2] It may be that the honored burial will display other elaborate traits, helping us to distinguish this pattern from true collective burials. One other practice that would result in the burial of many individuals in one facility is that of sacrifices unrelated to a single honored individual, perhaps as part of a dedication ceremony.

When communal burial is practiced, contemporaneous burial groups will represent social groupings of considerable importance, most likely kin groups (although cross-cutting associations might also be so marked). Among the few examples I found of the practice of collective burial, groupings were always "family" based, either extended family or lineage. This was true for Easter Island (Metraux 1940:116) and for the Tlingit. Tlingit dead-houses would be problematic archaeologically, since they held cremation ashes (Krause 1956:91), but it is significant that they were family based. The Arawak collected heads in baskets which they kept in dwellings (Rouse 1948:532). The groupings were family based, and while not exactly collective burial, bespeak the same relationship. Among modern Western societies individual inhumation is common but collective burial in large vaults is also known. These almost invariably represent families.

Most correlates designed for the study of individual burial can be applied if we use the tomb as the unit of study rather than the individual. Indeed the fact of collective burial itself might suggest that status is not graded on a purely individual basis, but that social groups (such as lineages) are ranked. The ability to relate status to groups may sometimes be an advantage. In a study of Enkomi (late Bronze Age Cyprus), Keswani found that inclusion of Mycenaean pictorial craters correlated with other indicators of the higher statuses. Two tombs (known as Swedish Tomb 3 and British Tomb 12) yielded examples from several periods, suggesting that "two or three such craters were being deposited every generation" (Keswani 1989:65). Of course on this information alone it remains plausible that they were all deposited in one grand burial at the end of the time span, some of the craters having previously been kept as heirlooms. But if the craters were included with several burials over a long period, Keswani's conclusion is striking.

> The disproportionately large number of pictorial craters in these tombs reflects the repeated use of similar symbols from one generation to the next, redundancies which in turn suggest a close connection between status and descent group, or at least tomb group, affiliation.
> (Keswani 1989:65)

Assuming tomb group affiliation was kin based, this is evidence that high status was hereditary (Keswani 1989:69). The importance of heredity (or at least social group affiliation) in determining status is already suggested by the fact of collective burial, but high status and leadership positions might still be achieved (with one's new status influencing that of the whole kin group). Thus evidence that status was maintained and marked in the same way over several generations is of great significance.

Change over time from individual to communal burial (or the reverse) is an important clue to the character of the status system for each period. A de-emphasis on collective burial indicates decreasing need to mark groups and reinforce membership claims, which may mean a decline in the importance of the association, perhaps a decreasing emphasis on descent as a determinant of status (Keswani 1989:70). This particular trend is well documented for parts of Europe, and based on a correlation with other lines of evidence, Gilman argues that "the very passage from collective to 'individualizing' burial rituals, a change occurring at the start of the Bronze Age over much of Europe, suggests the development of social stratification" (1981:1). The reasoning is that this qualitative change in burial practice represents an increasing emphasis on the individual. Renfrew also made use of the distinction between collective and individual burials as one of the features distinguishing his individualizing and group-oriented chiefdoms (1974:74). He found that communal burial and/ or burials with minimal wealth inclusions correlated with other evidence of an emphasis on group purposes, while elaborate individual burials correlated with factors emphasizing personal status. This is plausible for changes over time, but the relationship is not readily generalized to all societies with elaborate individual burial. Individual burial seems the most common form worldwide and is found among peoples with no apparent social stratification, and no emphasis on wealth. Also, collective burial may be an alternative practiced along with individual inhumation, something true of *all* examples mentioned earlier (Easter Island, Tlingit, modern Western cultures).

In a semi-popular piece meant to introduce the concept of material culture as text, Thomas observes that the widespread trend in Europe from megalithic tombs to individual graves in the later Neolithic was at one time interpreted as a consequence of invasion and population movement. The explanations I have just recounted (centering on the rise of prominent individuals) are then presented as the more recent view, but he then offers his own textual explanation as a third alternative.

> In contrast, I should like to suggest that this period saw the emergence of a signifying practice which concentrated less upon monuments, and more upon the human body itself . . . With megalithic tombs we can argue that the monument was the dominant element within the symbolic order . . . By contrast, the situation was now one in which the body itself had become the "text" to be read, and the funeral was a performance in which a certain reading of that body had to be produced.
> (Thomas 1991:11)

The items used in individual burials and their arrangement, become relatively standardized. They do not give a full picture of a person; the assemblage apparently "existed not to reflect the individual's identity in life, but to construct a highly formalized and impoverished kind of identity in death" (Thomas 1991:11). The assemblage was meant to make a statement, to represent rather than reflect the social context, and based on his introductory comments, Thomas may be interpreting this practice as the dominant group representing (misrepresenting?) or legitimating their own position.

While this is both a plausible and a productive way of looking at the evidence, it does not counter the conclusions of cross-culturally applied middle range theory. Quite the contrary, by drawing attention to the contrast between a focus on the monument (with its connotations) and the later focus on the body, it adds strength (and depth) to these inferences, for the obvious question raised by Thomas's analysis is *why* the great shift to emphasis on the body? It may be a change to an emphasis on the person as an individual rather than as a descent-group member.

Much the same can be said for another interpretive model for the move from communal to individual burial, that of Ian Hodder (1990b). He states that individual burials in large tombs "cannot be read as a simple expression of hierarchy," for they are likely "concerned either to represent the group through the individual or to play on a structural tension between individual and society (the latter represented by the collective construction of the tomb)" (1990b:309). It is possible, even likely, that such concerns are expressed in the practice of burying people in tombs that require a collective construction effort. But this too confirms the view that personal status has grown more important, since inequality is one very good reason for a tension between the significance of the individual and that of the group. Further, if those performing the burials are representing themselves as a group through the "honored" individuals, there should be a reason these relatively few people are considered representative of (and adequate symbolic substitutes for) the whole. This would better describe a leader than someone whose status was largely economic, but Hodder's interpretation of the move from communal to individual burial is not in opposition to the inference of hierarchy. He continues:

> The individual burials under round barrows in the late Neolithic may well look "richer," with more individual variation, but the change may be only apparent, caused by transformations in the domus–agrios structure. The earlier domus concerns with linear sequence, with body boundaries and the transformation of the flesh, with the durability of dry bones, and with the constraint of the individual within domus structures are replaced by an agrios emphasis on the individual. This social and conceptual change does not necessarily imply a greater or lesser degree of social ranking in the late Neolithic.
> (Hodder 1990b:309)[3]

I agree. But we can infer ranking from other features[4] (e.g. energy expended on tomb, grave associations) so the question is not so much whether the new individual burials show ranking because of being individual, but whether the change from collective burial indicates a change in the *nature* of ranking. The correlation of communal burial with specific social features is not clear-cut, but I believe there is some validity to these propositions:

1. Communal burial indicates that an important aspect of status in death (and significance for the living) is being part of a social group, probably with unambiguous kin-based membership.

2. Individual burial indicates either that group membership is not as important a part of status in death, or that it is important but not marked by the practice of communal burial.

3. A change from communal to individual burial may mean a change in how social group membership is affirmed, a social change reducing the importance of marking this aspect of status, or both. Since few other ways of marking social-group affiliation at burial are as clear as group burial, and since this is a major qualitative change, it would not likely take place without a change in the importance of group divisions relative to other aspects of status. It may mean a growing assertion of the individual, particularly certain individuals, over the group. The status system may be moving toward greater emphasis on personal achievement, toward social stratification, or both.

Variation in the quantity of grave associations

This dimension of burial practice is often used to infer inequality. But while it is important to single out, since one of my goals is to construct an overall outline of variables that may be the source of correlates, it is closely related to the energy-expenditure criterion discussed earlier. Also, while status differences can be inferred from major variation in quantity of grave inclusions, it is interesting that among ethnographic examples consulted (all of which were hierarchical), inclusion of a great number of items with burials is not common even for the very highest statuses.[5]

The inferential value of an overall count of items in different burials will depend on the range of variation and on the complexity of the assemblage. In many cases, counts of items of a given type will be at least as useful. In a study of the Predynastic cemeteries of Naqada on the Nile, Bard (1989) used four variables (and cluster analysis techniques) to determine patterns of differentiation, all of which concerned quantity – total number of undecorated pots, decorated pots, hard-stone vessels, and soft-stone vessels respectively. A simple quantity comparison would have been less useful for at least two reasons. First, slate palettes and beads were also common (Bard 1989:228) but would weight the overall count, reducing differences in vessel quantities to insignificance. In addition a study of the clusters resulting from the different variables made it possible to confirm additional substantive associations. Sir Flinders Petrie, who excavated the cemeteries in the 1890s, singled out wavy handle ware which, it has since been confirmed, evolved as a local emulation of the ledge handle jar used to import goods from Palestine. These were found in graves of high-status clusters, confirming their status-related significance (Bard 1989:240–241). The clustering also correlated with location – again suspected on other grounds – reinforcing, for example, the conclusion that the "T" cemetery was for very exclusive high-status use. Finally, the clusters did not reveal a simple pattern, suggesting perhaps personal ranking rather than a small number of clearly formed "levels," significant in light of the Naqada cemeteries being in use during the time the Egyptian Early Dynastic State was forming. The core of Bard's analysis is an assessment of relative quantities of artifacts, but the sophisticated data handling and correlation of results with other variables helped produce more significant conclusions than one might at first expect from a study of quantity.

Inferences based on the type of goods included

Variation among artifacts placed in a burial is one of the most important sources of social inference. Depending on the nature of the evidence, any of the following variables might be considered:

*Differences in type of artifact as an object (e.g. knives versus bowls, or bowls of different types).
*Differences in quality of workmanship among examples of the same type of object.
*Differences in raw materials among specific objects or between burial lots (a gold versus a pottery cup or a grave with, versus one without, gold items).

*Differences in source of materials, especially whether or not of local origin.
*Differences based on the inclusion of utilitarian or non-utilitarian artifacts, or
    proportions of each.
*Sacrificial victims accompanying an honored burial.

Once burials are sorted chronologically, we can assume the remaining variation in grave inclusions marks differences in status. In a review of ethnographic examples, Binford found that form of grave goods was regularly used for gender distinctions, and less commonly to mark social position. Variations in quantity were only used to mark social position, so, not unexpectedly, social position was the only aspect of social persona distinguished by both form and quantity (1971:22). A good way to begin an analysis then, is by checking for correlations between each artifact type and sex or age. Variation that does not correlate with either can potentially be related to some other social variable by means of any of several lines of inference. To gain further insight into the status system, King (1978:228) suggests distinguishing between utilitarian and non-utilitarian artifacts. Variation among burials in quantity of utilitarian items may be used to differentiate statuses, something we can infer most reliably if differences are great. Variation in type of utilitarian items might also mark ranked status. While this may more often mark gender or activity-related statuses (as with the inclusion of tools for specialized occupations) whether ranked or not, O'Shea found (1981:41–49) that among the Omaha, Pawnee, and Arikara, utilitarian artifacts vary with rank. The potential of this burial feature for the inference of rank will naturally depend somewhat on the artifacts involved and correlation with other variables, but apart from that sort of "context," it is somewhat tentative because of the likelihood of the alternative cause.

Variation and distribution among burials of non-utilitarian items offers greater potential for the inference of social hierarchy. An artifact might be recognized as ornamentation (hence non-utilitarian) but a wide distribution suggests most people wore it, in which case it would not mark status (Hole 1968:257), while if it were associated with one sex it would be a marker of status but not necessarily therefore of rank. It is differential distribution not just presence of non-utilitarian artifacts that is most helpful, something true of nearly every ethnographic example studied, so it also appears to be a common way of expressing status.[6] Even people who include minimal quantities generally differentiate *what* they place in different graves.

In some cases, the material used may be more important than type of artifact per se. For example, there is reason to believe that as iron replaced bronze in Central Greece around 1025 BC it was not just of superior practical advantage but was controlled by the elite, symbolizing status and the new order they were creating.

> By controlling iron and making it the only metal appropriate for grave goods
> in formal burial, the symbol of membership of the elite, the leaders of Greek
> communities could solidify their powers, creating a ritual gap between
> themselves and those excluded from iron and the formal cemetery.
> (Morris 1989:507)

The fact that at this time bronze went into disuse as a burial inclusion might not imply developing scarcity, but decline in elite ability to control it so that it could no longer function as a status marker. People continued placing the same *kinds* of items in graves – weapons and jewelry – but it is clear that there was a change in the meaning attributed to different materials. In this example, the change over time alerts us to the significance of the material, and comparing type of artifacts over time would presumably do the same. And as Okauchi's study of the mounded tombs of Japan shows, it may also provide clues to the changing character of the statuses so marked. Burial inclusions changed during the late fourth and early fifth centuries AD from an emphasis on ritual to practical and military-related objects (Okauchi 1986:145) – just when the Yamato government was reaching its peak of military and political dominance.

To infer ranking from burial inclusions it is not necessary to show that an object, or class of artifacts is used as a symbol of rank in general, since distribution can make a strong case for an item as a marker of rank or authority in any particular case. While an artifact found in just one burial may well represent a special, unique status, it may instead be just an exceptional piece of work. And if common it must have been widely available. But if found in just a few contexts it is likely an item subject to restricted access, in which case those with whom it was buried enjoyed some form of restricted status (Wright 1978:213). There is no way of restricting access to an item without presupposing a distinction among people as the basis for deciding who has access and who does not. Of course, this need not be a ranked distinction, so while useful for uncovering social distinctions among people, this is not sufficient to infer inequality apart from additional details of context or parallel lines of evidence.

At the Etowa site, Larson found that a number of attributes clustered together in a few of the burials. From the nature of the artifacts and the fact that one attribute is location in the mound, he believes the attribute cluster marks high status.

> all of the individuals included in the group of final mantle burials appear to have been wearing what almost amounts to a uniform. The differences in particular costume and paraphernalia would perhaps seem attributable more to differences in rank rather than differences in personal taste. The same type of headdress, axe, ear ornament, for example, appear with monotonous regularity.
> (1971:67)

The conclusion that any one of the burial features marked status is strengthened by their regular co-occurrence. In most ethnographic cases where type of artifact is used to mark ranks, status is also marked by other means (burial in mounds among the Tongans and Natchez, for example). The consistency of the association may relate to the distinctiveness of the rank being marked, or perhaps the degree to which the markers were meant as status symbols. Taken together these markers offer a fuller picture of status, and once we establish that they are symbols of high status, any smaller differences among burials possessing most of the attributes can be taken to represent rank distinctions, a conclusion otherwise much more speculative.

When there is great consistency in how those of high rank are distinguished, it is not so much the individual as the status, rank or office that is being celebrated. Those carrying out the ritual view the deceased (and intend that he or she be remembered) as an example of a certain status. This may be a way of distinguishing office-holding chiefs from self-made big men who do not succeed to existing offices but create for themselves a status which otherwise in many ways resembles that of a chief. It also suggests an interesting approach to interpreting the much-publicized Easter Island statues. Many of the statues are associated with structures that served as burial places in addition to (or as part of) their important religious functions. They all have much in common, and while something must be said for stylistic preference, it may be that this emphasis on similarity was desired because the statues were not simply portraits of individual chiefs. Each may indeed represent an individual but emphasizes not his uniqueness so much as his identity as a representative of office, or taken together, as representatives of an hereditary line.

But this is something of a relative measure, both from the perspective of ranking (the rank is always important even if the person achieved it) and from the perspective of the burial itself (burials are unlikely to be identical no matter what the regard for fitting into a mold). Even when a burial sample fits a pattern broadly, there may be less consistency in the details. Among the Cuna (Steward and Faron 1959:225) chiefly burials differ consistently from the rest, but at a more detailed level they reveal some of the underlying competition which also characterized chiefly affairs (despite chiefs holding stable, well-defined ranks). Thus all chiefs were buried with human sacrifices, but records suggest the actual number was by no means set (Steward and Faron 1959:225). The exact nature and amount of ornamentation also varied, although again within consistent guidelines (e.g. always items of gold with chiefly symbols marking them). This variation within a pattern does not detract from the major distinction between chiefs and others, nor from the fundamental consistency with which chiefly status was marked, but it does indicate that chiefs were negotiating their status, however firmly it was held.

Another way grave inclusions vary is by source of materials. While items made from exotic materials may just be luxuries or "primitive valuables," they may well be status markers, for often they are not things which just anyone can have, given enough yams to trade. It is valuable, methodologically, that we can know a material is exotic apart from assumptions about cultural attitudes toward the items, yet it is really only from the distribution of exotics that we can infer status inequality. Comparing Etowah with other Southeastern sites, Larson (1971:66) notes that in some cases exotic materials were distributed among otherwise "subordinate" burials, while at Etowah they were heavily concentrated in just a few burials. Only here is centricity in regional exchange indicated. Central economic control presupposes status hierarchy, whereas neither a regional exchange system nor the presence of exotics in themselves requires inequality. Among the ethnographic examples I studied, those of high status (or just chiefs) did receive a very large portion of exotic items. When scarce, chiefs may get them all.[7] This pattern holds for practical items (as with metal tools obtained by the Tikopia), status items, or items obtained through greater wealth (as among the people of Hasanabad).

Symbolic items may be widely distributed, as with the Chavin style of the Andean "Early Horizon" and markers of the Southern Cult of the US Southeast. Concerning the Southern Cult, distribution and context indicate that whatever else it may have been, its symbols were used as elite status markers. Peebles (1971:69) notes that when we are fortunate enough to have these "supra-local" symbols, we can use their association with local symbols to determine what status distinctions the latter represent. That people sometimes use symbols without also adopting the social realities (originally) symbolized does add a note of caution, but if patterns of association remain consistent (of symbols with each other, and with other features such as religious structures) we may infer at least a general similarity in meaning and purpose.

If a kind of artifact is found only among burials – not in the settlement or middens – this will strengthen the conclusion that it is a status marker. Some items function partly as symbols along with more mundane purposes while others serve as status symbols only, a distinction we might determine by context: "items that functioned *exclusively* as symbols of offices should be recovered archaeologically only in contexts associated with their manufacture or with their ritually sanctioned disposal" (Braun 1979:67). Such items may be kept in one's house, may accompany a person in death, or if the status had religious import, may be deposited in a sacred context regardless of where the body is put. Of course it does not follow that items found only in these contexts can automatically be taken as symbols of status, but this distribution is reason for believing they were special in some sense. Among the Arawak personal ornaments and status symbols (stools and gold pieces mainly) were buried with high-status people (Rouse 1948:532). They were also inherited (p. 526), usually upon marriage. I have found no other discussion of disposal, but it may be asking too much to expect statements that they never threw away broken high-status items, like goldwork. Who would think it worthy of special comment that they did not?

There is other evidence, also indirect, for the conclusion that status items are always disposed of carefully. Often the variety of status items used will correlate with the amount included in graves. Among the Tikopia, few items were included in graves, but very few items among their material culture were status symbols only. Among the Cuna many specific kinds of artifacts (especially goldwork) were used as status items only, and it is also the case that Cuna high-status graves were well stocked (Steward and Faron 1959). This correlation of quantity of status items in use with quantity of items placed in burials is at least consistent with the hypothesis. The question might also be approached by studying the archaeology of historically known peoples. The few explicit statements I have found concerning careful disposal of items of material culture actually refer not to status but to sacred items. The Tikopia and Tahitians possessed some ritual items so sacred that normal disposal was not possible. They would either be deposited in a proscribed manner in a special part of the temple, as among the Tahitians (Oliver 1974:101–102) or were never thrown out at all, but kept in the temple permanently, as with the kasoa necklets of Tikopia chiefs (Firth 1940:16). Few of these items would preserve well, but the approach to their disposal is still relevant. In both cases these sacred items were also important status symbols used only by chiefs, and while the remarks about special disposal concern their ritual importance, this is not easily separated from their peculiar relation to status.

Mortuary distinctions which cross-cut age or sex

Substantial differences among burials which cut across age, sex or social group affiliation may well be marking status hierarchy. This correlation makes sense because apart from ranked status, there are few other aspects of status commonly marked by burials which cross-cut these factors, and because for the most part these alternatives (e.g. occupation-based statuses) are readily distinguished. Of course mortuary variation which marks rank will not necessarily cross-cut age, sex, or social group categories. Rank indicators may be restricted to males as among the Omaha (O'Shea 1981:43) or adult males as among the Arikara and Pawnee (O'Shea 1981:43, 44). Among the Cuna, wives of chiefs did not receive the same type of burial as chiefs; some indeed were accompanying sacrifices (Steward and Faron 1959:227). But if status markers *do* cross-cut these other aspects of status they will very likely indicate rank.

Through more specific correlations along the same lines, it may be possible (under favorable circumstances) to determine if ranking was hereditary or achieved. Gilman interprets an increase over time in the proportion of rich female to rich male burials "as reflecting the progressive separation of high status from achievement, since the importance of female activities relative to male ones is unlikely to have increased over that time" (1981:1). It is rather common that where high status is achieved, this avenue to prestige and power is open only to males, while when ranking is strongly hereditary, women are often included in a more comprehensive rank system, and are more likely to hold the higher statuses. To the extent that this is so, the greater the predominance of adult males among high-status burials, the less likely it is that status is hereditary or the less important hereditary factors are in determining a person's rank. Likewise a more equal proportion of males to females in high-status burials suggests that heredity is important in determining rank.

This may represent a general tendency, but it does involve certain assumptions about the lot of males versus females. Gilman's penchant for thinking in economic terms may be appropriate for Europe's Bronze Age, where "rich" burials are distinguishable on the basis of quantity (although also type) of grave goods. But the questions of how wealth is inherited and of how prestige or leadership is obtained do not always have the same answer. If important aspects of prestige, and especially leadership, are achieved, it is likely to be more socially approved for men to be the ones to achieve it; or at least, to judge by known examples, men will find it an easier route. Yet an important "man of means" may easily have his mother or wife buried with great ceremony regardless of her achievement in this sense or her kinship background. Therefore, the correlation is tenuous when indicators of status are specifically measurements of wealth. We might be on safer ground applying these criteria to evidence consisting of symbols of rank or authority. But even so ambiguity remains, for within the context of inherited rank, there is room for varied emphasis on the male versus female line. If positions of prestige are inherited, but men in general are accorded much higher status than women, they will likely also be over-represented in high-status burials, which this correlate would read as a system of achieved status. Likewise, even if status is largely achieved and mainly by men, if women are accorded status by association with male relatives, they will also tend to receive high-status burials. Finally, although I have been unable to find even one example, we can at least imagine the possibility that achievement of high status was as open to women as to men.

   While the proportion of high-status male and female burials may be related to whether status is ascribed or achieved, we must conclude that the association remains ambiguous. Ethnography bears this out. Among the Shilluk, for whom rank was hereditary, burial treatment for all women differed from men, and there really was no true high-status female burial. The same can be said for the Pawnee, another people with an hereditary status hierarchy who restricted elaborate burial to high-status males. In some cases, women were buried with chiefs, and thus did not receive their own high-status burials even though status was inherited (as among the Cuna [Steward and Faron 1959:227]). Rouse (1948:529) notes for the Arawak that women could inherit high authority positions if no reasonably close male heir was to be found. Yet, they were typically buried with their high-status husbands. The Natchez, however, present an interesting complication. While the chiefs' wives were buried with them, their sisters, because of matrilineal inheritance of authority, were of very high status and received elaborate burial (Swanton 1911). This pattern would "work" as an example of Gilman's correlation. The Arikara (and to an extent, the Omaha, among whom there was room for achieved status mobility) also demonstrate this relationship by associating achieved status with elaborate burial for males only.

   But if generalization from Gilman's original idea does not take us very far, his model is quite sound in context. He was addressing change over time in one social tradition which is far more likely to have a simple social basis than any broadly comparative version of the correlation. But even this must be somewhat tentative. Altogether, not much can be said from a study of variables cross-cutting sex lines.

   The correlation of mortuary variability with age turns out to be much more rewarding. This is because certain social aspects of age seem to be more cross-culturally valid than culturally ascribed gender attributes. One correlate may be the most important line of inference available for distinguishing hereditary from achieved ranking. Basically, when burials differ in ways which indicate ranked status *and* infants or children are among those receiving high-status treatment, we can infer that status is at least partially inherited. The reasoning behind this is clear, and the correlation reliable; the minor objections which have been raised are all avoided by this careful, if admittedly cumbersome, phrasing of the proposition. An adult of high rank may have attained that status by ascription or by some activity which is an approved pathway to achieving status. But a child cannot possibly, in its short life, have done enough to affect its status greatly. If some children are accorded higher status than most adults, the basis for determining this status must be other than personal achievement.

The reliability of this correlate derives from the fact that an archaeologically recognizable configuration can be the result of only one social configuration but there are some important limitations. As Peebles and Kus point out (1977:431), the presence of *rich* child or infant burials is not sufficient evidence to infer ranking as such. Indications of wealth such as quantity of goods or even energy expenditure cannot "distinguish between systems of rank ascription and systems wherein a child's treatment at death instead simply represented the achieved prestige of its surviving family members" (Braun 1979:68). Brown (1981:32) notes that the inference of an hereditary basis for status from child burials is stronger when most children are buried in a different location from adults (not at all uncommon [Binford 1971:22]) or are otherwise treated differently from adults, yet a few are accorded prestige treatment. The inference will also be stronger when based on information concerning younger children, although this is unlikely to be a significant problem. While in some cases even children under ten may attain sufficient status to be given adult burial (Alekshin 1983:140) it is unlikely that they will have accomplished what would be needed to earn the right to *high* status compared to a majority of their elders.

Burial treatment for high-status sub-adults (or children in general) is not often mentioned in ethnographic accounts, but the few examples I found do support the correlation. Among the Tikopia, while an infant or very young child would be buried with no rites at all, Firth (1970:93–94) found two examples of still-born sons of chiefs who received burial treatment similar in most ways to regular chiefly burial. Among the Omaha (O'Shea 1981:43), people would be put on a scaffold for "burial" if they died during the annual bison hunt, while the son of Big Elk, a principal chief, was returned to the main settlement for burial. O'Shea's archaeological study of historic-period Omaha burials (1981:49) also uncovered several sub-adult males with the grave form and inclusions of high-status adult males.

Orme (1981) adds another dimension to the use of age in the study of inequality, by considering the treatment of old adults compared to other age groups. This might help distinguish among differing *non*-hereditary ranking and leadership systems. Unlike hereditary chiefs and some non-hereditary leaders (e.g. Cherokee White council elders), the "Big Man" will tend to maintain this status only in his prime. They will often die "as ordinary members of the community" (Orme 1981:141). We should expect evidence of hierarchy, but high-status burials would lean heavily towards not just adult males, but adult males in their prime, as distinct from older adults. This seems reasonable in theory, but it may require an unusually full data set. Also, Chapman (1987) cautions that big-men societies may be less visible archaeologically than we imagine. Extending the conclusions of White's (1985) archaeological study of big-men societies in New Guinea, he argues that leaders are not readily distinguished, in part "because their social position is based upon their use and disposal of wealth rather than its permanent accumulation and display in immovable capital investment" such as large houses (Chapman 1987:203). White concentrated on houses and associated refuse, but it is entirely possible that "the same argument can be made in relation to their treatment on death" (Chapman 1987:203). This caution of course, simply means we may miss recognizing real hierarchical societies archaeologically. It does not contradict the view that the pattern of differentiation Orme outlined (if found) represents achieved status inequality.

Spatial relationships among burials

Spatial organization is not, for the most part, something we can use for inference on its own, indeed except for the discovery of multiple burial locations, it is not even likely to be observable except in relation to some other dimension of mortuary variability. There are many levels of spatial organization, from arrangement of artifacts in a grave to the regional pattern of cemeteries (Goldstein 1981:57). If a difference among burials (those with large gold statues versus those without) correlates with a spatial pattern (burials "with" clustered in the center of the plot) this arrangement, by redundantly marking the same social distinction, reinforces any conclusion.

This is the thrust, I believe, of Palumbo's argument that Early Bronze IV Jericho was characterized by hierarchy rather than being egalitarian, for his main point is a correlation of body treatment and positioning "primary extended, primary crouched, secondary disarticulated" with differences in grave inclusions (Palumbo 1987:43). Positioning of the individual within the grave (outstretched or crouched; on the back or side, and if the latter, which side; orientation in relation to cardinal directions or architectural features) is often mentioned in site reports and ethnographies but has been little used in attempts to infer status. This is not surprising, for while it is clear that some people took great care in placement of the body, it is rarely more than speculation to suggest what was meant. The Jericho sample offers two advantages here, for the variation in position was *within* the sample (and so marks some distinction among the individuals involved), and bodily position correlates with artifact distributions. Thus to choose just one conclusion: "Individuals buried in extended position are perhaps members of a ruling class, considering the care given to body treatment and grave goods" (Palumbo 1987:46). The correlation of the two lines is particularly important for neither is strong in itself; the variation in grave inclusions is not great,[8] and of course, there is no independent reason for believing an extended position marks high status. To be sure it is easy enough to concoct an after-the-fact rationalization – crouching being a more humble position, extension a posture of grandeur – but this is hardly the basis for a firm conclusion. The value of the spatial pattern is rather its affirmation of the tentative conclusion on grounds of artifact inclusions, that certain burials were seen by contemporaries as a distinctive group.

If kin groups were ranked with respect to one another, spatial groupings should correlate with some of the markers of ranking discussed throughout this chapter. In addition to reinforcing the importance of the distinction in general, it would also be a clue that ranking is not a purely individual matter, but that social groups are ranked. It is possible also that the contemporary, spatially distinct groups of burials do not correlate with distinctions in other mortuary variables. If the groupings cross-cut other variables, that is, the spatial groups are similar to each other in range of variation, they most likely represent some "horizontal" (not hierarchical) social distinction, again kin groups, or sodalities. One can distinguish between these on the basis of age and sex proportions.

On a broader scale, regional integration can also be detected by the spatial distribution of certain mortuary variables. Steponaitis notes that the region around Moundville can be viewed as a hierarchy of three settlement types with only one major center, Moundville. This could mean valley-wide unification with Moundville as the capital, an interpretation supported by the spatial distribution of burials.

> Moundville's function as the highest-order center has been documented on grounds other than its relative size. Burial analyses have suggested that while persons of elite status were associated with both Moundville and the lower-order centers, individuals of the highest rank were interred only at Moundville.
> (Steponaitis 1978:438)

Many other spatial distinctions would be hard for the archaeologist to detect if not correlated with some other variable. Thus, if all richly stocked burials are located in the center of a burial ground, the spatial patterning reinforces the status distinction, yet if people marked status only by placing high-status people in the center of the plot, we might never know it.

6

The form and distribution of artifacts

From archaeology's beginnings, indeed from well before the study of antiquities attained the rigor implied by the term, artifacts have been central to our understanding of the prehistoric past. Using mobile products of human activity to infer status is also a time-honored practice. One basic approach attempts to infer inequality from the presence (and quantity when possible), of certain items in the assemblage, a line of reasoning that depends on our ability to recognize status, elite, or wealth items apart from a distributional context. Another basic approach makes use of the unequal distribution of artifacts in such contexts as burials, hoards, residences, and regions. This chapter covers two additional topics because they relate more to artifacts than burials or architecture: iconography and the inference of stratification. Further approaches to distinguishing stratified from non-stratified ranking are elaborated in the next chapter.

Status markers: elite goods and sumptuary items

Is it possible to show that something was a status item apart from distributional context, and so infer ranking from its presence alone? Hodder is certainly correct in saying that "to look at objects by themselves is really not archaeology at all," that material objects alone are mute and it is context that provides clues to their meaning (1991b:4). But while Hodder has in mind the traditional view of an artifact's context – the spatial associations of careful excavation – I suggest that knowledge of how items are used among other people constitutes an alternative context appropriate for drawing inferences from artifacts. Context is important, Hodder continues, because it helps constrain the interpretation of meaning. Any context that helps eliminate alternative conclusions is an aid to inferring social organization.

The basic starting point for the use of artifacts as evidence of status is neatly summarized by Sanders, Parsons, and Santly: "Gross differences in rank are usually reflected in the quality and quantity of dress, housing or burial furniture" (1979:301). Although quality and quantity will also vary for other reasons, it may be possible to isolate aspects of material culture that regularly vary only with status. Concepts like "elite goods" and "sumptuary items" provide links between artifacts and the nature of the former status system. The notion of eliteness is useful because of its vagueness; "a reference to elites suggests an image of inequalities and the wielding of power in interpersonal relations while remaining moot about whether an elite is an empirically more or less self-reproducing fixture of social organization" (G. Marcus

1983:7). It is vague, too, about such matters as the privileges and powers of being elite and the limitations and deprivations of not being elite, but is clear in one important respect: "[i]t evokes the image of specifiable groups of people rather than impersonal entities such as formal organizations and mass collectives" (G. Marcus 1983:7,8–9). We can thus begin discussions by using the terms elite, or elite items, in reference to inequality, without committing ourselves prematurely to ideas about the nature of these statuses or their level of institutionalization. A sumptuary item differs somewhat in being anything having the purpose of distinguishing one status from another. For Levy "the term 'sumptuary' refers to social rules that limit access to specialized artifacts to certain groups within the society. Restrictions are based on criteria of rank, political authority, occupation, or religious authority, but not directly on wealth, although sumptuary symbols of rank are often of great value" (1979:51). Thus while elite or prestige items mark the higher of ranked statuses, sumptuary items might also distinguish, for example, among unranked occupations.

To tell if an item was used to symbolize status, it is not necessary to know what a symbol meant; it is sufficient to know that something *is* a symbol and to tie it to status or rank. Many sumptuary items will be in some sense non-utilitarian – perhaps personal ornamentation, works of art, adornment of functional objects, or artisanry of unusual quality. The crafting of otherwise utilitarian artifacts in a range of sizes may also suggest "non-utilitarian considerations" (Bradley 1990:57), as would use of an unusual material. At this level the distinction has little value for distinguishing statuses (except perhaps within a distributional context) since not all non-utilitarian items mark status, and not all those that do represent ranked statuses. Context of *discovery* may also provide a clue. If something is made and used solely as a symbol of rank it would not be the sort of thing disposed of as trash but would be kept in a person's house, placed in a burial, or deposited in a ritual context (Braun 1979:67). Such items may also be the most clearly symbolic, this being their basic purpose. Perhaps then, many artifacts useful for the inference of rank will be found in contexts where they can be related to individuals (or families) and for which the study of distributions is possible. But context can be lost, and in any case many items functioned as status markers, though not exclusively so, and might receive a more "profane" disposal.

Joseph Michels relied heavily on artifacts in his study of household rank of Kaminaljuyu, concluding that some represent high status independent of context. But he warns that it is not easy, for even artifacts known to represent rank in one culture do not necessarily mean the same in all, or even at different periods for the same culture (1979:100). Despite the difficulties, Michels interprets several artifacts as elite items largely unaided by distributional context, although in each case this is based on frequency as well as qualities. Michels singles out items of personal adornment, gaming pieces, and weapons as relating to high-status activity and therefore as indicators of prestige, while Brown (1981:37) suggests seeking symbols not simply of rank but of authority, perhaps aspects of costume (e.g. elaborate headdress) or weapons, items with connotations of power. There are difficulties with compiling a set of things that can be taken as elite or high-status items whenever

Table 6.1. *A sampling of items restricted to those of high status*[1]

THE NATCHEZ	– seats or stools (e.g. the throne of the Great Sun)
	– feather crown
THE ARAWAK	– gold crowns and feather headdresses (chiefs only)
	– *guanin* pendants of gold/copper alloy (chiefs only)
	– gold objects in general
	– snuff (high status, incl. ritual specialists)
	– gold wreaths and turbans (high-status women)
	– litter for travel (chiefs only)
THE CUNA	– chiefs put marks or insignia on goldwork, other property, and slaves
	– gold ornaments in general
THE CHIBCHA	– stools
	– gold-covered litters (chiefs only)
	– insignia of priestly office included robes and calabash to hold coca
THE CATIO, NORE, ETC.	– gold plated litter (chiefs only)
THE TIKOPIA	– palm-frond necklet (used by chiefs only)
	– sacred clamshell adzes (large, well finished, handled only by chiefs)
THE TAHITIANS	– headdresses
	– royal insignia (unspecified, high chiefs only)
	– mask of the main mourner at chiefly burials
	– certain sports, hence presumably the equipment needed for them
THE SHILLUK	– special robes of antelope skins

found, but Table 6.1 provides insight into the kinds of things we might expect. It is no surprise that most common are items of clothing (especially headgear), personal adornment (distinctive in materials, design or both), and seats or stools. Although frequent enough to form a pattern, even those items most commonly restricted to people of high status are not always used in this way. Stools, seats, and many kinds of personal adornment are obviously in more general use among other peoples. While certain items are commonly used as status markers, we need more than their presence to infer ranking.

Without a distributional context, the inference of inequality from artifacts will be inconclusive except when the finds are so remarkable that we can say the workmanship is just not found among egalitarian peoples. But a tentative conclusion can be strengthened if the items are rare. If stools or elaborate headgear are found, but in small numbers, that fact would be good (not conclusive) evidence for ranking. The case would be much enhanced if, in addition to being an item commonly restricted to high status and rare in the sample, it displayed features often associated with elite items – elaborate decoration, fine workmanship, special designs or insignia, or materials widely considered valuable (exotic, rare or otherwise exceptional). It is important to consider how each factor can affect the reliability of inferences.

The presence of exotic materials is always important, but the inference of ranking also requires distributional information since regional exchange systems are not unique to hierarchical society. And even if the items clearly are not necessities, we cannot assume they are luxuries reserved for a privileged few. It is likely that where ranking is more important, rare and exotic goods will be also. With more extensive ranking we could expect exotic goods in greater quantity, variety (to continue to have "rare" items despite increased quantity), and quality. Another attribute is quality, fineness, or effort in manufacture. Some items that are not rare overall nevertheless exhibit great variation – with those of higher quality being rare. Limited variation could follow simple personal preference, but items of fine, elaborate manufacture will indicate ranked status differences, an inference strengthened if they are found along with a majority of simpler items, if we can document the pattern in several artifact categories, and if they are very elaborate. It is possible (if unlikely) for a person of talent to produce a few items of exceptional quality even though not a specialist doing one of many tasks, and even though making the object for personal use. But if we find a few very fine chipped stone tools, *and* delicate, finely decorated pottery it is far less likely that one or a few people did this just for aesthetic reasons.

Among my ethnographic examples I found variation in quality of workmanship (especially elaboration of design and fineness of execution) to be regularly associated with differences in rank.[2] On the other hand, while the Tikopia may make greater quantities of an item, they are not given to elaboration of design or improvement of quality (Firth 1947:70–71). And while the chiefly artifact inventory differed from most, it was not in having high-quality or more elaborate versions of the items everyone used. The Tahitians also present an interesting case. Chiefs used sleeping mats of fine quality (Oliver 1974:171–172), whose manufacture required exceptional skill (and time) but which are not striking to those unfamiliar with the culture. Even what appear to be small differences in quality could be associated with ranking. Of course small differences could also derive from ability and personal standards among unranked people producing for their own requirements, and an element of subjectivity may be inevitable in archaeological attempts to distinguish among these alternatives. But there may be ways of getting around having to justify objective definitions of relative quality. Patterned differences in one artifact type, for example, would help us distinguish between someone simply having done a better job, and a culturally-accepted "high quality" or "chiefly" version. Parallel variation in several artifact types will also help. Copying is another clue that an item served as a symbol in addition to being desired for itself (Fleming 1973:579). Dever notes, for example, calcite vessels from Middle-Bronze sites in Palestine made locally in imitation of alabaster and faience vessels imported from Egypt (1987:166). Copies fashioned in less costly (in this case local) material, or exhibiting poorer workmanship, indicate that originals were both restricted and desired for their symbolic value (so that a copy, though not remarkable in itself, could still satisfy the desire) and therefore were status markers regardless of what practical or aesthetic purposes they also served. On the other hand, copies which are not inferior in any of these senses (e.g. the elaborate copper versions of stone objects characteristic of the Early Bronze Age of Europe

[Bradley 1990:86]), reinforce the symbolic importance of the originals while also participating in their prestige value. Possession of even an imitation is a boost to status, suggesting an element of competition. At the same time, the social significance of artifacts can change, and emulation of any kind contributes to the instability of status markers. Access to imitations can dilute the value of the originals, and the emergence of new status items in succeeding periods would strengthen the association with desired status, as well as the inference of competition and most likely an element of achievement.

Another approach to weeding out alternate explanations is to objectify the distinction between elaborate and normal artifacts. The production-step measure of pottery crafting developed by Feinman is an assessment of relative labor investment in the manufacture of different ceramic vessels. It works by scoring one point for each step in production, "and can be used to weigh the relative costliness of those kinds of ceramics which are distributed differentially" (Upham, Lightfoot, and Feinman 1981:826). This is an elegant and conceptually simple means of recognizing pottery as high quality without assuming status symbolism, and at the same time sidestepping the subjective element of "quality" by picking out artifacts which result from a more lavish outpouring of effort. It is, in fact, a sophisticated application of the energy-expenditure principal. The order into which artifacts are arranged by production effort will correspond roughly to the relative value placed on them by those who made and used them, simply because people are unlikely to put extra effort into making an item if the result is of lower value than one produced by a known process consuming less time.

Craft specialization and status

Craft specialization is a form of social differentiation in that even part-time specialists differ from non-specialists. It is also widely associated with inequality, but this is largely an empirical observation, and the question of why craft specialization should be tied to the presence of elites is still a matter of debate (Peregrine 1991:1). Given our current understanding of specialization I do not believe we can use evidence for craft specialization unquestioningly as evidence of ranking as though we were confident that it never occurs apart from inequality. But recent work on how craft specialization and elites are related may lead to a reliable (if more specific) association. The problem is that specialists are not themselves elites (though they may gain respect through their skill); the close connection can be explained either in terms of centralized direction making specialization possible or in that elite use of crafts increases "demand" for the products of specialization.

Specialization is a way of increasing the efficiency or quality of production, but for people to devote time to making things they cannot eat, they need some level of assurance that they can obtain life's necessities, whether through exchange, elite patronage, wage labor or otherwise. Elite coordination of exchange encourages specialization by providing greater stability than ad hoc arrangements. Everyone can reap the benefits of quality craft products and improved subsistence stability. An alternative model considers elite strategies for maintaining and increasing political authority (Peregrine 1991:1). Rather than indirectly encouraging specialization through a dependable exchange system, leaders increase the need for specialized products by using them for their own purposes. Often leaders employ the artisans themselves. Ethnographically Peregrine found that among peoples with greater political centralization, labor devoted to personal ornaments increased significantly, as did decoration. Another way of limiting access to status-signifying items is to use materials that are rare, hard to recover or non-local, but Peregrine found "that acquisition labor is almost randomly associated with political centralization" and in the more centralized societies "raw materials for personal ornaments are more likely to come from a local source than a non-local one" (Peregrine 1991:8). Elites among the more centralized societies in this sample had come to rely more on control of the skills and labor of craft specialists than on control of imported materials, indicating "a political strategy in which increasingly powerful elites employ specialist artisans to produce exotic personal ornaments that the elites use, in turn, to further differentiate themselves from the rest of the society. Craft specialization, seen in this way, is as much a political activity as it is an economic or artistic one" (Peregrine 1991:8).

These two models of the association of craft specialization with elites are not necessarily opposed. They assume different emphases not just on why specialization increases with centralization, but on *what products* the specialists will produce. Chiefs could conceivably regulate a regional exchange system encouraging specialized production of subsistence and utilitarian items, while at the same time assembling a group of skilled artisans to produce fine crafts, particularly ornamentation, for their personal use, and as honors for loyal followers.

But how does this help us infer inequality? While highly elaborate personal ornaments could be interpreted as status items, and serve as evidence of ranking on their own, recognition that items were produced by specialists can be useful in two ways. In this case when the artifacts themselves already indicate ranking, it would offer further insight into the nature of statuses. For example, if status items are religious in nature, inference of craft specialization adds evidence of significant economic control, showing that the statuses were not purely ritual in nature. But recognition of specialization may be even more important for confirming tentative conclusions when personal ornamentation is not sufficiently elaborate to demonstrate inequality on its own.

Hoards, residences, and regions

The burial context is so central to the inference of rank using artifacts, that scholars using non-mortuary contexts have mentioned lack of burial data as either motivation for the study (Levy 1979:49–50) or a reason for the results being unusually important (Michels 1979:99). But this work in turn makes it clear that other distributional contexts do offer insight into ranking, and being largely independent, greatly enhance the depth and reliability of any conclusion. Here I consider two special contexts, hoards and household artifact distributions, while the next section covers approaches to inferring rank from regional artifact distribution patterns – where the site rather than grave, house or hoard will become the unit for comparison.

Hoards

Hoards are intentional deposits of artifacts not primarily associated with burial, and while a comparatively rare phenomenon worldwide, they are often a major part of the archaeology where encountered at all. Such finds comprise a substantial number of artifacts recovered throughout Europe, and although they have had a strangely marginal role in archaeological writing, except in a descriptive or typological sense (Bradley 1990:4), Bradley makes the intriguing observation that acts of hoarding play an important role in European literature. *Le Morte d'Arthur* and the *Nibelungenlied* are two such works which engage Western thinking at a deep level and presumably express something important from ancient tradition. This alone is justification for the view "that such collections are of fundamental importance to our perception of early society" (Bradley 1990:4), a point confirmed by the more pedestrian observation that much effort was expended in the deliberate removal from circulation of artifacts, "among them some of the most elaborate ever made" (xiii).

Hoard deposits may be approached in ways parallel to burial study, except for interpreting the purpose of the hoard, and the problem of associating items with individuals (or even with a particular society). We must determine which hoards were ritual, since accidental deposition, or that for the purpose of hiding valuables (with the intent of recovery) naturally bring very different meanings. To investigate Denmark's Bronze Age hoards, Levy used ethnographic studies of ritual, plus historical data peculiar to Denmark, to formulate criteria for distinguishing ritual hoards from other finds of buried objects. Broadly applicable indications of ritual include signs of purposefulness in deposition (e.g. neckrings encircling other items [Levy 1979:51]), supporting the assumption that different hoards are somehow instances of the same phenomenon. On analogy with Early Bronze Age burials (before cremation was common) many Danish hoards contain what appear to have been the possessions of a single person, objects with status-related social value. With this established, use of hoards in social inference proceeds very much like burial analysis.

But of course this is not always easily established. It can be difficult to distinguish ritual from non-ritual hoards, and not all ritual finds can be related to personal status. Single finds may be chance losses (although the fine quality of so many pieces does suggest otherwise) and while Levy (1979, 1982) offers means for determining if items were deposited together, the nature of recovery often makes this difficult. Context is rare among European hoards; most river finds, for example, were uncovered by dredging (Bradley 1990:6). Ritual hoards are intended as permanent deposits, making it worthwhile to distinguish intentional, non-recoverable, from unintentional deposits and those meant for retrieval (Bradley 1990:11–12). The latter might include unintended losses (shipwrecks, items dropped from bridges, weaponry never recovered from battlegrounds), personal items hidden during times of uncertainty, the wares of merchants or materials of founders. These deposits are sometimes recognizable, for example bundles of identical swords, or more commonly, collections of scrap metal pieces which may well have been intended for recycling.

Hoards of personal items deposited with intent to recover would represent wealth perceived to be in danger of loss, perhaps through confiscation or capture. It may even be possible to recognize dangerous eras, when individuals could easily lose their wealth, or suffer other personal loss because of their status, by what Bradley calls hoarding horizons, times represented by more hoards than usual.

> Material may have been hidden or stored in the ground during many or most periods of prehistory, but only when circumstances prevented the recovery would it have stayed in the archaeological record. Peaks in the frequency of such deposits tell us most about the conditions under which those collections were lost. We have less idea of why they were hidden in the first place.
> (Bradley 1990:20–21)[3]

For our purposes, though, a high frequency of roughly similar deposits would strengthen the inference that they are examples of lost personal wealth and that major status differences existed (assuming that not everyone possessed items needing this sort of protection).

It is probable that many river deposits were ritual in nature. Some groups of weaponry could be the result of battles at fords and others may have been dropped or eroded from riverbank settlement sites, but such explanations do not account for the magnitude of the finds, or that in many cases deposits were made over a long time span (Bradley 1990:24). The quantity, fine condition, and narrow range of artifact types compared to settlement finds further suggest offerings (p. 23). Some items found in hoards are not only elaborately made but, like the large bronze "lures" of Scandinavia, are found only in watery locations or depicted on rock art (Bradley 1990:29), a context indicating that they were intentional deposits, and probably made just for this purpose. They are not directly associated with personal status, but the elaborate and skilled manufacture along with their use indicates craft and ritual specialization. This indicates status inequality, but there is still the question of relating the finds to peoples in place and time. Assuming we are correct to infer status inequality, of whom are we speaking?

Several models have been proposed concerning the place of votive offering hoards in a social order, and while speculative, these models do have implications for status organization. Levy (1982:117) proposes that votive offerings promote social solidarity by preventing too much wealth from being controlled by too few people. Like many modern reform movements (perhaps not coincidentally) this solution levels resources by making the wealthy less so rather than by raising the lot of the poor. A mechanism of this sort would be of value in stratified societies, particularly when, as in modern Western society, profound wealth differences are juxtaposed with a deeply egalitarian ideology. Whether the elite of Bronze Age societies faced a similar incongruity, and needed to appear not to hoard wealth, is another question. A more important difficulty with adapting this perspective for status inference is that the idea (in itself, that is) assumes rather than serves as evidence for stratification.

Bradley notes that ritual destruction of artifacts, or deposition such that they could not be recovered, would "provide the ideal arena for conspicuous consumption" (1990:138; cf. Gregory 1980). This allows direct competition for social standing, and since the offerings are permanently removed from circulation, makes it difficult for a rival to regain lost ground. These offerings might serve the same social purposes as gift exchanges but with less tendency for escalation than when gifts can be recirculated. Although it is not clear if this can be generalized as a correlate of status it can certainly help in some cases. For Bronze Age Britain Bradley offers several reasons for this approach, in essence correlating the space and time distribution of river deposits with "other" evidence of rivalry. And, for Southern Germany, it may have been a form of "military posturing" in which consumption of large numbers of weapons "might be regarded as a form of surrogate warfare" (Bradley 1990:139). Because apparently similar artifact collections could have been deposited for different reasons it is clear that examination of the context in this broader than usual sense, is an important step in using hoards for fine social inference (Bradley 1990:192).

Residences

Domestic architecture is another productive context for correlating archaeology with society. Architectural variation is often the most obvious way dwellings differ, but artifact distributions can provide insight into the relative status of the inhabitants. We could proceed much as with burial data, except that residential artifact inventories relate not to an individual, but to all members of the household. As with collective burials, it will be difficult to associate variations with any age or sex-based category, a significant area of research in the mortuary context. Site-formation processes also differ substantially from burial deposits or even from architecture and permanent features of residential study. As Bradley (1990:33) observes, only the production and final deposition stages of the lifecycle of an artifact can be observed. I would add that exchange events can also be inferred if they have resulted in movement of an artifact from a known source to a recognizably different place of deposition, although it may not be possible to uncover the specific nature of the exchange event(s). Middens will pile up with broken items and valuables will be removed whenever possible upon abandonment. On one occasion when the Natchez abandoned their village, they took many of the chief's household items with them, despite a distinctly hasty departure (Swanton 1911). Observers mistakenly believed that even the chief lived in a sparsely furnished, albeit rather large house. Although hardly surprising, this could lead us substantially to underrate the differentiation present were we to use excavated household artifact inventories alone for inferences.

Household studies might also yield different kinds of data. Artifacts found in dwellings (and associated middens) will differ from those placed in graves. Because of not having gone through the filter of mortuary ideology, they may cover aspects of status not considered important in the mortuary context, providing a picture more closely based on a person's place in day-to-day activity (status-in-life). For instance, among the Tahitians (Oliver 1974:169), Arawak (Rouse 1948:525), and Tikopia (Firth 1936:80, 1939:243) chiefs kept in their homes a number of important ritual objects. This would not only distinguish them but indicate the ritual importance of their status. Household furnishings may also show to what extent life style differed among ranks.

Regional artifact distributions and status

Understandably, much of the work using artifact distributions to infer status has involved pottery, and while that medium will also be central to this discussion, most correlations between artifacts and status could be adapted to any artifact found in sufficient quantity and with sufficient variation.

In any hierarchical society, there will be *more need* for items to display status than in non-hierarchical societies. Because there are limits to the status-demonstrating value of hoarding great quantities of normal pottery, it will not be possession of pottery as such, but of some special type that will best serve the need to mark status. And since not all pottery is used to demonstrate status, the distribution of some forms will remain largely unaffected by the status system. Yet we may learn something about status from distributions on a regional scale. Depending on the nature of the status system, the use of pottery to mark statuses may result in a distribution of a uniform decorative style over large areas, or in other cases may actually result in great differences within a region of similar size.

The following examples might help us correlate a distribution pattern with a specific type of ranking. In one European example, Gilman (1981:1) relates a wide distribution of elite artifact styles (bell beakers or swords, for example) "to the existence of upper classes whose recruitment was sufficiently stable for them to establish a web of widespread, mutually supportive partnerships." But for a different European context Sherratt notes (among a number of other changes) that a "large number of distinctive pottery types gives way to uniformity, suggesting that pottery was no longer a competitive or prestige item" (1982:23). Sherratt suggests that with competition for rank or among those of high status, the fine quality artifacts used to mark a status would not be uniform. People would seek innovation (probably also conspicuous quantity), perhaps an ever-heightening elaboration of those aspects of style considered prestigious. But the distribution pattern Gilman found is quite different. He relates this wide geographic distribution to a group of high-ranking individuals in stable, peaceful contact with each other, people who attain their rank by established, widely-accepted means. Broad distribution of uniform elite artifacts requires that over this area people have similar ideas about how status ought to be symbolized. This itself implies interaction, although it may not be possible to specify whether in the form of common cultural background, trade, or elite interaction. The uniformity suggests that the items are standard symbols of a certain status, one that is fairly uniform and standardized, so implying a stable ranking system as Gilman argues.

But this says little about recruitment, except that however people attain status they do not so much make their own unique position as fill pre-defined positions or offices. Widely held ideas about statuses are only likely if people view them as a continuing part of the social order. Evidence of temporal continuity leads to a similar conclusion, and broad distribution, whether geographic or chronological, indicates that those involved are not strongly competing for prestige, that social approval is more easily won through conformity than by trying to outdo others. A region wherein there is little variation in status markers will represent either the geographical extent of a society, or if made up of separate societies, ones whose elite are in significant contact, but not competition. Alternatively, a variety of contemporary elite artifact styles within a region indicates either cultural heterogeneity or that elites are in competition, alternatives that can be distinguished by studying variation in more mundane artifacts. That is, if the overall artifact inventory suggests little cultural similarity, variation in elite styles may simply be a further expression of cultural diversity or limited contact, while if there is evidence of cultural similarity within a region, the variation in elite artifacts argues either for competition, or for lack of a coherent definition of what a rank ought to be. Here it is not as important for elite to prove membership in a definable rank or office; emphasis will be on demonstrating the ability to do high-rank things. Status competition is most prominent when rank is based heavily on achievement or when a region comprises several distinct social orders with local leaders in competition with each other. Rank may be hereditary in the latter case, for leaders are representing their social group in competitive interactions with others, and are not necessarily competing for rank among their own people. Distinguishing among these alternatives would depend on recognizing socio-political boundaries within a region of cultural similarity. This is not easy, of course, but where possible we may have a means of distinguishing achieved from hereditary ranking.

Practical application is further complicated by the problem of defining "similar-ity" and by the possibility that broadly similar artifacts will nevertheless vary in detail. Hierarchical groups of Central and nearby South America symbolized status with worked gold (local or imported from the "higher" civilizations), a trait found throughout a large region of competing hierarchical societies. Also widely shared was the great value attributed to quantity. But there was, over the same area, variation in just *how* goldwork marked a status. Cuna chiefs decorated theirs with personal insignia, which therefore differed (in detail) even within the Cuna area. The similarity is evidence of the broad cultural similarity throughout the region, an underlying factor which no doubt helped make competition meaningful. At the same time the variation in details would help us recognize the status competition so well documented in ethnographic records. This combination of variation among elite artifacts alongside a background of similarity over a broad region, can be very helpful but because of the range of interacting factors – social boundaries, cultural boundaries, recruitment to statuses, interaction among leaders of different social groups – each influencing the distribution of artifacts, specific conclusions remain ambiguous. It does not seem possible as yet to make reliable connections between the nature of the distribution of artifacts, and specifics of ranking (e.g. ascribed versus achieved; stratification), without supporting evidence from other correlates.

Implications of an uneven distribution within a region

It may, however, be possible to infer ranking with relatively little ambiguity from the extent to which an artifact is distributed *uniformly* throughout the area in which it is found. I have argued that some artifacts can be considered status items on their own, but fine ceramics are not always among them, making distributional evidence very important. Cordell and Plog (1979:420) observe that some ceramic types of the Anasazi area are found only at the larger and more complex sites, indicating that they were restricted to use by certain people who lived only at some of the sites. Restricted use in turn suggests status markers, which (especially in light of their quality) indicates ranking. An uneven artifact distribution also indicates a regional basis to the status system, a point elaborated by Upham, Lightfoot, and Feinman, who also note that not all uneven distributions result from ranking. Uneven distributions might well be functional or temporal differences (1981:826).[4]

A non-egalitarian settlement system can be recognized by the concentration of exotic and costly items at certain settlements. Costliness could be determined by Feinman's production-step measure, which rather than requiring one to presuppose the ceramics in question are status items, is a means of demonstrating it. Upham, Lightfoot, and Feinman suggest that in non-egalitarian situations "certain fine, highly decorated types will be unevenly distributed throughout a region" in the sense of occurring at administrative centers but not at all settlements, while "the less decorated vessels with low production step measures should be distributed more evenly" (1981:826). If each village had its own local chief, it is possible that elite artifacts would be found at each site, but even so quantities may vary, and the most elaborate artifacts could still be concentrated at a few settlements.

Variety of an assemblage may be another way of relating artifact distributions to status differentiation. Rice observes that "in complex societies, producers, production means, and the products themselves reflect the inherent internal variety of a diverse or segmented social system" from which she concludes that "the existence of variety in kinds of goods or services and in elaboration of their appearance or composition should vary more or less directly with social status" (Rice 1981:220). For example, household inventories of a plantation site in the Southeast USA were found to reveal a greater variety of materials in higher- than in lower-status dwellings (Rice 1981:221). This is positive evidence of the correlation, although since status differences were great (owner and overseer versus slaves) it does not show how precise the correlation might be. Study of more specific aspects of the assemblage can be useful, and making use of Rice's analysis for purposes of status inference, I see three major possibilities:

1. Greater variation and complexity in the status system will lead to greater variety in artifacts.

Some artifacts mark statuses, and many statuses, especially those differing greatly in prestige or privilege, will be marked by distinctive artifacts. With a greater range of statuses will come, overall, greater variety of artifacts. Some of these, particularly non-utilitarian artifacts used to mark high status, can be conceived as additions to what a hypothetical artifact inventory would have been like without ranking. In general, it seems reasonable to expect a greater variety of artifacts when there is ranking than otherwise, yet this cannot be used as a specific measure of rank, as in saying that an assemblage of more than a certain number of artifact types can only have resulted from ranking. A cross-culturally valid scale for relating variety of artifacts to complexity of the status system may not be possible, and is, at the least, a practical matter of some difficulty. But theoretical and operational problems are both largely avoided when considering change over time. If the number of different types of artifacts increases, we have evidence that the status system is also growing more complex – probably, but not certainly, in the sense of increasing hierarchy. Among the Cushite-speaking Booran Oromo, for example, it was traditional for different kinds of leaders to be associated with specific ornamentation (Kassam and Megersa 1989:25). It is true that aspects of status which do not figure in the basic hierarchy (broad gender distinctions and age grades or "life stages") were also marked with distinctive ornamentation, but it is not clear that these social categories were free of hierarchy. There is also the question of whether each status would have been marked with such care in the absence of an underlying ideology stressing the importance of distinctions among people. If the proliferation of status-marking artifacts is a consequence of ranking even though many sumptuaries do not mark actual ranks, this would not really serve as a counterexample to the correlation.

Development of technology (growth in number of crafts practiced or crops cultivated), of specialization, or of special-interest groups are all part of the complexity of a status system, and could contribute to complexity in the artifact inventory. Arnold found that artifact variability (at least in the sense of variation in design) may be affected by historically specific rather than socially based aspects of the practice of a craft. A ceramic study among potters in Quinua, Peru showed that "the kinds and amount of design variability produced by a community of potters is greatly affected by the vessel shape layout type and design zones" and because different vessel shapes carry different amounts of variability, "decorations and spatial units that cross-cut vessel shapes may give behaviorally spurious results" (Arnold 1984:147). Similarly, Bradley observes that one advantage metals had over stone "is that they can carry complex decoration, a feature which had previously been confined to pottery and rock art, among those forms for which archaeological evidence survives" (1990:82–83).

It is possible largely to eliminate such alternative explanations. Knapp found an increase in the range of pottery types during the Middle Bronze Age of the North Jordan Valley, particularly resulting from a growth in the range of imported goods, and from the appearance of fine wares through specialization in manufacture (Knapp 1989:141). The inference of increasing status hierarchy from the increased range of artifacts is strengthened by the nature of the diversification and the context of wide-ranging change.

2. Higher-status individuals will possess a greater variety of artifacts than those of lower statuses.

This follows closely from the well-documented observation that in hierarchical societies, some artifacts are restricted to the higher statuses. Whether the restriction results from their use as status markers or their costliness, those of higher status will have access to a greater number of different types of artifacts. Indeed, household pottery inventories of the modern Mexican village of Metapec suggest that diversity of styles may even be a better indicator of status than numbers of vessels or of imports.

> The wealthiest household . . . has neither the largest number of vessels nor the largest number of "tradewares." This may be a telling point, given archaeologists' predilections for assuming that tradewares are signs of status. What the wealthiest household does exhibit is the highest diversity (richness) statistic . . . and the highest evenness statistic. [It has] both more different kinds of vessels and more equitable access to acquisition of each of those kinds than do any of the other households.
> (Rice 1989:115)

This correlation is consistent with other ethnographic examples. The Natchez are of particular interest. While some items were used only by chiefs, including his "honors" and dishes (Swanton 1911:150), there were not many and material culture in general was not extensive for anyone, not even the Great Sun. As chiefs were largely relieved of manual labor we may assume those of lower status were in possession of the tools needed for these tasks. This would counter the tendency of this correlation and since Natchez chiefs did not possess many types of status artifacts, may cancel it out in this instance. But the point is not that in hierarchical society those of high rank inevitably have a greater range of artifacts, only that if we do find a significant divergence among individuals in variety of artifacts possessed, we can reasonably infer ranking – unless all of the additional items were equipment for specific tasks.

3. The artifact variety in (1) and (2) can be studied from several perspectives and scales.

I have been considering the correlate on an individual-to-individual basis, but if it is not possible to associate the artifacts recovered with this context, any other distributional context could potentially help us infer status differentiation. We might instead compare variation in the total artifact inventory or study each artifact category (e.g. pottery) on its own.

The use of iconography to infer status

It does not take a deep reading of the current literature to see that the archaeological study of symbolic systems is in a period of ascendancy. The study of social organization has not been a major thrust of this work, however. Indeed, some of those who have done most to further interpretive archaeology are among the most deeply skeptical of cross-cultural approaches to status inference (e.g. Hodder 1990b, 1991b). This posture may simply be the second phase of an Hegelian progression, and while I do not attempt a synthesis, I note that the study of symbolic systems as represented in material culture (particularly in art), and cross-cultural methods of status inference can be useful to each other.

Interpretation of symbolism offers rich insight into what it would have been like to be part of a former society, and could enhance our understanding of status even when the interpretive program does not seek this goal. Likewise the findings of middle range theory might provide a context or foundation from which interpretive models can be developed or refined. But if scholarship which begins by viewing artifacts as symbolic representations is not easily applied to questions of status inequality,[5] a more specific focus on explicit artistic expression holds more immediate promise. The study of iconography – the symbolism or imagery of an artwork, or perhaps the pictorial illustration of a subject – has long been important in the fine arts, and can be quite useful here (Willey 1976) in several ways. Consider: (a) the presence of iconography in an assemblage, (b) its distribution and (c) insights from the intended symbolic meaning.

The presence of iconography in an archaeological assemblage is significant, but there are several possible reasons people might choose to use iconography. Concerning San Lorenzo Phase (Olmec) ceramics of the Mesoamerican Gulf Coast, Grove (1981:377) states that the major change from the previous phase is the addition of two pottery types with iconographic motifs. While scholars agree that such a development must be significant, Grove has encountered a range of ideas on what it implies socially. It "may have functioned in rituals of sanctification ... as status markers ..., or to identify descent groups" (1981:377). Finally he offers his own more general conclusion:

> The presence of iconography on ceramics reflects a higher level of
> sociocultural complexity, although it is not necessarily a "marker" for
> Olmec culture nor should its appearance imply external influences.
> (Grove 1981:377)

Distribution of iconography may also be useful. How widespread (or localized) is it? In what contexts is it found? What materials or media are used? Symbolic representation of sufficient complexity to be called iconography may be found on permanent structures or mobile art. Distribution on buildings and other structures (including what types of structures and which particular ones) may provide clues to its purposes and possibly to the status system. Among the Arawak, iconography was used on stones lining central "ball court" embankments, on other stones in ceremonial areas, and in cave shrines (Rouse 1948:507). The consistent ritual purpose does not speak directly to status, except as another element justifying the inference of central leadership in planned constructions, and as evidence of ritual specialization. Among the Tahitians, several carved *ti'i* poles or images were placed around chiefly dwellings to warn travellers of the area's sacredness (Oliver 1974:1042–1043), and among many Northwest Coast groups totem poles and other carvings were associated with dwellings. Variation among the carvings, or a presence/absence distribution as among the Tahitians, would differentiate the dwellings and the status of their respective inhabitants, although whether we could recognize these as ranked differences is not clear.

Iconography may be found on ornaments, as with the insignia used by Cuna chiefs to mark valued possessions (Steward and Faron 1959:225), the distribution of which may offer a means of inferring inequality. If found on pottery it may be another means (along with production cost and fineness) for recognizing status-based access to prestige items. In the Olmec example it becomes more apparent in the next phase that iconography is associated with high status, as it is found more commonly on exotic greenstone, an important item in the growing long-distance trade and the "increasing differentiation of access to goods at major centers" (Grove 1981:378). Iconography helps in recognizing the extent of ranking, being another distinguishing characteristic like rarity and quality. Of course, to contemporaries iconography would say a good deal more than this, but to get any further, we need to move toward the meaning of the symbols themselves.

In *Emblem and State in the Classic Maya Lowlands* (1976) Joyce Marcus derived important inferences about Maya social and political organization largely from an interpretation of certain glyphs. Each glyph is a symbol, and the early stages of decipherment are much like the study of any iconographic system. But this is an unusual case, for although not yet fully readable (and much less so in the 1970s) the complement of Maya glyphs at a site amounts to a written language. Unlike simpler iconographic systems, the great quantity of symbols and the fact that they are ordered and combined according to linguistic rules, make interpretation less a matter of speculation than it might be, allowing newly interpreted glyph meanings to build on (and check) previous inferences.

Trigger attempts a more generalized approach to symbolic interpretation in his use of iconography to infer political organization (hence also leadership statuses). He notes widespread ways of symbolizing certain ideas and argues that whenever these elements of iconography are encountered, we can reasonably infer the general meanings even when we cannot produce a full and reliable reading at a more specific level.

> Among the most obvious themes are the following: (1) the relative size of figures and elaborateness of costumes tend to correlate ... with their political importance; (2) defeated enemies are shown simply dressed or naked in the presence of their elaborately-costumed conquerors (examples from Egypt, Mesopotamia, Maya, Mochica culture); (3) a king is often

Table 6.2. *The symbolism of egalitarian and hierarchical art*

Egalitarian	Hierarchical
Repetition of simple elements	Integration of unlike elements
Much empty or irrelevant space	Little irrelevant/unused space
Symmetrical	Asymmetrical design
Figures without enclosures	Enclosed figures

portrayed dominating a supine enemy (Egypt, Maya, Aztec).
(Trigger 1978a:165–166)

To these representational approaches Cook (1987) adds location of figures (e.g. center versus sides) within the overall composition, and there are no doubt other possibilities. These examples are from a complex social situation and elements may be useful in determining if a society was a state. For simply inferring inequality, or even political centralization, the iconography found on the pylons at Karnak for example, would be largely redundant with the impressive structures themselves. But in other cases – including the Andean Middle Horizon pottery studied by Cook – iconography is an important clue in itself. This "iconography of power" is also, in its way, somewhat of a specialized case, for as Trigger points out, it depends on formalized symbolism in representational art. The more abstract forms of art may have even greater potential for carrying symbolic meaning, but will generally be more difficult to interpret.

Assuming that a person's view of the world is affected by the organization of society, and that these modes of thought will influence artistic expression even when (unlike the examples above) it is not the explicit purpose, suggestions have been made concerning how this might allow interpretation of even the most abstract works. Following Fischer, Fairservis (1975:172) relates four broad aspects of composition that might be affected by whether the artist was steeped in hierarchy or the world view of an egalitarian society. Art, whether or not we can interpret the symbolism, could be evaluated according to whether it tends toward the characteristics listed on the left or the right of Table 6.2.

Approaching art on these terms could prove interesting when symbolic expression is not obviously an iconography of power, but when the actual meanings of the art remain unknown. Of course, we would uncover "tendencies" not unambiguous status inference.

The archaeological recognition of social stratification

The importance of stratification for the character of life has been affirmed, and any means of distinguishing a stratified hierarchy from one that is not will be important, the more so because few such methods have been developed. Under stratification there will be a qualitative difference between those with the greatest (most direct) access to critical resources and those with the least (most indirect), and recognition of this difference is sufficient for the identification of stratification. By far the most systematic and thorough attempt at identifying stratification archaeologically that I am aware of remains that of Jonathan Haas (1981, 1982), who identifies two steps in the process: determining which are the basic resources, and developing ways of recognizing differential access to them from as many kinds of data as possible.

It turns out that identification of a people's basic resources is not at all straightforward. "'Basic resources' are essentially all the goods and products that are absolutely necessary for, or significantly contribute to the probability of, survival and reproduction" (Haas 1981:84). The list of items meeting these criteria will vary "depending upon environmental, technological and historical circumstances" (p. 84) since people will have different approaches to survival and may require different resources. Still, it might be possible to distinguish a minimal list of *general* categories of resources that are basic in all societies. Haas suggests "food, tools used for the production and preparation of food, and protective devices for coping with the physical environment and an antagonistic social environment. Everyone needs something to eat; everyone needs to have some means of obtaining food and making it edible; and everyone needs protection from the elements and potential enemies" (1981:84–85). Status markers (and luxury goods generally) play an important role in maintaining and even generating status, and are thus important for the reproduction of the social order. Indeed, they are likely to be essential for the maintenance of stratification. But because they are not needed for personal survival, they are not essential resources in the sense used here. Socially condoned differential access to luxury goods does not have the same consequences as differential access to the means of obtaining things which are basic to survival. In particular, it does not offer those of high status the endlessly expandable source of "control" over people's lives provided by genuine control of essential resources.

In formulating the concept of basic resources, Fried emphasized capital resources, and because he had several good reasons for doing so it is important to explain why Haas's list (which I follow closely) consists of consumer goods. These are produced through the use of capital basic resources, and are emphasized not from a low view of the importance of unequal control of capital resources, nor because there is any difficulty determining what the basic capital resources are. The problem is rather with the archaeological recognition of differential access to these resources, for "[a]ccess to capital resources can only be determined ... indirectly through the distribution of the consumer goods derived from the capital goods" (Haas 1982:93). Haas then adds, "or directly in those cases when a group is clearly in a superior geographical position in relation to the capital resources," but this is not sufficient, for mere proximity to a resource does not prove differential access.[6] For that we need evidence of distribution of consumer goods requiring those capital resources (Haas 1982:93). The inference of stratification can be approached by searching for unequal distribution of any of these basic resources or anything else that can be identified as a basic resource in the particular society under study. It is probable that some uneven distribution of these resources can occur without the aid of a social mechanism of stratification, but differences will be neither great nor stable, for there are no effective ways of accumulating resources beyond varying personal ability and energy without preferred access to capital resources. Also, while differential distribution of any one of these products implies stratification there will likely be a pattern of differential distribution (Haas 1982:93).

In general, the distribution of prestige items might be expected to parallel inequities in the distribution of basic resources (Haas 1981:85) so one way to begin a search is to see if those individuals who are known, on the basis of status markers, to be of high status are also associated with greater quantities of the basic resources. This is important from the perspective of interpretation and not just method. In more complex societies, characterized by specialization and even ethnic or cultural diversity, it is possible that some basic resources will be unevenly distributed for reasons other than stratification. If high-quality foods, for example, are consistently associated with individuals otherwise determined to be of high status, it is most likely because of stratification, and not a voluntary, ethnic, or religious preference for a vegetarian diet. The correlation of basic resources with status markers helps tie differential distribution to the status system. It may also provide a check on our own ethnocentricity in making interpretations.

Loosely following the outline for the inference of stratification developed by Haas, I review a range of specific approaches to recognizing the differential distribution of each type of resource.

(a) Food items that contribute to basic subsistence and adequate nutrition.
Unequal distribution of foods may be evidenced in either trash deposits or skeletal remains (see Chapter 5), but the association of storage facilities with high-status residences is not sufficient, since this may represent a redistributive system (Haas 1981:85).

> The upper stratum's diet should have a higher nutritional content (protein, vitamins, minerals, etc.), and include more types of foods and perhaps higher quality items and better cuts of meat. Thus, a stratified society based on unequal access to foodstuffs should have trash deposits with qualitatively different comestible assemblages.
> (Haas 1982:94)

This is entirely reasonable, although in some unusual cases there may be a problem deciding what constitutes a better diet. Thus in the Hindu-influenced diet patterns of India there is in fact a differential distribution of animal protein; only those of the lowest strata will stoop to using meat. Goody has also found that the development of a differentiated cuisine – an *haute cuisine* compared to the normal low cuisine – often (but by no means always) accompanies stratification. Importantly, the gulf between the elaborate tables of the rulers and the simple diet of the lower classes was "not simply a matter of quantity, but of quality, of complexity and of ingredients" (Goody 1982:99). Although this is not itself differential access to essential resources – there is nothing essential about the complex combinations of ingredients and modes of preparation of ancient Egyptian cooking, nor the more than thirty forms of bread and cake found on the Egyptian Papyrus Harris of about 1200 BC (p. 100) – it is evidence of access to a different order of agricultural produce, trade items, culinary effort and skill, and cooking equipment. It is conceivable that an elaborate cuisine would be associated with a leader in a non-stratified society (given perhaps a close association of foods with the sacred person) but Goody found that it has not been universal even among state societies, and probably requires a large "upper class" and certain qualities of agricultural production to develop. Such a differential cuisine might be recognized by variety of food types and both utensils and facilities for preparation, although I suspect that it would have to be quite highly developed for reliable inferences.

The experience of the modern West is one of a vast difference in distribution of food among people, something closely related to variation in personal wealth and a result of social stratification. Among Tahitians, foods were also restricted, chiefs getting much more in general and the totality of certain highly-valued foods. Meats especially (and pork more than fish) were severely restricted to those of high status (Oliver 1974:223, 258, 273–274, 782–789). But among Hawaiians, while chiefs had the right to demand what foods they wanted without regard for what was left the rest, in practice there was enough satisfy everyone (Sahlins 1958). Equally to the point, differential distribution of foods does not appear to characterize non-stratified ranking. In some cases (the Natchez [Swanton 1911] and Cuna [Steward and Faron 1959]), even when there was considerable ostentation in status display, and great reverence shown to chiefs, records give no indication of significant differences in foods apart from the first-fruits donations common among redistributive systems.

In a study of the changes in pre-state social organization of Jutland, Parker Pearson (1984a) observes that as the variation among households in cattle keeping increased, it was not just that some individuals accumulated greater wealth, but at the same time some experienced a decrease in wealth; despite the growing wealth of some, their poorest contemporaries were now poorer than anyone in earlier periods. This strikes me as a good archaeological indication of developing social stratification, for it is most unlikely that we are just seeing a scattering of ambitious or fortunate individuals managing to raise a few more cattle. Growing wealth and economic control are being maintained even as others in the same settlement experience an eroding economic position. Some individuals appear to have had greater access to this important basic subsistence resource than others.

Drawing from this example, it is possible that this represents a more general relationship; when disparity in status and living conditions grows as a consequence of stratification, it will be characterized not just by the higher statuses becoming yet higher, but also by an actual decrease in quality of life among a certain segment of the population. We should not just concentrate on a search for evidence of more elaborate living, but also evidence for a decline, specifically a focused decline coinciding with increasing prosperity elsewhere. A general decline, of course, could as well be due to environmental degradation.

(b) Tools for acquiring, producing or preparing foods.
Among tools for food production, Haas emphasizes small agricultural implements. Since these are typically kept in or around one's homestead (or placed in burials), it is possible to determine whether or not they are evenly distributed. Immovable items like irrigation works, and less durable "properties" like draft animals, probably have an even greater effect on ability to produce food, but it is much more difficult (at least at present) to relate these to individuals using archaeological data alone. (One exception would be when we can identify stables or pens and determine how many animals were held by each.) There are many possible differential distributions of tools depending on the specifics of a stratified system, but they can be grouped into two basic patterns: when tools are widely distributed, but differ in quality; and when they are found associated with only some individuals.

> [C]ertain types of tools may be technologically superior to other types of tools (for example, metal vs. stone plows), and bestow an advantage on their possessors in the production of food. In this case, finding the superior tools in association with only a portion of the population, and the inferior tools in association with the remainder, would constitute evidence of a form of stratification.
> (Haas 1982:97)

The other pattern, a distribution of agricultural tools such that some individuals have them and others do not, can surface in either of two ways.

> One possibility is that the persons in possession of the agricultural implements have greater ability to extract basic subsistence resources, and constitute an advantaged upper class. Another possibility is that some persons without agricultural implements have some means of inducing those with implements to supply the requisite subsistence resources.
> (1982:97)

Smaller tools will more often follow the latter distribution, while large capital resources (land, irrigation access and the like) will more likely concentrate in the hands of high-status persons. However, there may be some problem inferring social stratification from unequal distribution of tools. This pattern will be found whenever leaders are relieved of the manual labor of food production, an arrangement which, while not found among all hierarchical societies (Tikopia chiefs cultivate their own gardens [Firth 1936]) does characterize some societies not otherwise considered stratified (the Natchez [Swanton 1911]). It is possible to argue that this custom of some people having access to the labor of others itself constitutes stratification. Yet differential access to the labor of others in general is not necessarily *itself* differential access to an essential resource; it can be a luxury, depending on what this labor accomplishes. Among the Hawaiians it was clearly an aspect of stratification since the differential access to labor was integral to the land tenure system; cultivation of chiefly fields was a condition for receiving land for one's own use. Chiefly control of status items may involve differential access to the products of semi-specialized artisans, but this kind of activity can take place in the absence of true differential access to basic resources.

Most of what was said about tools used for food production would also apply to those used for the *preparation of food*, which include items necessary for cooking, processing, eating, and storing foodstuffs. But in this case, unequal distribution may also assume another pattern; while everyone may have access to the tools needed, obtaining them may be more difficult for some with the consequence that they will be more intensely used and re-used. Rather than finding a distribution such that some had an item and others not, we may find variation in patterns of disposal and of wear (Haas 1982:99).

(c) Protective devices for coping with the environment.

Differences in clothing and housing, means of protection from difficulties brought by the physical environment, may also be evidence of differential access to a basic resource. The means of recognizing differential access to clothing are similar to those for tools; some individuals may have access to the products of specialists or improved access such that they need not use any specific item as intensively. Admittedly, this is all rather optimistic about preservation, and it is important to consider that those of high status received access to special kinds of clothing through the work of specialists, something which does not in itself constitute improved access to basic resources. Housing as evidence of social stratification may be indicated by differences in size and quality of construction, but as discussed in the next chapter, variations in size and quality of residences may be found among ranked but unstratified peoples. Haas says that "in a stratified society there should be 'palatial' architecture clearly different from other lower status residential architecture" (1982:101–102).

Although it is not clear that these larger, better-made buildings represent a greater or more direct meeting of the basic need for protection from the physical environment, some at least would constitute evidence of stratification for a different reason. If a residence is distinctly superior – especially one requiring labor far beyond what an individual and obligated relations could provide – it indicates greater wealth, the means to obtain much labor from others for personal ends. And substantial wealth differences would only be possible under a stratified system. Even here, though, ambiguity could remain, except when the scale has become quite grand, for chiefs may be provided an exceptional dwelling as a sumptuary item, not based on wealth.

Protection from aggression by another social group – as with weapons or defensive architecture – is also basic to one's well-being (Haas 1982:103). Of course, it is not necessarily the case that stratification was lacking if these evidences are not found, or even if they decline in importance. This point was brought home with force through Costin and Earle's study of consumption patterns among the Wanka just before, and just after they were conquered by the Inca. During the Wanka II period (AD 1350–

1460) the region was controlled by several independent and mutually hostile polities, whereas it was united under the Inca, and subsequently at peace during Wanka III (AD 1460–1533). Costin and Earle (1989:694–700) distinguished elite and commoner households based on architecture, then studied artifact distributions in relation to this classification. Elite household artifact inventories of the Wanka II period were characterized by a greater portion of (a) foods highly valued for nutritional or symbolic reasons (maize and most meats); (b) highly valued utilitarian craft items (based on labor in manufacture, distance from sources, limited distribution); and (c) non-utilitarian wealth items. This indicates notable stratification, but with the Inca conquest, access to most of these items grew more equal. Hastorf found a similar leveling when the Inca conquered the Sausa (1990:285). It appears that the Inca demand for tribute did not have a strong adverse effect on diet, and wresting control from local elites actually broadened access. We know better than to conclude that stratification was absent from the Inca state, or that states are on the whole economically benign. It is merely that the study area no longer represented the whole story.

In addition to recognizing unequal distribution of basic resources (capital or consumer) it might be possible to infer social stratification by recognizing its secondary effects. By secondary effects I mean any aspect of economy or life style that is a consequence of differential access to basic resources. Based on discussions in Chapter 3, these would include accumulation of wealth, extension of central economic control to the household level, and possibly also a decline in the economic well-being of certain individuals while wealth is being accumulated by others.

The inference of wealth

Although I have used the term frequently, discussion of wealth was deferred because of its distinctive implications. Wealth refers to items of value anyone may possess if they have the means, in contrast to sumptuary goods, symbols of status which may be owned or used only by those of appropriate status. Wealth is also more of a comparative concept. As major wealth differences probably would not develop, and certainly could not be maintained without stratification, they constitute evidence of this element of status.

Clearly, then, there is great value in being able to recognize wealth items in this sense. Among peoples with ranking but not stratification, those of high status may use finely made (often exotic) items possessed by no one else. These are not wealth but status items. Other finely made items may not be pure status items, but high-quality versions of utilitarian items. These *could* represent wealth. Stratification can be inferred from major variation in artifact quantities among individuals which cannot be attributed simply to the use of status-marking items so common with unstratified ranking. It seems that wealth differences, measured by great variation in quantity of possessions, are common in stratified societies. Among the Tahitians for example, everyone possessed some cloth, while chiefs enjoyed much greater amounts than required for physical needs. Among modern Westerners much material culture is available to all who can afford it, and there are great differences among people in quantities possessed.

However, the problem of distinguishing wealth items and their accumulation from status markers will often make this a difficult correlation to use. If an item's distribution is due to its being a status item it should be restricted to specific statuses. If its distribution is based on wealth differences resulting from stratification it will be found more commonly or in greater quantities among the wealthy/high-status people even though it is available to anyone. Thus wealth can be inferred by substantial variations in quantities, where they are not restricted in distribution to certain statuses. But while a valid correlation, this presupposes that we already know something about the status system. Even though status items in a non-stratified society are restricted to certain statuses they may still be widely distributed. It may be that an item marking high status is possessed in greater quantity by those of highest status than by those of intermediate rank. While it will be restricted to those above a particular rank, the result will be a fairly broad distribution accompanied by variation in quantity. And one could expect that, in general, artifact distributions based on wealth variation would be similar, some people possessing more, some less, and many not having any at all. Even though it would be socially acceptable for anyone to possess such items, the poorest in a stratified society will lack certain items entirely. Thus unless we knew the nature of the ranking system and could correlate the distribution of artifacts to it, we could not use such a distribution to distinguish wealth – hence stratification – from restricted access in a non-stratified situation. This does not mean distributions lack value in efforts to infer stratification. It may be possible to learn enough about the rank system by other means to meet this stipulation. Also, the type of artifact is important. It is likely that differential distribution of fine and luxury items will be the most obvious effect of wealth differences. These would ultimately be the result of differential distribution of essential resources.

7

Status, settlements, and structures

The "built environment" is typically studied at three levels. For the field archaeologist these might be the structure, site, and regional settlement pattern; for the analytical archaeologist the micro, semi-micro, and macro levels (Clarke 1977:9); and for the geographer, the household, community, and region (Hodges 1987:133). The first perspective emphasizes what we as archaeologists have to work with, while the latter reminds us of real people living together. And while Clarke's terminology is not widely favored, scale is clearly central to the use of structures, sites, and their distribution to reconstruct households, community life, and regional interaction. Although these levels tend to blur when applied to the study of inequality, they are useful for ordering the discussion.

The distribution of communities across the landscape

Early studies of settlement archaeology often emphasized the relations "between human groups and the natural environment" (Trigger 1989a:282). This was an important theme, for example, in Robert Braidwood's Iraq Jarmo Project, and Richard MacNeish's Tehuacan Archaeological-Botanical Project. Without ignoring environmental interaction, however, Gordon Willey altered the course of settlement study with his pathbreaking *Prehistoric Settlement Patterns in the Viru Valley, Peru* (1953), by investigating settlements and their distributions as a reflection of available building technology and "various institutions of social interaction and control" in order to "reconstruct cultural institutions insofar as these may be reflected in settlement configurations" (1953:1). The distribution of communities across a landscape reflects (in addition to environmental and other historical contingencies) primarily "the impact of trade, administration, and regional defence" (Trigger 1989a:285). Therefore, insight from the regional perspective is not redundant with settlements and structures, which tend more directly to reflect community structure and family organization. A single community might be largely undifferentiated even if part of a regional hierarchical organization (as with modern "Shahabad"; Kramer 1979b:144), in which case we could not easily infer ranking except from the regional perspective. Another advantage is the possibility of making inferences based on survey data even in the absence of detailed investigation of individual sites (Kowalewski 1990:40).

The settlement hierarchy

Identifying settlement hierarchy is the most important means of inferring inequality from regional data. Any differentiation among settlements sufficient to indicate the dominance of one or more is a settlement hierarchy. This in turn is evidence of rank because whatever the nature of this "dominance" it means there is at least one individual in one settlement with leadership functions extending beyond a local community. Assuming we can identify a settlement hierarchy, then, we can infer social inequality apart from any other evidence for personal status. Differentiation among settlements may take the form of size variation (measured in area or population), or "complexity," a concept encompassing any number of aspects of plan and construction. Yet this rather indirect connection (settlement hierarchy as evidence of authority patterns directly, then of status) sets limitations. It is not true that the ranking of individuals correlates with the ranking of settlements in the straightforward manner described by Price: "Site stratification – the contrast in size, plan elaboration, and contents of communities which comprise a network – is the material isomorph of all non-egalitarian society" (1978:168).

There is no solid theoretical basis for the idea that all non-egalitarian peoples lived in a settlement pattern involving a contrast in size, plan elaboration, and contents of the communities. More importantly, ethnographic counter-examples are known. When Raymond Firth visited the island of Tikopia, he found it dotted with twenty-one villages plus a few scattered houses (Firth 1959:182). Villages were all very similar in size and plan, so unless we stress the scattered houses, Tikopia is not characterized by site stratification. The scattered settlement pattern of the Tahitians (Oliver 1974) adds further complication. Non-residential structures such as *marae* (temple areas) and archery platforms were typically separate from dwellings. The dispersed distribution accommodated the entire built environment of a hierarchical society without the need for anything that would fit our notion of a village. Certainly it was neither simple nor uniform – importantly, chiefly homesteads were larger than those of common people – but it does not approach what could meaningfully be described as a hierarchy of settlements. In one interesting case, archaeology suggests that settlement hierarchies are not always found even when there is other evidence of personal status inequality. Bernard Wailes notes that while "the enormous henges, megalithic tombs, and stone alignments of northwestern Europe certainly require immense labor and so, by implication, control of people" there is no evidence of settlement hierarchy, indeed "we are hard put to identify even hamlets for the societies responsible, let alone anything remotely approaching the urban." (Wailes 1990:354–355). Of course we can no more deny the large number of people whose labor was required, than the need for leaders to direct their work – reason for caution with conclusions based on the meager settlement evidence.

But the point is not to deny the reasonableness of inferring inequality from settlement hierarchies when found; it is only that high statuses, even those with a substantial leadership component, will not predictably lead to settlement hierarchy. The social basis for site stratification is the centralization of certain activities. This results in the concentration both of the physical structures used directly for these activities, and of the further material consequences of their taking place in only one of the settlements. At least one settlement will differ from the rest, probably in size, but in other ways as well. Since central authority presupposes status differentiation, it is safe to infer ranking from the presence of site stratification.

What differences among sites would constitute site stratification or settlement hierarchy? Size is the most widely used attribute, in part because this information is often ready at hand. Reporting on a survey of the coastal plain of Israel, for example, Gophna and Portugali (1988) identify "strongly hierarchical settlement systems" largely on the basis of relative size. They further calculated population size, and since this was not based on a simple formula assuming the same number of people per area for all sites, it did give a somewhat different (although not genuinely independent) picture of variation among sites. But settlement size is a largely continuous variable, raising the question of what degree of differentiation is sufficient to justify inference of a hierarchy of settlements. As Price makes clear, site stratification is not simply variation in size. This is possible in any social situation; even seasonally migrating bands will live in different-sized groups from time to time, which will leave their mark as sites of different sizes. Settlement hierarchies will involve a patterned variation in size and complexity, which would be distinguishable from size variation resulting from factors not directly related to social organization (e.g. different resources available to independent settlement groups). Clearly, inferences will be stronger when we can discern such patterns, substantial differences, or both. Possehl, for example, distinguishes the Pre-Urban and Urban Harappan Phases of the Indus Civilization by contrasting the lack of "clustering within what would be called a tiered hierarchy of settlement patterns" (1990:270) among sites of the Pre-Urban phase with the two very distinct tiers found among Urban Phase sites. This latter hierarchy consists of three very large sites (Mohenjo-daro, Harappa, and Ganwariwala) plus the rest, and the inference that these are "regional centers or 'capitals' developing as part of the emerging Urban Phase" (Possehl 1990:271) is strengthened by their even spacing within the Harappan domain.

A "tiered" or "multi-level" hierarchy refers to patterns of variation where sites fall into clearly distinguishable clusters based on size, clustering which indicates a qualitative difference among the settlements. Naturally, sites might vary more continuously and it still be the case that one was an authority center. Also, administrative seats, the physical loci of centralized power, are not always the largest settlements. Compare, for example, Washington, DC with New York City or Augusta with Portland, Maine. But while an exact correlation of settlement size, political importance, and economic importance cannot be assumed, their interrelation can to some extent be sorted out through excavation (e.g. McAnany 1989), and even my "counter-examples" were from a social situation characterized by both settlement and status hierarchies. And who could mistake Washington for anything but a ceremonial center of the first order?

To the extent that size variation is a consequence of (multi-community) authority patterns, it is because of the *centralization* of leadership functions and typically also the presence of functions not found in less complex political organization. Chiefs can become surrounded by specialists, and high chiefs, princes, and kings by several orders more of administrative functionaries. To the extent that leaders control the economy (even just a redistribution system or the flow of prestige goods), residences will have a wealthier aspect. Often, too, the settlement will be more cosmopolitan. It may be stretching to apply that word to the chiefly villages and *bohios* of Ancient Panama for example, but Helms (1979) demonstrates that the intellectual life, not just wealth and artistic patronage, was centered around those of high rank, that travel to exotic places (physically and through trance) to obtain esoteric knowledge (and almost anything from abroad) were much cherished, and that all of this comprised a significant dimension of prestige. Through functionaries and specialists directly, and urbanity and prestige indirectly, the settlement in which a leader lives could become larger than others quite apart from any special environmental endowment. Webster provides ethnographic evidence supporting "a high degree of correspondence between administrative and settlement hierarchies" (1990:338–339), a major link being the number of supporters of the leader in residence. He also uncovered several African examples which support the notion that settlement size differentiation increases with administrative centralization or number of administrative levels. Thus a "Yao petty chief's" village is much larger than the average, and among the Lovedu, the paramount's village might be over ten times the size of a typical village.

> Similarly, the massive size of royal towns in some intralacustrine kingdoms, with populations in the tens of thousands, is in large part explained by great numbers of royal family members, military, craftsmen, slaves, and other courtiers, retainers, and dependents in resident service to the king. (Webster 1990:339)

It would be reasonable to expect these settlements to vary in other ways as well. In the southern Mexican Valley of Oaxaca it has been found that (especially after AD 250) "[l]ower-order towns were not small versions of larger cities, and the cities were not small centers writ large" (Kowalewski 1990:49). This he calls "vertical complexity," and defines it as "a measure of the degree to which central places differ in composition depending on their hierarchical level (Kowalewski 1990:49).[1] It may be a way of confirming that there *is* a hierarchy, and where a given site fits within the hierarchy. Concentrations of public architecture, particularly that related to authority (plazas, major storage facilities, government buildings, craft specialists) at some sites would indicate multi-village authority. In general, greater vertical complexity would correlate with a stronger, more centralized or more extensive authority system (extensive in area and/or range of matters over which authority is centralized).

Through an interesting chain of inference, Stephen Shennan concludes that political centralization had developed in Central Europe by 2000 BC, the close of the Early Bronze Age. He takes the appearance of a two-level settlement hierarchy as primary evidence of political centralization (1986:119). The higher-order sites were not major population centers; rather, several other factors suggest hierarchy (1986:120–122): (a) fortification of some sites; (b) aspects of distribution, especially the fact that there were only one or two per valley; (c) a large number of storage pits (relevant, perhaps, to tribute collection or redistribution); (d) indications of craft activities; (e) hoards of metalwork, as well as amber beads from the Baltic; and (f) equipment (sometimes elaborately worked) for horseback riding. There is evidence from later periods that equestrian pursuits are associated with high rank. The pattern of some defended settlements (including labor-intensive construction as well as location) and scattered undefended settlements is also known ethnographically, for example among the Maori (Firth 1929:92). An illustration of somewhat greater complexity comes from the Valley of Oaxaca where Kowalewski found that until about AD 650, primate centers "possessed by far the greatest concentration of civic-ceremonial architecture, art related to state ideology, exotic goods, and craft manufacturers; and they had the best access to the widest range of utilitarian goods" (1990:49). Lower-order centers were also distinctive, based on size, extent to which these features were exhibited, and (unlike primate centers) lack of ties outside the region (p. 49).

While there may be any number of ways in which settlements vary due to status inequality and authority patterns, Hodder cautions that some kinds of variation could instead "represent different expressions of wider social and symbolic structures" (1990b:309). This may in part come from his tendency to view social organization and symboling as opposed explanations, but his examples are also a reminder that some variation in size, and some specialized structures are possible without implying inequality.

Number of hierarchical levels

Kowalewski sees the number of levels in a settlement hierarchy as a useful measure of complexity, noting that in the Valley of Oaxaca, number of levels (as measured by architecture) "grew from the chiefdom through the state periods. The former had up to about three levels, while the latter had between four and six" (1990:47). Although Kowalewski does not use this as a basis for deciding whether a period was characterized by chiefdoms or states, Henry Wright and others (see H. Wright 1986 and his extensive bibliography) have suggested exactly that, arguing that the chiefdom can be inferred from a settlement hierarchy of two or three levels (the latter corresponding to more complex chiefdoms), while additional levels would indicate a state. The idea is not without merit in a basic sense, but as with the type concepts themselves (perhaps even more so) there is rather too much fuzziness for such specific, clear inferences. One problem is methodological in that even when a settlement hierarchy is clearly evident, it may not be easy to determine an exact number of real levels, as distinct from levels produced (or ignored) as an artifact of method. There is also the matter of relating settlement levels to social or political organization. Why should each level in a political hierarchy be expressed in a distinguishable level of settlement? Yet even a rough number of levels in a hierarchy is a valuable thing to know, offering insight into the complexity of the ranking system, and to a certain degree, the range of differentiation among statuses as well.

Settlement and population distribution across the landscape

In the absence of political control, de Montmollin suggests, it would be reasonable to expect "a spatially 'efficient' distribution of the population with reference to agricultural fields" (1989b:299). This may mean settlements of a location and size allowing all food producers ready access to their fields. Then, substantially divergent population distributions would be evidence of political control above the household or village level. I believe there is much potential in this ingenious proposal, but it is not without problems. The main concern is that this is an approach to middle range theory which involves (in the first step) a prediction about what people would do in certain circumstances. Earlier, in defending middle range theory I largely conceded to Hodder that attempts to predict what people would do are incompatible with the view that humans are active and creative "agents." A purist in this matter would likely reject this inferential method out of hand, allowing that there is too much room for misunderstanding if we try to attribute modern, Western, secular-materialist "rationalizing" motives to people of markedly different cultures. And I would agree to a point, for correlates depending on assumptions predicting human actions (which cannot be true all of the time) have a built-in weak spot. But I add also that the behavior predicted by this approach to inferring political organization from population distributions is neither specific nor unreasonable.

The practical problem is that it will be difficult to settle on the null hypothesis; what would be an efficient distribution that we can reliably contrast with a politically enforced – or at least organized – alternative? Subsistence productivity and available transport affect the number of people who could cluster and still conveniently exploit their fields, while both culture-specific preferences and features of the "human" regional environment also affect how people would settle uncoerced by leaders: the relative preference for dispersed versus aggregate living conditions and relative need for defense being two influential possibilities. Whether under the strongest central control, or under no intervillage control, the actual settlement pattern of a complex society will be a difficult-to-predict compromise among several incompatible goals, a configuration unlikely to be optimal for any single factor (Conrad 1978).[2] For example, minimizing agricultural effort will often conflict with maximizing arable land, because to locate one's dwelling near a field could mean locating it *on* another potential space to produce food. Also, aggregation into any but the smallest of villages means some people will live further from their fields than if they lived in dispersed hamlets. The fact that villages, towns, and cities are so common across cultures suggests that for whatever reason (innate or culturally-based sociability, real or imagined defensive need) people are often willing to put in a bit of extra effort to live near a larger number of other people.

Nevertheless, it may be possible to isolate the effect of "maintenance of sociopolitical control" as de Montmollin argues. Conrad tested for the relative importance of arable land maximization, minimization of agricultural effort, and maintenance of sociopolitical control in the Viru Valley of Peru. Based on a set of assumptions (including control of settlement by the Moche State) he compared for each factor what the optimal settlement pattern "should" be if that was the sole guiding principle in deciding where settlements should go, with the actual configuration of Moche Period (AD 200–700) settlements. He found that villages tended to cluster around "tertiary centers" which indicates a concern for sociopolitical control and no apparent attempt to restrict settlements from arable land. Even under strong central control, settlement patterns are compromises, and while it may be possible to sort out which factors were more influential in each case, and thus infer the presence (even perhaps the strength) of administrative control, Conrad's reminder that "sub-optimal behavior" is inherent to compromises must be kept in mind (Conrad 1978:296).

Other features of the built environment

Demarcation of the landscape into fields and house lots might also yield evidence of ranking (possibly differential access to essential resources) but moving from information like field size, distribution of improved or higher quality land, and relative permanence of landholdings to "causal" social configurations is not easy.

> "Proximity" arguments come into heavy use; the inhabitants of houses or the persons manning political facilities closest to agricultural features were most likely to control them. Such reasoning raises some problems, given the possibility that control was exercised at a distance, but it is difficult to see how one might proceed otherwise in a regional archaeological analysis. (de Montmollin 1989b:296)

It is possible to imagine archaeological scenarios that lead us to envision stratification. Suppose that within a region, larger sites, or those with high-status and public architecture, were found adjacent to a large section of improved land (perhaps terraced and irrigated) while most settlements were less elaborate and located by unimproved land. By the "proximity" argument we could conclude that the concentration of high status (as measured by other factors) in these settlements is related to access to the presumably higher-productivity land and the essential resources produced by it. Social stratification comes easily to mind, yet even though this example is carefully contrived to reduce ambiguity, a clear inference still eludes us. One would hope that with all the effort expended on "improving" the land, it had grown more productive, but this would still not answer the crucial question of whether it was substantially more productive than other land in the region. This may be stretching a point, and if we *can* conclude that some people are becoming "wealthy" from bumper crops, this is indeed "unequal access" to basic resources, and can significantly affect status and other aspects of social interaction.

The level of individual settlements

As early as 1881 Lewis Henry Morgan presented a formal correlation of quality, scale and variation in architecture with complexity of culture (Abrams 1989:49), a correlation which has apparently been made, if only implicitly, by many people throughout the world who have chosen to build distinctively or on a larger scale than their fellows. If the plan and architecture of a site are not homogeneous it may indicate a differentiation in function among buildings implying activity specialization among residents. This is direct evidence of differing statuses, although not necessarily of ranking (Renfrew 1972:399). Nonresidential construction has been seen as evidence of inegalitarian social structure (S. Pozorski 1987:18; Pozorski and Pozorski 1987:42; Cliff 1988:206–207), although not in itself sufficient. Cliff, for example, is unwilling to conclude for a Late Preclassic phase at Cerros (northern Belize) that status inequality had developed despite "the community effort implied by the construction of structure 2A-Sub;" probably a public dock (p. 207). The problem is that specialized, non-residential structures (and plans) may be found in non-hierarchical societies. Adler and Wilshusen (1990) found that social integrative facilities[3] were quite common in "tribal" societies. Of the twenty-eight groups studied, twenty-two (or 79%) used a structurally-separate communal building. Apparently, productive community effort is possible with no more than transient leadership to get the idea going and provide direction, something perhaps especially true of facilities for group activities like dance or clan houses, plaza structures and men's houses. This sets a limit to the correlation of intra-settlement complexity with social hierarchy. Many specific configurations, and any really substantial differentiation imply ranking, but there remains a wide range of "borderline" cases. This is because while the need for special buildings increases greatly with central authority, this construction need not be extensive. Tikopia villages are not obviously complex, and Kramer (1979b:144) found that while the modern traditional village she calls Shahabad is an integral part of a vast and ancient civilization, it is essentially a small peasant town with little non-domestic architecture.

Another aspect of settlement complexity that suggests ranking (also by way of centralized authority) is organization and planning. Arawak villages were differentiated, with a ball court in the center surrounded by communal houses and the chief's house. At least one settlement was also carefully planned, to the point of having right-angled streets (Rouse 1948:524, Steward 1948:24). Chibcha and Uraba settlements (Steward and Faron 1959:213–215, 222) were carefully planned and organized as well as characterized by variety in constructions. Planning requires a planner whose directions are followed – a leader, a person of high status – and in these two ethnohistorical examples, chiefs saw to it that a village was set out according to their approved plan. But while planning is reliable evidence of inequality, the problem is determining what kind of settlement organization really indicates planning in this sense. For example, an observable "uniformity" in residences may imply no more than a common idea of what a house should be like, while constraints of topography and earlier building may create an artificial impression of order and design that was not accomplished at the hands of a designer. The following sections review the implications of several types of non-homogeneity in settlements.

Inferring stratification

Although attempts so far at relating "emerging stratification" to changes in settlement patterns and architecture have not met with great success, I believe some progress has been made. Gary Webster (1990), for example, argues that mature stratification may be a prerogative of an already established hierarchy of power rather than a major factor in its development. Leaders will accrue increasing control over labor, after which true differential access to basic resources and major accumulation of wealth will follow. One prediction would be the appearance of pronounced settlement and residence size differentials prior to the development of stratification. But it is clear, as several commentators have pointed out (Hodder 1990a: 350; Knapp 1990:351; Martinez Navarrete 1990:352–353; Wailes 1990:354–355) and as Webster acknowledges, that settlement hierarchy is not evidence for differential control of labor, however consistent with it. Hodder mentions some alternatives, that differences in settlement sizes "could well be the result of differential success in exchange (for which there is much evidence), feasting, and the control of ritual (especially in the heavily ritualized causewayed enclosures)" (1990a:350).

Major internal divisions within a settlement have also been proposed as indicators of social stratification by way of being "evidence of internal stress and class conflict at the site" (Topic and Topic 1987:49). Haas (1981) for example explains the "great wall" at Galindo (a Moche V site in the Moche Valley of Peru) as a social barrier meant to mark off upper- from lower-class residents. Topic and Topic, though, argue that this wall is actually for external defense rather than a reflection of internal conflict "since elite architecture is on the outside of the wall, and storage, as well as lower class residences, on the inside" (Topic and Topic 1987:49). But while the Topics reject neither the correlate in general, nor even the conclusion that the residents of Galindo were divided into social classes, Hodder (1987a) is more wary of generalizations of this sort. A boundary cannot be taken to have a defensive (or physically protective) purpose unless it would suffice to provide protection. And, while it might be a social barrier without being one meant to protect people from physical harm, the assumption that it distinguished (and/or protected) one class from another must account for other possible explanations. Hodder (1987a:138) points out that boundaries around a settlement may well be meant (symbolically) to separate culture from nature. Extending his point to the present concern, internal barriers might also have symbolic connotations; for example separation of sacred from mundane. It may separate an elite compound without implications of stratified classes, or it may simply have once marked the edge of a growing settlement. These are important cautions but by recognizing them, a careful study of the nature of the barrier and of the configuration of the settlement on either side may well allow us to discover the purposes of any specific barrier. Does it mark off a temple, a major elite residence, or a "neighborhood" of large, well-built residences from the rest of the settlement? Symbolic "statements" might be harder to sort out, but are not necessarily incompatible with an alternate conclusion. As with a low Victorian cast-iron fence, easily seen through or hopped over, the separation of upper-class residences may itself be more symbolic than a matter of physical protection.

The analysis of residential architecture

A residence is a structure used for human shelter, and we may usefully contrast "residential" with "public" architecture. To be sure this is rather rough; in what sense can a cave be described as a "structure" for example, and given this definition, it is clear that there are important aspects of the built environment that are neither residential nor public (e.g. field boundaries, storage facilities or other "industrial" structures for use by a family or segment of the community). Finally, structures used to shelter humans may serve any number of additional purposes. But while this may muddle what had seemed a clear distinction, differing cultural conceptions (and practical expressions) of what a residence is can be very useful for understanding former lifeways, including personal ranking (Trigger 1978b:170, Cordy 1981:viii). Cliff summarizes – clearly and to the point, if perhaps a bit optimistically – how domestic architecture may serve as evidence of status: "Dwellings are viewed as complexes of architectural features that (a) individually symbolize the social status of the occupants, (b) collectively symbolize the social structure of the community of which they are a part, and (c) change in recognizable ways as the social structure of the society changes" (1988:200, 202). This inferential process can also be quite complex since the character of residences may be affected by any of a large number of factors (environment, history, utilitarian considerations, social factors other than status). Size, for example, may be related to family organization, especially whether a nuclear or an extended form is the rule (Trigger 1978b:172–173). Building materials may be related to environment (e.g. the importance of mudbrick at both ancient ChanChan and modern Trujillo, and of stone in the early hill-country settlements of the Southern Levant [London 1989:47]), while construction may be influenced by materials. Aesthetic considerations will make their own demands on design, engineering, and materials. Other influences include characteristics of the social environment; general complexity, need for defense, engineering knowledge (and access to this knowledge), people's conception of the functions of a residence, not to mention how each of these has been shaped by history. The influence of these factors should be felt throughout the settlement, so within-site variation will tend to be more helpful for status inference. Not all variation among dwellings at a site will be the result of status of course, but "variation between houses within a village can be one of the best sources of information about the variation between families – variation in subsistence, division of labor, craft activity, social status, and so on" (Flannery 1976:16). The major variables of residential architecture are reviewed in the following sections but actual structures depend on the myriad possible combinations of these, and recognizing inequality will likely be more complex and subjective than the theory suggests.

Scale, prominence, and energy expenditure

One of the most important ways in which residences vary within a settlement is size – important because it is common, often recoverable archaeologically, and because major size differences frequently represent ranked status differences. Two related measures are energy expended in construction, and the more subjective variation in scale or prominence. These perspectives take advantage of different kinds of evidence (energy may go into different materials rather than size, while "prominence" might be achieved largely by location), but in each case variation relates to social hierarchy in a similar way.

Energy expenditure correlates all work in much the same way, varying primarily in the specific features used, and in how data are translated into energy terms. Much that was said of the mortuary energy correlates also applies here, although dwellings generally reflect family rather than individual status (and so will be less helpful in, for example, the study of gender relations). Cordy (1981:86) summarizes the main points of an energy-expenditure correlate first developed by Tainter and Cordy (1977).

> Labor expenditure involved in permanent housing construction positively covaries with the social rank of the household's highest ranking member. Households whose ranking members are in the same social rank level have similar amounts of labor expended in the construction of their permanent housing.

People of higher rank will be entitled to greater disruption of daily activity for house building, and those to whom more people hold social obligations will be entitled to more labor. This general connection is reasonable. In addition, Cordy tested its reliability with an ethnographic sample of fifty-six cases with impressive results; the hypotheses were confirmed without exception (Cordy 1981:86–87) or even any ambiguous cases (see chart pp. 233–235). But some correlations are fairly broad and Cordy observes that in most cases labor expenditure and ranking will not correspond one-to-one (1981:234 note C). The correlation may actually work at a detailed level, but Cordy's second point (correlating rank *levels* with energy *levels*) is important. In my own much smaller sample (which also supported the correlation)[4] much of the energy difference was expressed in size, chiefly houses being similar in materials and construction, just larger. But other uses of energy were observed. The Natchez Great Sun lived in a dwelling that was not only large but built on a mound, a striking qualitative difference which consumed far more energy than the larger size of the house itself (Swanton 1911:59). The houses of Cuna leaders were not grand in size but were built on a stone paving, thus distinctly more energy expensive (Steward and Faron 1959:227). In the village of Shahabad, Kramer (1979b:153–154) found that wealth (the most meaningful measure of status) correlated with house size. But the correlation was skewed by the exceptional wealth of a few; in detail, house size did not always vary precisely with wealth.

Magnitude of variation may be even more limiting than when using mortuary evidence, for while people rarely contribute labor directly to the construction of their own tomb, members of a family may well participate in the construction of their dwelling. In some cases, those of high rank are required to abstain from labor, and in highly specialized economies, many people, regardless of status, will lack the necessary construction skills. But not uncommonly, families provide a significant part of the labor, and much variation can result from differences in skill, attention to detail, aesthetic sense, and family size among unspecialized individuals, quite apart from systematic status differentiation. Further, it would not be unusual for many people to draw their "labor force" from among relations or neighbors, and additional residential variation could result from differences in family size, popularity, and influence. Thus among the modern Kekchi Maya, the more important individuals could have larger houses because there is "a direct correlation between the status of the individual, the number of relatives he could call upon, and the amount of building materials he was able to collect" (Cliff 1988:219). This was the case despite it being an ostensibly egalitarian community, and the fact that although only relatives helped collect materials, all community members participated in much of the construction.

But there will be limits to this variation, for even though peoples with little or no ranking recognize some individuals as more important, and even though they have differing kin groups to draw on, they are unlikely to recognize an obligation to build someone a house twice the size of their own. *Major* differences in size require qualitatively different statuses. They will appear only when the range of people with social obligations is extended *and* the idea of one family deserving a more energy-intensive residence is acceptable to those doing the work. Such a person will have a different kind of access to energy: access to the labors of people out of the normal set of relatives, and possibly also differential access to specialists. People may be expected to contribute to a chiefly residence regardless of their relationship, or perhaps because everyone is a relative of the chief. Among the Tikopia, people helped chiefs with construction, but helped each other in similar ways, so that despite the matter of rank, and the fact that chiefly houses were commonly temples as well, they were only slightly larger (and not otherwise more labor intensive) than normal. Clearly an argument from the negative would be unsound. Someone with an achieved high status may also have an energy-expensive residence, but while the outcome fits that predicted by the energy correlate, it would be due more to personal industriousness than a structural access to labor.

Nevertheless, if a settlement boasts a few distinctly energy-intensive dwellings, we can safely infer inequality. Energy *will* correlate with rank, but with other reasons for variation we cannot safely infer it from minor differences – despite ethnographic precedent (e.g. the Tikopia). How we measure energy can also affect the outcome. Problems can be minimized by accepting only large differences as evidence; otherwise ignoring one variable could easily throw off the order in which residences are ranked by energy expenditure (compare, for example Arnold and Ford's [1980; Ford and Arnold 1982] approach to differentiating Mayan dwellings with that of Folan *et al.* [1982]).

Variations in the scale or prominence of residences relate to social hierarchy in basically the same way as energy expenditure, indicating that some people have greater access to labor than others. But while there is much overlap (particularly since size is central to energy measures) energy could be invested in alternative construction materials, arguing that when possible we should not compare structures on the basis of size alone. If size is the only evidence at hand (e.g. floor plans) constructing an energy measure could be unrewarding, even misleading.

Important to Renfrew's individualizing chiefdom model is the ability to distinguish those of high personal rank or who are leaders. Archaeologically this may be done either through personal possessions "or by the scale and prominence of his residence" (1974:79). A few residences will, he argues, be out of proportion to the rest. This might mean being so much larger as to be on a different scale, as with chiefly dwellings among the Arawak (Rouse 1948:525) and the wooden "palaces" of Chibcha leaders (Steward and Faron 1959:213–214) or, as among the Natchez, standing out for their placement on platforms, mounds or in a striking area of the settlement (Swanton 1911:59, 102). Arawak chiefly houses were not only of an unusual design and exceptional size, but were prominently located at one end of the ball court in the center of the settlement. And among the Palenque of Northern Venezuela, one chief is said to have had a large palisaded stronghold with a mound in it (Steward and Faron 1959).

But while this correlate appears to bring reliable, almost obvious conclusions, cautions have been issued. Visual impressiveness, we are warned, can be misleading as an indicator of rank (Arnold and Ford 1980:715; Lightfoot and Feinman 1982). Yet these concerns have more to do with the limitations of a negative conclusion. Thus Lightfoot and Feinman found that while Mogollon pithouse villages were simple and unimpressive, there likely was some ranking among those who produced them. I have noted much the same for the Tikopia and Tahitians, and a cross-culturally valid correspondence between degree of status differentiation and range of residence variation does not seem possible. The relation of scale and prominence to status inequality is imprecise (and somewhat subjective) but inferences will often be sound, since if there are major differences in prominence, some families simply must have had greater resources to draw on. We can also conclude that it was a legitimate use of labor and resources – which raises the question of whether the expression of status through prominent dwellings may indicate not just ranking but an element of self-aggrandizement and indulgence.

One practical caution should also be mentioned. Clearly this line of inference assumes we can distinguish personal dwellings from other structures. Prominent buildings do not demonstrate ranking unless indicative of corporate labor (see below), whereas the mere presence of prominent residences would. And reliable identification of a structure's purpose may well be a difficult task. Witness the continuing debate – of nearly one hundred years – over the function of tripartite pillared buildings in Iron Age Palestine (Herr 1988). Fortunately, distinguishing a special function or public building from a residence is often easier than identifying the exact function of a non-residential structure. Yet there are confusing possibilities. Consider this description of an Island Carib settlement: "In the center of the village was the mens' house, where all males slept, ate, and were attended by the women ... The women's houses surrounded the men's houses'' (Steward and Faron 1959:322–323).

Although obviously related to prominence and to energy measures, variation in size requires separate discussion because there are at least three social bases for some dwellings being unusually large: status display and luxury, number of residents, and use for "additional" functions not typical at the time. It may be common that size variation is related to status display or luxury, in which case it would have the same social "cause" as scale, prominence, and impressiveness, even when no examples are genuinely prominent. Among the Arawak, chiefly dwellings were easily distinguished by size, but served no special 'public' function. And while chiefs had more wives, the greater size was not for the utilitarian purpose of housing more people, since other Arawak dwellings were multi-family, yet smaller nonetheless. High-status dwellings of the Chibcha, too, were probably large only for status display or the pleasure of the inhabitants.

But size variation may also relate to number of inhabitants. Such dwellings may be distinguished by spareness of detail and furnishing, or use of much of the space for basic functions of a large family. Yet even if some variability can be attributed to household size, it still might involve differential status. Orme relates the large houses of big-man leaders and village-level chiefs to their larger households. "The material manifestations of polygamy, and some other facts of big man status, may be visible archaeologically: housing to accommodate the family, and shelter for extra animals, or storage for the extra crops that a big man is expected to raise in order to give away" (Orme 1981:141). Among the Palenque of Northern Venezuela, the chief with a large palisaded stronghold is said to have lived with a harem of two hundred women (Steward and Faron 1959:244). For the modern traditional village of Shahabad, Kramer (1979b:148) found at least a small correlation of house size with social hierarchy, but this did not account for all variation; house size also correlated well with family size. Second stories, which greatly increase house size, are typically built for additional family members such as married children.

A leader may also require more space to house crafts, food, and equipment, and indirectly because of the larger household needed to out-produce others. This brings up the third major social basis for residential size variation: some structures which are basically dwellings, serve additional purposes or accommodate greater intensities of normal household functions. Lightfoot and Feinman (1982) argue that if larger houses are associated with intensification of certain activities – surplus storage, subsistence intensification, regional exchange, redistribution, and other forms of central coordination – they were the households of high-status individuals with leadership roles. This is important because when dwellings are not *much* larger, size alone makes a weak case for inequality. When status is reached by achievement in normal activities (and the ideal of creating obligations by generosity), high-status dwellings may well be large, but not on a different scale. They will be large versions of normal residences and will evidence intensification of some basic activities.

In other circumstances, a few dwellings are larger because they are used for additional functions, not just intensified normal household activity. Among the

Tikopia most chiefly houses are also temples (Firth 1936; 1940:30, 136). Much the same is true for the Natchez (Swanton 1911:59, 102); chiefly dwellings were important religious centers, and the Natchez Great Sun's house had many features in common with the main temple. In both cases, chiefs were important to the religious-ritual system. Among the Natchez, the chief's house was also used for meetings. Trigger observes that among the Huron, "the most important chiefs in a village occupied the largest long houses, which served as gathering places for meetings and rituals" (1978b:173). Use of a residence for a meeting place may well be common (although separate meeting and ritual facilities are also widespread) and will be one reason for a larger high-status residence. Even when the scale of elite dwellings makes it reasonable to call them palaces, much of the space is used for public duties. Dever summarizes residential variation for several sites of Middle Bronze Palestine as follows.

> Most private houses are simple mudbrick structures, with only a few earthen-floored rooms ... rather closely crowded together around communal courtyards and narrow lanes. A very few large, multi-roomed structures, however, resemble "patrician villas," such as those at Hazor, Tell-Beit Mirsim and elsewhere. Finally, we have a growing number of even more elaborate buildings, such as the two-story colonnaded structure near the Northwest Gate at Shechem. These are almost certainly the palaces of local dynasts.
> (1987:164)

Our confidence in Dever's understanding of the social basis for each level is enhanced through contemporary parallels and documentary evidence (Ebla is one of the sites with an MB palace), but some version of the archaeological argument itself might be more broadly applicable. This three-tier residence hierarchy is relatively clear because of *patterned* variation and the substantial difference between tiers; the clarity of the distinction among tiers makes for stronger evidence of distinct ranks.

Variation in the plan of residences

By plan I mean a complex of variables, including number of rooms (or buildings), proportions, specialized rooms and arrangements (association with shrines, audience rooms, workshops, storage facilities, military constructions), and differential segregation and defense. While any variation in plan may potentially relate to ranking, details of layout might reflect instead personal preference in design,[5] available space (influenced by natural topography, or the history of re-building in a compact settlement) or any number of other factors. Dwellings of Arawakan chiefs were rectangular and gabled where others were round with conical roofs (Rouse 1948:525). This may relate to size, since large buildings are easier to make in rectangular form. But since there is no structural reason that the other dwellings could not also have been rectangular, the difference may have signalled rank. As plan comprises a number of variables, several examples might usefully illustrate their potential relation to status.

Additional and special function rooms   For Loma Torremote, Sanders, Parsons, and Santly (1979:319–320) concluded that certain variations in plan (together with artifact distributions and size) allowed the inference of ranking. One dwelling was distinctive in having a greater roofed area per capita, an annex identifiable as a shrine, and a much larger grain storage capacity. Shrines were not associated with other residences, suggesting that this served the entire community, and that one aspect of this family's distinctive status was as religious specialist. High status also had an economic side. Some of the evidence comes from artifact data, but the architecture itself indicates the family's economic importance. More than 2.2 times the family's annual grain needs could be stored in the pits within this compound, while the storage capacity of neighboring compounds indicates their annual needs would be just barely met. It is not clear what either the source or use of this "extra" grain might have been (1979:320–321). It may not be beyond an industrious household to fill this storage, but the architectural feature shows at least an unusual economic position in the community which, in light of other evidence, may well be redistributive in nature.

Number and configuration of buildings   Among contact-period Hawaiians, high-ranking families had a greater number of separate structures within their household compounds (Cordy 1981:75), something also true for the Tahitians (Oliver 1974), Cenufana of Columbia (Steward and Faron 1959:222) and Shilluk (Dempsey 1955). There are many more houses on Tikopia than are necessary for mere accommodation "and a man of rank may have three or four in different parts of the island" (Firth 1939:35). Yet many others also have more than one house, and in any case, such a pattern would be difficult to recognize archaeologically. The typical Tikopia "house" included a dwelling, cook-house, and canoe shed. Not all possessed all three, but variation was not associated with rank (Firth 1936:58). This variation is not great, so it remains reasonable to postulate that major differences in number of buildings per homestead will evidence ranking.

Platforms, fences, and barriers   Platforms are among the most commonly mentioned architectural features distinguishing dwellings. They absorb copious effort and rarely have mundane practical function. If they were utilitarian in nature, one could reasonably expect all residences, or perhaps all those on land prone to flooding, to be on platforms. The purpose might not be clear, but certainly one of the most obvious effects is raising a dwelling to relative prominence. A fence or palisade around some dwellings clearly marks them as distinctive. More elaborate versions might be for defense, indicating greater access to external defense or a need for some people to be separated from fellow residents. Either would be evidence for social stratification (Haas 1982).

These examples offer concrete perspective, but clearly some of the ways in which residential structures might vary, while good working clues, would not result only from ranking. These examples suggest that it is more difficult to accept an unambiguous relationship between plan and status differentiation than, say, for size variation.

Aspects of residential construction

Variation in the nature and quality of construction may also be evidence of inequality. Several dimensions (quality, finish, materials, unusual features) are relevant to energy measures, for effort and expense are their most direct and objective connection to status. But they are also independent qualitative features, and may help us uncover the nature of status, or strengthen a basic conclusion when the magnitude of energy variation is not decisive.

"Quality" denotes a complex of factors, some more objective and observable than everyday use of the term suggests. "Finish," for example, may mean use of cut versus field stone, squared timbers, or plaster to smooth a wall (while not improving its strength). Ethnographic examples of construction quality distinguishing high-status dwellings are common; well-done thatching among the Tahitians (Oliver 1974:165–167), frequency and quality of floor refinishing in the village of Shahabad (Kramer 1979b:148), or plastering among the Natchez (Swanton 1911:59). No doubt some variation in quality and attention to finish can be traced to differing skill or personal fastidiousness. One observer of Tahiti noted differences significant enough to call some wretched, unwholesome, comfortless huts (Oliver 1974:168), a condition attributed to indolence or lack of tools (the latter not unexpected per discussions of stratification).

The use of different materials in contemporaneous buildings cannot have an ecological basis in the same sense as variation across regions or time periods. Materials may require varied labor expenditure, even special skills; either way, one's choice may depend on status-related access and skills. High-status houses might use additional materials (Cuna stone pavings; imported glass for windows at Hasanabad), or might differ overall (Chibcha chiefly houses being of wood, others of wattle and daub). Among Classic-period Maya structures in the Valley of Copan, Hendon found that finely-dressed tuff ashlars predominated in the Main Group while wattle and daub was most common in the outer zone (1991:905). In one group (which included both residences and ritual buildings) most structures made use of a combination of tuff ashlars and cobbles with the worked stone "generally placed on the front of the building ... suggesting a desire to display the tuff as prominently as possible" (1991:905). Labor differential may be central to archaeological inference, but for contemporaries the materials no doubt had other meanings as well. In the Mesoamerican Early Formative, wattle and daub was the nearly universal construction material, and Flannery suggests that the first use of adobe, probably in public buildings, established meanings and associations which emphasized its importance (1976:24). Rather than assume that the importance of adobe resulted from the extra labor required, perhaps an historically conditioned cultural perception made investment of the extra labor acceptable. Materials which do not differ greatly in labor or skill requirements may still mark different statuses, as when some dwellings are more like public structures. Without suggesting it as an invariant correlation, the observation could strengthen conclusions otherwise more tentative. The decorations of Tahitian chiefly houses, for example, were found also in public buildings (Oliver 1974:165–167). They were no more than braided cords on rafters, hardly a great distinction to an outside observer, but the difference was qualitative, required specialists, and served to tie these houses to public buildings. Among the Natchez, too, aspects of design and finish made the home of the Great Sun differ from ordinary dwellings in being more like a temple (Swanton 1911:59).

One final construction variable is differential presence of specific features including decorative details, functional features, or complex construction techniques. Special features like decorative braiding among the Tahitians (Oliver 1974:165–167) or sacred carvings in one Tikopian house/temple (Firth 1940:212), consume labor but produce a building which functions no better as shelter or comfort. We might also discern the work of specialists, differential access to which is consistent with ranking. If variation falls into a pattern (but does not involve differences in quantity or quality) we might instead suspect symbols of kin group affiliation, and the differential presence of functional features (a paved versus dirt floor as among the Cuna, built-in furniture or storage, and any number of other internal features) may represent additional labor but not such that can be separated from industriousness and differing aesthetic attitudes. Kramer (1979b:148) found for Shahabad that variations in built-in features of houses (hearths, ovens, storage bins) do not reliably predict either wealth or number of residents, correlating better with the time a house has been in use. Differential distribution of complex or sophisticated construction has more promise, but the chain of inference is not from variable through labor to status; implied instead is differential availability of special skills (e.g. Moore's discussion of the Chimu site of Manchan, Peru [1981:116]).

Change in features of residences over time

A few very large, finely-constructed dwellings in one period would lend weight to the suggestion that the much less marked variations of a previous phase indeed expressed inequality. A study of change can also offer new insight into the social relations at any given time. For example, throughout the building levels of Loma Torremote, all features indicating higher status were consistently associated with the same house compound (A-1). This was rebuilt several times and remained distinctive throughout the sequence. Sanders, Parsons, and Santly (1979:321–322) conclude that status was maintained by heredity. This assumes dwellings were occupied over time by people related by descent, which does not always hold true for residences of leaders (e.g. the White House), nor for very mobile peoples like ourselves whose houses are bought and sold, although it does seem reasonable for many archaeologically-known peoples. Compound A-1 is a large, elaborate example of normal housing (at first only barely distinguishable from the rest) which appears to be the home of a family that grew in status over time.

Gerontocratic status can ... be rejected because here we would expect variation to occur only within a single building level and the overall pattern should be more cyclical in nature, corresponding to the growth and decay of individual families. In contrast, if these patterns [increase in storage, roofed space and other features] are related to emerging ranked distinctions, then they should appear to a greater extent over several generations and remain in evidence regardless of fluctuations in population size.
(Sanders, Parsons, and Santly 1979:319)

Any non-hereditary ranking should show the same cyclical housing pattern that these authors expect for gerontocratic status. If someone achieves high status and builds a suitable dwelling, this can be used by his or her descendants regardless of their status. But when it comes time to rebuild, this could only be done on the same scale if the high status had been maintained in the family. This is sound and useful, though its reverse will not do, for residence location may well shift even if status remains in a family. A Natchez great chief's cabin, for instance, was demolished at his death and a new one built for his successor (Swanton 1911:103). Among the Tikopia, building sites were inherited and chiefs in any case wanted to remain near their *marae*. But old houses sometimes became shrines, and burial under the floor encouraged moving after a time. Firth found that between his 1929 visit and his return in 1952 some buildings had been repaired or rebuilt in place, while some were new and others abandoned (Firth 1959:187).

Non-residential construction

"Non-residential" refers to any construction not typical of domestic architecture even if part of a residence, and just what qualifies will depend on the range of activities people define as domestic. "Public architecture" is also useful (and largely interchangeable) even if it is not always clear whether or in what way a structure was public. The relation of residential to public construction is important, for if the physical contexts for religious or economic activities are associated with particular dwellings, we can infer that the relevant social categories were also associated with the residents. Among the Natchez, Cuna, Chibcha, and Tikopia, chief's houses were closely connected with the main religious structure, while Cenufana chiefly house compounds were surrounded by several large storehouses.[6]

Social complexity generally correlates with settlement complexity. If there are more different activities carried out or if they are more distinctive or institutionalized (craft specialization, certain individuals functioning as priests), the social order will embrace a greater range of statuses (although of course, not all will be ranked). Complex society will also require public buildings, structures reflecting the activities held to be important (Renfrew 1972:402), and both the activities and work organization required are clues to status. Particularly important are scale (with corresponding implications for organization) and among structures of a certain scale, what kinds of non-residential structures were emphasized.

Monumental and corporate labor construction

Although we cannot infer ranking from the presence of non-residential architecture as such, if some structures are monumental or the products of corporate labor, there must have been some level of inequality.

> The amount of energy expended during single episodes of construction reflects the involvement of very large numbers of people, an organization capable of orchestrating those individuals, the political power requisite for mobilizing that labor force, the presences of craft specialists sufficiently trained and skilled to contribute to the construction process, and a system that can afford to lose the energy that otherwise would have been produced during the period of construction.
> (Abrams 1989:60)

This important and long-established line of argument can sometimes be applied in much this form; Dever for example says of the massive (and architecturally complex) defenses of Shechem, Gezer, and other Middle Bronze sites that they "simply could not have been built by an egalitarian society with voluntary efforts" (1987:163). And after even a brief look at the plans, it is hard to imagine anyone disagreeing (Dever 1993, figs. 1, 10, 14, 15, 17, and the photographs in Dever 1987:156–159). The inference of inequality through monumental construction is logically sound in that it unambiguously connects a material characteristic to one social configuration. But it is not so obvious what, exactly, would qualify as monumental. The defensive works of Gezer tell us of an established social hierarchy, but what of a structure half the size? Feldman (following Moseley 1975:79–80) draws on the concept of "corporate labor" as distinct from just "group labor," to clarify this point. Corporate labor is

> group labor that draws its work force from separate households, either from within a single community or from separate communities. The laborers work together in a collective, integrated manner for a specific purpose, which is defined and sanctioned by an authoritative body that coordinates the project, and to which the will of the individual is subservient while the laborer is participating in the project. Corporate labor is an organizational concept that implies the existence of an authority with the rights and ability to mobilize people and direct their actions.
> (Feldman 1987:11)

Thus the major structures of the Cotton Preceramic (ca. 2500–1800 BC) of Aspero on the Peruvian coast "could possibly be interpreted as the products of an *ad hoc* organization," says Feldman, "but their size, detail, and continuity of formal concept through time show the hand of organized control" (1987:12). Both massive building projects, and smaller projects which display either complexity or coordination of specialized skills (in the arts, or in engineering) require the effective centralized direction of a large number of people. As evidence of leadership, it is also evidence of ranking, for while we can conceive of ranking with more prestige than authority, central authority without a distinctive status to bear that right makes no sense. Importantly, this adds to the list of real structures which are clearly projects requiring authority for completion. Yet ambiguity remains, for the question has always been just how much could be done without a leader; what is a minimum combination of size and complexity from which we can safely infer central authority? Also, what could be accomplished by simple ranking and what would require stratification? A common and productive approach involves translating constructions into the amount of work or energy it would have required. Progress has been made, and pitfalls are well recognized (see Abrams 1989:63–68 for a summary). Archaeologists, Abrams reminds us, do not excavate energy but "material embodiments of energy" (1989:63), so most questions concern translation. A labor–time measure (e.g. person-days) is common, and one use of such calculations is determining how many people would have been at work at once. Correlating this with population estimates can indicate if workers were recruited from one or many settlements. But this all depends on knowledge of (or assumptions about) length of construction period, how hard people worked, and what really can be accomplished with a given "level" of social control. It does not take a productivity expert to recognize that knowing someone was "on the job" eight hours tells us little about the amount of work accomplished. Yet if we are careful to define "person-day" or develop standard measures (Abrams suggests basing them on ethnographical, experimental, and physiological data) this will allow us better to compare structures.

To claim that a particular structure is solid evidence of inequality means knowing that it could not have been accomplished by an egalitarian society, but just what might an egalitarian society accomplish? It might be useful to survey the architectural accomplishments of ethnographically and historically known non-hierarchical peoples, particularly the more populous and well-integrated groups. To my knowledge this has not been done in any extensive way (although the Adler and Wilshusen [1990] survey does help). I believe this would allow more dependable inferences from a certain range of constructions even though we could not fully trust the tempting conclusion that anything more substantial than the largest structure uncovered in the survey was built by a hierarchical society. The question of what is *possible* for an egalitarian society (or one with a certain kind of status system) must remain ambiguous because of the great importance of motivation, work ethic, and other culture-specific factors we are unlikely to discover.

This is the crux of Webb's (1987) argument, as he takes issue with the idea that the state had developed on the Peruvian coast by the Initial Period. Haas had argued that Huaca La Florida (Rimac Valley), with a volume of over 400,000 cubic meters, represents work of a magnitude not seen among non-state societies (Haas 1987:32). Webb's calculations seem to support this; by comparison, the largest *marae* of Tahiti and Hawaii are only about 14,000 and 15,000 cubic meters. But do we know this was the limit of the organization's capability? The figures themselves do not account for priorities. For example, Webb found that the effort needed to raise the 2,200 pigs slaughtered at the dedication of one Hawaiian temple would, if directed otherwise, have made it possible to double the temple size (Webb 1987:162). This is still a trifle short of 400,000 cubic meters, but Webb calculates that such a project could be accomplished by a large-scale chiefdom (population 15,000) in a little over fifty years if that was a priority for them, and concludes, "It all depends on what one likes: Haas and I as New World archaeologists, enjoy hauling rocks about in the hot sun; the Polynesians favored feasting on pig and dancing" (1987:162). Haas counters that there is more than just negative evidence to support his conclusion. Webb's argument draws on the important question of motivation. If motivated to concentrate their energies on a temple mound, a chiefdom of 15,000 *could* build Huaca La Florida in about fifty years. But what would provide such motivation, and how likely is it? Motivation is a major difference between a chiefdom and a state when it comes to corporate labor projects, for state leaders have a "qualitatively greater kind of economic power base not found in chiefdoms" (Haas 1987:32). It is this greater control of resources and of people that makes large-scale construction possible. "People," Haas concludes, "simply do not go out and merrily build platform mounds without being told to do so by some authority figure" (1987:32).

This brief exchange has not answered the question of when the state first appeared on the Peruvian Coast, but it usefully draws our attention to the concerns we need to address. The basic inferential argument itself is simple; this structure is evidence of a certain pattern of authority because it is too large or complex to have been undertaken with less central control. Thus Webb's approach addresses the argument much more directly than would an ethnographic survey. If an egalitarian (or ranked) people could produce a monument, it cannot be taken as evidence of hierarchy (or the state). But while this is also simple enough, Webb's calculations raise their own questions. Is there reason to believe a mound was built over a period of fifty or more years? Is it likely that energies were concentrated on this one mound? It may be possible to answer these kinds of questions archaeologically. And Haas also has a point. On the surface, his position is simply common sense contrasted with theoretical possibility. There is no evidence that chiefdoms produce monuments like Huaca la Florida, and there are innumerable examples of states having done so. Further, this is exactly what we would expect given the differences in the authority patterns between chiefdoms and states. Certainly we can envision chiefdoms producing larger monuments than on Hawaii or Tahiti, but more than twenty-five times the volume? And where would we stop in such hypothesizing? The same 15,000 could, in about one hundred years, produce a monument fifty times the largest ever produced by the Hawaiians or Tahitians. At some point it is fair to ask, if all this is possible, why has no known chiefdom or stratified (non-state) society produced anything even remotely like it. At some point the answer must be, insufficient political coercion. But at what point? Because we do not know how much work 15,000 people would be able to sustain regularly over fifty years motivated only by religious fervor, village pride, or a succession (over fifty years) of unusually persuasive chiefs, inference of state organization will only be fully reliable when based on works which by any calculation would have been impossible. So, back to our original question, what could be sustained by a non-hierarchical people with only ad hoc leadership?

But it would be inappropriate to end on this pessimistic note. The inference of hierarchy – or some specific form – from major non-residential constructions will not always be as firm as the direct logic of the basic correlate suggests. But this correlate was already unusual in offering (if only sometimes) unequivocal results in isolation from other lines of evidence. And reasonable, if not irrefutable inferences can be derived from many equivocal examples. It may even be possible to infer specifics of ranking. Shelia Pozorski suggests that the large mound and successively smaller mounds at Sechin Alto (Peru) "argue for an intrasite status hierarchy with at least three or four levels including the main mound and the domestic occupation" (1987:23). We may also be able to draw inferences from the characteristic types of construction at a site. Corporate construction may emphasize projects supporting group activity; meeting places, temples, and other ceremonial architecture, or perhaps specialized works related to subsistence pursuits benefiting the whole group. But the focus may instead be on high-status individuals themselves with constructions serving to emphasize their glories or provide them with comforts and pleasures (Trigger 1978a:160). These alternate emphases correlate with Renfrew's (1974) group-oriented and individualizing chiefdoms. The main features of the group-oriented chiefdom appear to fit a social order of ranking without stratification, while features of the individualizing chiefdom better represent social stratification.

Access patterns and status

Access patterns are useful for inferring inequality from non-residential constructions. Thomas Pozorski uses some interesting aspects of the plan of the Huaca de Los Reyes at the site of Caballo Muerto in Peru's Moche Valley (T. Pozorski 1980, 1982) for this purpose. Particularly important is the division into areas of very different size, but potentially similar function.

> Plazas I and II could hold a great quantity of people and were probably used by common people, visitors, and pilgrims. The awe-inspiring giant friezes found there ... would certainly be in accord with this view. The restricted Plaza III and the plazas of mounds C and C', being smaller, held fewer people and were probably used by a more elite clientele, persons of higher status. The variety of friezes in Plaza III and the distinctness of the feline figures of mounds C and C' argue for a more complete knowledge of the religious pantheons ... perhaps restricted to certain status groups. Furthermore, the inner sanctum of the mound F summit could very well have been restricted to the most elite members of the society. (1982:250–251; see also 1980:109)

The temple of the Fincenu of Colombia must have been similar, in both structure and intent. While the main part of the temple (which held twenty-four large gold-covered figures) could accommodate about 1,000 people, "Temple guards prevented ordinary people from entering the inner sanctum while the priests were communicating with the gods" (Steward and Faron 1959:223). Indeed, religious-ritual structures with small, restricted, inner rooms are not uncommon ethnographically, being mentioned for the Natchez (Swanton 1911:65), the Lache of Venezuela (Steward and Faron 1959), Cuna (Steward and Faron 1959:227), and Chibcha, access to whose temple was restricted more by a palisade than by size (Steward and Faron 1959:215). The Hebrew temples (including the earlier tabernacle described in the Pentateuch) were built as a series of more and more restricted areas (for basic references see Kenyon 1974). Temples of similar plan are known archaeologically from Shechem (the so-called "Middle Bronze Age palace"); Middle Bronze Age Ebla (Tell Mardikh); Canaanite Hazor (Late Bronze Age); and Phoenician Tell Tayinat (ninth century BC) (Dever 1990:110–111). This division of space which included special, restricted rooms, was also a feature of Roman oracular temples. Those at Didyma, and probably also Kedesh included a cella housing the cult statue (Apollo). Although most likely unroofed, these spaces were only accessible to priests (Magness 1990:174–175).

For purposes of relating an architectural pattern to social organization, "restriction" could refer to (a) areas which are much smaller than others (can only accommodate a sub-group of those who could participate in events held in the larger area); (b) areas that could be used by only a small portion of the residents of the settlement; or (c) areas not capable of accommodating the number of people needed for the overall construction work. The degree to which access is restricted may also be a clue to its social basis, the nature of the exclusion. Portions of the Early Intermediate Period ceremonial area of Cerro de Media Luna (Chillon Valley, Peru) appear to be marked off by degrees of sacredness but "there is little sense of great separation between the different levels of participation" (Quilter 1990:78). For example, the different spaces are terraces rather than closed-in areas. By contrast, access to different portions of the West and Middle Temples at Tarxien (prehistoric Malta) is through barred doors and blocked-off sections (Bonnano *et al.* 1990:200). The means of access might be as good an indication of differentiation as relative capacity. Pozorski observes that passage from one area to another at Huaca de los Reyes was through "narrow restricted entrances" which suggests status differences. "If this were not the desired effect, then wider, more accessible passageways would have been built for easier traffic flow" (Pozorski 1982:251).

The slightly earlier Cotton Preceramic site of Aspero (Supe Valley, Peru) illustrates another way in which access and decoration can reinforce observations from the "capacity crowd" argument. Feldman describes "a pattern of graded access ... reflected at least partially in doorway width," and in the central rooms, a concentration of ornamentation and cached artifacts. Together these "suggest levels of ceremonial space open to selectively more and more restricted groups of people" (Feldman 1987:11). Neither Huaca de los Idoles nor any other Aspero mound was clearly monumental, and they appear also to have been built in several phases (p. 10) making the access argument and other aspects of plan (e.g. continuity of formal concept through time) all the more important to the inference of ranking.

These divisions distinguish between the more public events of one area and what took place in more restricted and exclusive areas, but does this reflect social divisions of a sort we could call ranking? The large areas suggest that a great many people were concerned with what went on at the temple – highlighting the specialness of the smaller areas. This plan does suggest that the inner areas are special places which in all probability were never entered lightly. And it is clear too that no event could be held there in which more than a small part of the population could participate. This argues for ritual specialists with a distinctive status that was institutionally endorsed and reinforced through architecture. Ritual specialists are found in egalitarian societies (e.g. shamans) but when public architecture is planned and built to distinguish ritual that can only be performed and participated in by a very few, it is clearly a more distinctive role and status. The structure represents (and its presence continually reinforces) a separation, a hierarchy of ritual accessibility and importance, and by emphasizing it so concretely, advertises its social importance. This does not in itself demonstrate a pervasive ranking system, but an important hierarchy in which a few individuals are distinguished from the rest. The segregation includes trappings of differential prestige (even though it is in one sense a hierarchy of function) and thus can be considered structural inequality.

Taking a mildly postprocessual approach, Julian Thomas (1990) uses the concept of access to interpret Irish megalithic tombs as texts read by the people who built and used them. This offers further insight into the effects of spatial distinctions but (for reasons unrelated to the method itself) does not lead as clearly to the recognition of inequality. These tombs feature progressively smaller spaces, particularly between the inside and the courtyard outside, a distinction emphasized by entranceways that were small (requiring one to bend over), yet sometimes quite elaborate. Also important, Thomas notes, is the fact that you must pass through the other spaces to get there. This linear or sequential plan is an important aspect of access patterns. Comparing the early "portal dolmen" which was "effectively no more than a large stone box enclosing a burial deposit" (Thomas 1990:172) with the "court tomb," he notes that because of the spatial effect of certain refinements, the development is one that "deserves a better explanation than vague notions of evolution toward greater structural complexity guided by a competitive urge" (p. 172). The addition of a mound and court made the chamber approachable only from one direction and after crossing the court, while the court itself marked off a place for activity connected with the monument and the burials. Internally, many court tombs consist of a series of small chambers "subdivided by sillstones and septal slabs" (p. 173), and accessible only in serial order. In later tombs the courts themselves were enclosed. This clear division among segments (particularly the chamber-court–outside world) "might be taken to suggest some social division between those granted access to these different spaces" (p. 173). Although important, these divisions would not necessarily be ranks on this evidence alone.

In the "passage tomb," elaborate artwork was also common, and significantly, either decoration in general, or specific motifs would be found in ("restricted to") certain areas. Although we cannot reliably evoke the full meaning this spatial arrangement had for users, we can say something of how these features constrain movement and stage or frame ritual practice.

The journey from the outside world into the chamber space is thus a highly orchestrated one, in which the individual is constantly being made aware that he or she is passing between radically different spaces, by being presented with symbols and by being forced to bend down or squeeze through particular parts of the passage.
(Thomas 1990:175)

What can this tell us about status? As with Pozorski's use of access patterns, it is clear that for different ceremonies or different portions of a ceremony the outer areas which were marked off from the general landscape could accommodate far more participants than the inner. This in itself could indicate ritual specialists, and the distinction is reinforced by other features of the tomb. The greater the distinctiveness between areas (the more the distinctions are emphasized by design features), the more clearly distinctive (and important) are those who go inside compared to those who remain in the courtyard. This reasoning need not assume that access to the inner areas is at all times denied to the majority of people; we can infer a distinction among them in relation to ritual performance, which is enough to infer an important social distinction whatever people's rights vis-à-vis the tomb at other times. The sequentially-channeled movement, the small entrances, the presence and distribution of art all reinforce the importance of the contrast.

This is clear enough, but in the case of tombs, just what distinction is emphasized architecturally is not so certain. While it could be an expression of people who are used to thinking of each other in hierarchical terms, it may instead be that this "highly orchestrated" journey from the outside into the chamber is a way of separating the dead from the living. Likely enough it is a bit of both. The separation and hierarchical ordering among living people is more readily inferred from progressively exclusive areas and from access patterns in ritual structures than from tombs, but a distinction of this sort, particularly where so much skill and energy has been devoted to representing it architecturally, is important to consider in relation to other evidence of social distinctions.

Çatal Hüyük: a ranked Neolithic town in Anatolia?

Bold, mysterious, and endlessly fascinating, a few ancient monuments have profoundly shaped our understanding of the past, becoming, indeed, household words. Çatal Hüyük is not among these. But if not quite a Stonehenge or Machu Picchu in the popular imagination, Çatal Hüyük is in many ways just as striking, disturbing, enigmatic. And its singular importance for prehistory has not been lost on archaeologists, who have long appreciated the extraordinary social and intellectual life that flourished here nine millennia in the past.[1] The great murals of Çatal Hüyük have not yet aroused fantastical theories and tabloid revelations, nor have they entered the twentieth-century imagination so deeply as the cave paintings of Lascaux. But the site holds a fascination for archaeologists and other scholars of the early history of humanity which remains undiminished since excavations began, an interest, I expect, that will only grow as we ask ever more personal questions of the lives of early humans.

A precocious settlement and well preserved, Çatal Hüyük offers a vibrant picture of creativity and passion in the Early Neolithic, an era otherwise largely obscured by the passing of more than eighty centuries. The unmistakable humanity revealed here is all the more striking for the fact that excavated levels date from perhaps 7,500 to 6,700 BC in calendar years.[2] And yet, whether despite or because of the range of material preserved, this settlement remains somehow inscrutable and alien. The expressive art in particular leaves us feeling that we almost know what was going on here. Almost.

And all of this was quite a surprise. Only two years before the site was discovered, five before excavations began in the summer of 1961, Seton Lloyd could still write that "the greatest part of modern Turkey, and especially the region more correctly described as Anatolia, shows no sign whatever of habitation during the neolithic period."[3] But this 32-acre mound, rising 17.5 meters above the modern plain, was occupied for more than 1,000 years with no noticeable break, then abandoned – all before the Early Neolithic had ended.[4] Numerous Neolithic sites are known from the Konya Plain (south-central Turkey), but Çatal Hüyük is by far the largest,

> in extent larger than Grodion, the Phrygian capital, and as large as most Anatolian Bronze Age towns; about twice the size of Troy VI or Old Smyrna and from three to four times the size of pre-pottery neolithic Jericho and that on the Anatolian Plateau, an area supposedly backward. (Mellaart 1961:2)

Çatal Hüyük is not only unique in its region; it takes its place as the "[l]argest Neolithic town in the world" (Gimbutas 1991:419; see also Mellaart 1962:42).

Four excavation seasons (1961, 1962, 1963, 1965) uncovered approximately one acre of well-preserved buildings and courtyards, revealing a compact settlement plan often compared to the Native American Pueblo dwellings of the Southwest U.S.A. In many cases walls and not just floor plans have been recovered;[5] a number of these were decorated with paintings, earning the site a listing in the *Guiness Book of World Records* under "earliest murals." About 150 murals have been recovered so far, and walls were also decorated with relief sculpture, animal skulls, and horns. Mellaart identified some of the buildings as shrines – as many as fifteen in use at one time – the rest as residences. Available evidence indicates that domesticated cattle provided over 90% of the meat portion of the diet (Todd 1976:120). The people also engaged in hunting, cultivation of domesticated cereals, and collecting of a great variety of wild plants. The site's exceptional artifact inventory includes items of wood, cloth, and other perishables, as well as statuettes and quantities of jewelry. The artifacts of Çatal Hüyük represent highly skilled artisanry, executed on an extraordinary range of non-local materials.

Wide horizontal coverage – including full excavation of many contiguous buildings – along with exceptional preservation, offer an unusually detailed picture of early settled life. Yet the excavation, concentrated entirely in one area, comprises less than 1/30 of the mound. The extent of contemporaneous occupation is not known for any level, and speculation concerning the other side of town has spawned widely divergent interpretations of social life.

Çatal Hüyük in social perspective

From each excavation season emerged a consistent pattern of evidence revealing "a luxurious standard of living that fit no one's expectations for a neolithic community" (Settegast 1987:163). The extraordinary range of "imported" raw materials (extensive trade?), the fine workmanship of many crafts (specialization?), and the many non-utilitarian finds ("beads," Mellaart said, "were used in enormous numbers" [1964:95]), have led to varied but always enthusiastic assessments of the Çatal social organization. Çatal Hüyük has come to represent the threshold of civilization (Fairservis 1975);[6] the "domus" home-centered society that conceived and nurtured agriculture (Hodder 1990b), and the peaceful, woman-centered "Civilization of the Goddess" (Gimbutas 1991). In Gimbutas's model, the Civilization of the Goddess flourished throughout "Old" (pre-Indo-European) Europe from 6,500 to 3,500 BC, before "the transition to patriarchal and belligerent societies" (1991:vii–viii), and something like it was found at Çatal Hüyük a millennium earlier.

> Archaeologists and historians have assumed that civilization implies a
> hierarchical political and religious organization, warfare, a class
> stratification, and a complex division of labor. This pattern is indeed typical

of androcratic (male-dominated) societies such as Indo-European but does
not apply to the gynocentric (mother/woman-centered) cultures described in
this book [which include Çatal Hüyük, although the site is not central to her
point].
(Gimbutas 1991:viii)

To a war-weary century, whose own experiments with classless society have failed
in the most extraordinary manner, this model encourages hope that something of the
sort may nevertheless be possible – at least if it correctly appraises these societies both
in their claim to "civilization" and in their classless character, largely peaceful
orientation, and relative equality of sexes. Any conclusions that emerge from the
present study are relevant to this appraisal, and in outline, it may be that Gimbutas is
on to something.

Others have tried to find Çatal Hüyük a place in more conventional models of
prehistory or social evolution, models which have not gone unaltered by having to
accommodate this "premature flash of brilliance" (Redman 1978). Kirkbride
described it as "an immensely rich and luxurious city" (quoted in Settegast 1987),
and the excavator has described it as a town (Mellaart 1967) or as a city (Mellaart
1962:42). He also views it as a civilization, although I do not believe he is using any of
these as technical terms. In a summary for *Archäologischer Anzeiger*, he states:

> it is now abundantly clear that this site was not a village, but a city,
> inhabited by a community with a developed economy, social organization, a
> rich religious life, specialized crafts and a well-developed art. They were
> anything but self-sufficient, but traded far and wide to obtain the raw
> materials their economy demanded. But for the absence of writing they
> satisfied all the conditions usually demanded for the use of the term
> "civilization."
> (Mellaart 1963b:19)

For Renfrew however, the limited internal interaction suggested by the site plan
(c.f. Mellaart 1963c:722) indicates "the very antithesis of civilization" (1984b:89).
Maisels concurs, observing that "the earliest large settlements," such as Çatal Hüyük
and Jericho, "were not cities as they lacked urban structure – density and diversity of
activity manifested in the built environment" (1993:1). Certainly the "agglomerate
settlement" indicates some interaction, but even so, Çatal Hüyük strikes Renfrew as
an example of an early farming village that, despite almost urban size, did not reflect
urban organization. "There is no justification for taking a population figure of this
order [ca. 4,000] as an indication in itself of civilization or of cities" (Renfrew
1984b:90). Both the question of density and this lack of interaction might be debated
(Mellaart postulates considerable craft specialization) and I have also seen widely-
differing population estimates,[7] but the built environment is not in fact very complex,
and, indeed, the site has not often been called a city or civilization in the
anthropological sense.

What were social relations like at Çatal Hüyük? What principles of equality and inequality guided social interactions? Todd may be correct in asserting that "Çatal Hüyük is of the greatest significance in the development of Western Civilization" and certainly it is of the greatest significance to our understanding of this development (1976:IV). What kind of social organization allowed, inspired or drove this remarkably early technological and intellectual sophistication? Could this have been a civilization without stratification, without social classes, perhaps even without extensive inequality?

The examination of Çatal status relations that follows uses the methodology of the last few chapters, and excavation results as described in published reports. There is, I believe, evidence for inequality at Çatal Hüyük, probably a significant degree of non-stratified ranking. Thanks primarily to the rich corpus of art and the opportunity to correlate lines of evidence it may also be possible to infer, if rather more tentatively, several specific aspects of the status system. This chapter is meant as a preliminary investigation, but even this brief exercise in examining a body of data and illustrating the abstract discussion which makes up the bulk of this essay, has made it clear, I believe, that middle-range theory (if not applied in too simple and mechanical a fashion) can yield some interesting results.

Mortuary practices

The basic practice was secondary burial beneath "platforms," the built-in furniture common to houses and shrines. A few people were buried beneath other parts of the floor, but none were found in storerooms or courtyards. Since only the mound itself has been excavated, the possibility of outside cemeteries has yet to be explored (Todd 1976:65). Skeletal evidence indicates the flesh was removed before burial in houses, but since many skeletons remain articulated and largely complete, it may be that corpses were "exposed on platforms, accessible to the birds and insects, but not to dogs and other scavengers which carry off bones" (Mellaart 1967:204). The duration of exposure varied considerably, as indicated by differing states of excarnation, and as a plausible if speculative scenario, Mellaart suggests that burial coincided with an annual redecoration/replastering of houses and shrines, probably in spring or early summer. Skeletons were wrapped in cloth or skins, and in at least some cases this bundle was then wrapped in a twined, net-like fabric and tied with cord or woven tape (Burnham 1965:170). Usually they were laid directly in the earth, though some were placed on mats.

The sample is large, consisting of about 480 individuals from Levels XI–I (Todd 1976:64), and each burial is clearly associated with a specific building level. Levels VI A and B lasted about 150 years, but other levels were less enduring. Since chronological distinctions can often be made among burials in one house, groups of rough contemporaneity are readily established. Yet we also have continuous burial evidence spanning some 800 years, so it is worth looking for sequences of change. In fact, considerable continuity has been found (a characteristic of much of the site), and the small sample from some levels might hamper analysis, but this may be an avenue worth exploring. Exceptional preservation is another advantage. Burials were, one

might say, kept indoors for centuries and with a fire aiding preservation of some
levels, the unusual collection of organic items includes boxes and implements of
wood, and cloth of wool or flax (Burnham 1965:170 versus Ryder 1965:176). We can
learn much from the current sample, even apart from what we might find were more
of the site excavated, and a search for extramural cemeteries conducted in earnest.
And because the following inferences are quite suggestive, there is reason to look
forward to an in-depth study of the complete sample, allowing more effective use of
certain mortuary correlates.

Human osteology, paleopathology, and demography

In the late 1960s J. Lawrence Angel and Denise Ferembach undertook a study of the
skeletal material, making some interesting observations. As mentioned, those
analytical techniques with the greatest promise for social inference have mostly been
developed in the last decade, but the usefulness of further study would depend on our
being able to correlate it with other burial data, and with the structures. I am not
encouraged by Angel's observation that there was some confusion concerning which
actual skeletons were those mentioned in publications. He also noted some loss "in
cleaning," and only had skeletal material for 294 individuals, rather than the 480
indicated in reports (Angel 1971:77,79).

Osteological study has not yielded clear evidence of major status divisions and
while Angel did uncover some very interesting facts about the character of life, their
social meaning remains ambiguous. One of the most intriguing is the excess of
females among adult burials (136 of Angel's sample of 222), while among children the
ratio may have been about as divergent in the other direction (Angel 1971:79). This
has contributed to the view that women were particularly important in the religious-
ritual life at the site, but two cautions are in order. First, while the proportion was
higher among rooms with fewer burials, females do not appear to have comprised a
greater portion of the total from shrines than from houses. Also, while Angel says the
sex ratio "was almost certainly less biased" among the living (p. 79) the
preponderance of females among adult burials may have some demographic basis.
Excess deaths of boys could explain the ratios both among children and adults,
although "a more usual explanation would be some sort of social selection at death,
such as male deaths in hunting or trading or war or female preferment in a family-
centred society" (Angel 1971:79).

Also interesting is the finding that the population of just this one part of town
displayed significant morphologial variation indicating two different "racial
strains," among them "dolichocephalic Proto-Mediterranean and brachycephalic
elements" (Mellaart 1966a:8), and some variation within these types. For Gimbutas
"the point to be emphasized ... is that the bulk of the population was still close to its
Upper Paleolithic ancestry" (1991:9), but the diversity (perhaps also indicated by "a
group of black men among the otherwise pink-skinned celebrants in the Hunting
Shrine murals" [Settegast 1987:173]) may be culturally significant; "Such a
heterogeneous population accounts in large measure for the inventiveness and the

rapid advance in every field of cultural activity seen at Çatal Hüyük" (Mellaart 1975:99).

Diet and nutritional status
There is no osteological evidence so far of differential access to food. Nutrition was generally adequate; "The diet was a rich and varied one, but may have fluctuated in the meat protein ... needed for maximum child growth" (Angel 1971:89). Adult lifespan was on average one year longer for both males and females than for Upper Paleolithic samples (Angel 1971:80): 34.3 years for males and 29.8 years for females. This can be accounted for by the "completely settled and relatively secure life of the trading settlement rather than any real improvement in quality of diet or health" (Angel 1971:82) which, although better than among Mesolithic groups, may not have been as good as for the Upper Paleolithic hunters. The tendency for females who reach adulthood to not live as long as males probably relates to deaths in childbirth and should not be taken as evidence of lower status for women or of poor health for the population in general. This disparity is not known to have reversed until nineteenth-century Western cultures (1971:80).

Infection, stress, trauma, and workload
The Çatal Hüyük population did face disease and injury, most significantly the oft-noted incidence of malaria, which may have affected some 40% of the population. This "means that a trading town of over 5,000 people functioned efficiently, even with ebullient creativity as well as fertility, in spite of a great disease handicap" (Angel 1971:88). This incidence of just one disease suggests that the benches prominent in many shrines might be healing couches, like those of later antiquity, which also relate to a period of increasing malaria (Angel 1971:88; see also Settegast 1987:188–189 for elaboration).

Indications of childhood stress were low, although a few severe cases were noted and Angel also uncovered a range of wounds or injuries. Falling down the house ladder (all buildings excavated could be entered only from the roof) may account for some (Angel 1971:91) and others apparently represent unique events. About one-quarter of adult males had suffered major head wounds (27% versus 6% of females), a form of injury more common at Çatal Hüyük than for any other known example before Roman times. Ulna fractures are also common, although less so: 7% of males, no females. These may be "parry fractures," wounds resulting "from the direct violence of stopping a blow, probably a weapon" (Angel 1971:91). Although raiding and warfare come readily to mind, we may be able to relate these and other injuries to the games and festivities depicted in murals.[8]

Only rarely could the various bone reactions be attributed to specific activities, but Angel did conclude that "physical stress was heavy" (1971:91). Certain "postural details" also indicate an active lifestyle, an adaptation to rough country (p. 92), including running, walking, especially downhill (carrying heavy loads?). While it is not clear to what portion of the population this applies (Angel speaks of "hard work on the part of everybody" but his report does not indicate that all skeletons display this character), it is something to keep in mind when assessing whether excavations fortuitously hit upon a high-status area of a very hierarchical settlement. Not everyone (if even anyone at all) in this part of town lived a pampered upper-class life.

Combined or overall measures

Application of the energy-expenditure correlate, or any overall measure, depends upon detailed comparative study of each burial, or at least a tabulation of the contents of each and comparison on the basis of quantity, raw material, workmanship, and perhaps other variables. Nevertheless, even a few general observations turn out to be quite instructive.

While accepting that many burials are clearly secondary, Todd cautions that we must not rule out the possibility that some were primary. No proven examples were found, but "the occurrence of anatomically intact skeletons clearly indicates that the process of decomposition had not, in these instances, progressed very far at the time of burial, if, in fact, they were not actually primary burials" (Todd 1976:67). Secondary burial is distinctly more "energy expensive" than primary, and this could be a significant variable to consider if it is ever determined that some burials were primary. The shrines, or at least some portion of the activity held there, were related to the dead. Add the fact of secondary treatment, and perhaps also the building of charnel houses, and it might be said that treatment at death received considerable attention although it is not clear whether this rates as high "overall emphasis" in the sense used in the theoretical discussion.

Variation in tomb form; implications of collective burial

Burials were consistently placed below platforms or floors of the main room of shrines or houses, the only variation being that those found in an extended position or sitting upright required a larger hole (and more effort) than the much more characteristic pose of tightly crouched on the side. In some cases individual burial events can be distinguished (and grave goods associated with an individual) but Çatal burial must be studied largely as a kind of collective practice. Bones were often jumbled (Mellaart 1962:51), and incomplete burials are common. Disturbance of early burials by later ones is especially significant in Level VI where over time less care was taken to avoid disturbance (Mellaart 1967:205), but it is not always the last interment that is complete (Mellaart 1962:51). While this may be a product of secondary burial, it was sometimes intentional, as when several skulls are found in clusters apart from other bones.

The collective nature of burials, and their placement in dwellings, argue for the importance of the family as a social unit. House size brings to mind the nuclear family, and the burials "suggest a strong familial sense of kinship with the dead" (Mellaart 1962:52), something emphasized by the preservation of skulls. Number of burials varies considerably from house to house, and cannot be correlated with length of occupation of the dwelling (Mellaart 1967:205–206). It is clear that not everyone could have been buried here, and the fact that more than two-thirds of the burials were found in shrines suggests to Mellaart that shrines were not regularly inhabited as dwellings, and people buried there lived in nearby houses, "which confirms our opinion that the entire quarter was inhabited by priests and priestesses, who would naturally prefer to be buried in hallowed ground" (1967:206). Of course, there may simply have been cemeteries outside of town, but this is plausible and does raise the question of who received burial in houses, shrines or elsewhere. If Mellaart is correct, only "exceptional" members of nearby households would be buried in shrines. Of course, if they were instead people who lived in the shrine-dwellings, they would still be distinctive for that reason.

Variation in the quantity and type of grave associations

Many burials were not associated with any grave offerings, and none was "lavish," yet there is some variation in quantity. Certain grave inclusions are generally (sometimes exclusively) associated with one sex, although they do not appear to form a "set" of items found together if at all.

> Male burials were accompanied by weapons (stone mace heads, obsidian lance or spear heads, flint daggers with wood or bone handles), various flint and obsidian tools, clay seals, occasional copper finger rings, bone belt hooks and eyes, and a few beads and pendants. Female burial gifts consisted mainly of jewelry and items used for personal adornment (numerous beads and pendants, copper or bone finger rings, cosmetic palettes for grinding paint, and obsidian mirrors), together with various bone and stone tools. Where the body of a child accompanied that of a woman, additional goods included bone spoons, spatulas and ladles.
> (Todd 1976:69–70)

Some items (wooden vessels, baskets, various foods) are found with both sexes, while others, notably figurines and pottery, were never found in graves (Todd 1976:70). Conversely, some artifacts were found only in burials; obsidian mirrors and bone belt fasteners for example, were found only in female and male shrine burials (Mellaart 1967:208). Shrine burials are generally "better provided" than those in houses (Mellaart 1967:207). But while it is difficult to sort this out from the reports, we clearly cannot go so far as to claim that shrine burials are richer, more elaborate or higher status than house burials, something often implied in summaries of the Çatal Hüyük material. Yet there *is* variation among burials, and many of the more elaborate are in fact shrine burials, so there does seem a correlation of grave goods with architectural settings.

Consider some specifics. In a small number of burials (probably twenty-one per Mellaart 1966b:183) parts of the skeleton had been treated with red ocher. These are more common in early levels and may all be from shrines (several are from buildings of uncertain designation). They are not associated with the "richest" sets of artifacts. Many are women, but some are men and ocher was also found on children and one prematurely-born infant (Mellaart 1964:93). Two conclusions are suggested. First, at just over 4% of the sample, ocher burial appears highly restricted. But while there can be no doubt that such treatment carried important meaning, it is not clear who qualified (Todd 1976:71), or how we should define the status marked except that it is important, not necessarily wealth-related, and probably included a significant religious element. Second, the treatment of children, especially the infant, suggests heredity.[9] In addition, although several infant and child burials are mentioned in the site reports, it is clear from proportions of the burial population that "the people did not usually bury new-born infants, and probably not always those of 6–12 months" (Angel 1971:82). This infant, then, received treatment that was special in that few adults were so treated, and in that children that age were not as a rule buried beneath floors.

Perhaps even stronger evidence of social inequality at Çatal Hüyük is the marked variation among artifacts included with burials. Some are extraordinary pieces. A fine flint dagger (or hunting knife) was "the most usual male burial gift" by far (Mellaart 1964:94) but many male burials did not receive one (or anything else either), and they varied in quality, too. An exceptional example, finely flaked and with a bone handle carved in the shape of a coiled snake, was 10 inches long and most probably "a luxury weapon . . . used only ceremonially" (Mellaart 1964:95). This is reasonable although I have not seen mention of whether it has yet been examined for use-wear.[10] Characteristics of "rich" women's graves include bead jewelry (sometimes in considerable quantity) and cosmetic kits, a few of which included finely-made obsidian mirrors. Of the varied materials used for beads, "not a single one . . . could be found within less than several days' journey from the town" (Mellaart 1964:97).

On occasion, treatment with ocher, exceptional inclusions, and other indications of importance come together in the same burial. Consider two burials under shrine VIII.31. It seems the shrine was built over them, perhaps to house their remains (Settegast 1987:175). One is the disarticulated skeleton of a young male (approximately 21 years old) upright in a sitting position and wrapped in fiber.[11] "Enveloped" in the fiber and around the burial were the skulls and long bones of many mice and a shrew (Todd 1976:71). The man was wearing several necklaces and two bone rings, and had "a fine white-veined blue limestone mace-head" (Mellaart 1966b:182). Initially identifying this person as a woman, Mellaart remarks that she was buried with a macehead, "a symbol of authority" (1966b:182). This has, I expect, contributed to the recurring mention in the literature of the importance of women in the social and political organization of Çatal Hüyük. If we can use long-standing tradition preserved in Greek mythology to aid interpretation, this person might be seen as a healer (Settegast 1987:175), an association based on the symbolic significance of mice, the possibility that the benches in shrines were healing couches comparable to Greco-Roman *abata* (pp. 188–189), interpretations of certain wall paintings, and possibly also the mace head (pp. 178–179). A healer in this tradition is responsible for guiding the soul to the land of the dead not just for physical healing, so this "medical" interpretation would in no way counter the obvious religious-ritual nature of shrines. The role of healer would in both ways contribute to an honored position in society.

Also buried beneath this building (sometimes known as the Red Shrine, and itself rather unusual) was a young girl in a basket accompanied by a large quantity of jewelry (Mellaart 1966b:182, Todd 1976:71). Both burials were placed before the shrine was built, "and the unusual features, the painted platform and the orange panel with libation hole, mark the position of the graves" (Mellaart 1966b:182–183). Mellaart believes the shrine was built in memory of these two, "and the strange ritual, the rich gifts and the markers above the graves strongly suggest that we are dealing with members of a privileged class, maybe their chief priestesses and/or members of a ruling family" (p. 183). This is indeed a most unusual burial, in which several distinctions coincide (ocher treatment, amount of fine inclusions, association with unusual architecture). While religious and/or medical specialists (e.g. shamans) may hold a distinctive and honored status in societies which would not otherwise be considered ranked, the coincidence of all of these features suggests a greater level of inequality.

Distinctions which cross-cut age or sex

Three of the main mortuary variables – shrines versus houses, fine artifacts versus no artifacts (or fewer and less distinctive), treatment with ocher or not – cross-cut both age and sex, thus signifying some other aspects of status. The fact that women are found among the prominent burials indicates that it was possible for them to obtain what higher ranks there were more or less as readily as men. Further, several female burials involve strong symbolic references. I would not go as far as Gimbutas who states that there "are no male graves with such extraordinary symbolic items," an idea which may have its source in the symbolically distinctive male burial originally mistaken for a female. It is also stretching to suggest (and Gimbutas did merely suggest) that one from shrine E VII, 14 may have been a "queen priestess" (1991:9). But here the priestess part is entirely possible, and in any case this woman (as well as several others) "had a respected position in the society" (Gimbutas 1991:9). My objection is to the label "queen," not the idea that it is among the most distinctive burials in this large sample. To the extent that these burials indicate central leaders, women were as prominent among them as men.

Also significant for understanding status at Çatal Hüyük are the elaborate burials of a few children and even infants who, in their short lives, could not have achieved statuses higher than so many adults. However, unless these burials were distinguished with status markers (not just wealth), they may simply mark the achieved prestige of surviving family members. The case is weakest for those which are distinctive primarily in, say, number of necklaces and stronger for red-ocher burials. There was considerable variation among the child burials, from the inclusion of only "a chip of obsidian and a piece of shell" with the burial of a newborn under shrine E VI,14 (Mellaart 1963a:99), to that of the Red Shrine (VIII.31), a "female child in a basket, extremely richly adorned with funeral gifts, necklaces, bracelets, pendants, etc." She was also treated with red ocher (as was the associated adult male), and connected somehow with the distinctive architecture of the shrine. Of the double burial, Mellaart said it is "the nearest thing to a royal burial yet found at Çatal Hüyük" (1966a:4). Finally, while considering the case that whatever ranking we find was hereditary, this is a good place to revisit Mellaart's comment that the practice of intramural, and in a sense collective burial, "suggest a strong family sense of kinship with the dead" (1962:52).

Spatial relationships

Each burial is associated with a dwelling or shrine, and with more systematic presentation of the data, it may be possible to make more use of this spatial variable. But easy generalizations appear to be out, for while Mellaart does note a tendency for shrine burials to be "better provided for" (1967:207), it is not the case that burials which stand out for the artifacts included correlate well with residences or shrines that also stand out. For example, "there is no relation between the size of a building or the abundance of its decoration and the poverty or richness of the burial gifts of the dead below its platforms" (Mellaart 1967:82).

There are other spatial patterns, but I have been unable to relate them to status. Orientation to cardinal points is not consistent. Orientation to features of the room is much more so, the most common being feet toward the wall, head toward the center of the room. Most lie on their left side, in a contracted position, but some are extended on their backs, and some were to a greater or lesser degree jumbled (Mellaart 1967:205) The fact that there was something of a pattern – and that it was not always followed – may be important but, like most spatial relationships, only as a means of reinforcing conclusions from other variables.

Artifacts and their distributions

The two main approaches to inferring inequality from artifacts are to identify status, elite or wealth items from the objects themselves, apart from distributional context, or to demonstrate the unequal distribution of high-quality items.

Elite and sumptuary items

Most striking is the consistent high quality of the artifacts, generally (if not completely) overshadowing variation in quality. The chipped-stone industry, for example, consists of some fifty distinguishable tool and weapon types, and is "easily the most elegant in the Near East (with Byblos in Syria taking second place)" (Mellaart 1975:103). The ground-stone industry is also impressive and for Mellaart, some weapons, including the perforated maceheads "are clearly prestige objects" (1975:103). Other candidates for prestige objects include stone vessels, flint daggers, and ground-obsidian mirrors. Although none is unquestionably the sort of item owned only by those of very high status, each item listed (and others to a lesser degree[12]) display some qualities indicating use by high-status individuals.

Stone vessels were found rarely (fewer than a dozen in the first three seasons), perhaps because of the effort they require compared to the town's well-established traditions in basketry and wood (and to a far lesser extent, pottery). As Mellaart notes, the extensive use of rock at Çatal makes clear that neither material nor technical competence were limiting. But only rarely did they consider the effort worthwhile, and both the quality of these artifacts, and their association with shrines or "important burials" (Mellaart 1964:84) encourage the conclusion that they are ceremonial objects or items of prestige possessed by the few.

> The thin-walled marble bowl on crescent feet from Level IV; the four
> spouted dishes in fine veined red limestone from various shrines in Level VI
> A, the similar white marble dish found with the ceremonial dagger in a male
> grave of Level VI A in room 29, all show accomplished carving and rare
> materials and so were obviously either the possessions of the rich or used for
> ritual purposes.
> (Mellaart 1964:84)

Finely chipped flint daggers, and ground-obsidian mirrors are also candidates. Even in an assemblage notable for its skilled artisanry, these stand out for their quality, for the effort devoted to their production and, in the case of the mirrors, for the exceptional skill needed. The mirrors were most likely non-utilitarian. They are generally thought to have a cosmetic purpose (an idea supported by their association with palettes and related implements, in some cases including already mixed "rouge"). Whether simply a luxury, or of ceremonial value, is significant, but either way they are rare, difficult to make, and associated with only a few individuals.

No Çatal artifact is indisputably a status item (where are the giant gold statues that made my contrived examples so usefully unambiguous?), but they do stand out for effort[13] and quality, with placement in burials or shrines also suggesting status or ritual import. The mirrors were entirely non-utilitarian, but actually, many individuals were associated with some non-utilitarian artifact (especially jewelry). Thus there is a good, if not conclusive, case that certain artifacts were used as prestige items, in which case, inequality characterized at least some aspects of town life.

Craft specialization

The economy, Mellaart concludes, is based on trade and industry "with specialized craftsmen" (1975:105). The argument for specialization rests on the quality of the crafts, not, as is more common in such inference, uniformity indicating production by the same hand, or the mass production characterizing more developed specialization. Also important is a somewhat indirect argument for the concentration of production. No *direct* evidence of specialists has been found for any craft at Çatal Hüyük (no workshops or stockpiles of tools or materials), but very little evidence of production has been found at all. Loom weights were recovered from the upper levels, but not in quantity, and no trace of textile tools was found from Level VI, despite recovery of a number of textile samples (Burnham 1965:173). And apart from one house in Level III (A,III) which "produced a large number of stone tools as well as raw material" (Mellaart 1962:55), there is little evidence for the manufacture of the many chipped and polished stone tools found. Even after the first three seasons, Mellaart could say that evidence of stone chipping had not been found in any of the 200 houses excavated (1964:105). Indeed, despite the importance of agriculture and the regular presence of food preparation equipment (querns, pestles, and pounders) in both houses and shrines, few agricultural implements have been found.[14] There is, in other words, little indication of these varied artifacts having been produced by the people who consumed them.

It is conceivable that people from every household did make their own beads and chip their own obsidian, but did not work inside their houses, on their rooves, or in the courtyards of this part of the settlement. This leaves out-of-doors as the major site of craft production for all the people who lived in this area, somewhat unlikely in such a climate, particularly among agriculturalists. While I have little expectation that future excavation will uncover a stoneworkers' quarter or bead manufacturers' neighborhood, the near-absence of production evidence throughout the entire excavated area suggests at least part-time craft specialization, and that the specialists lived elsewhere. It also means that those who lived in the excavated part of town had access to the products of specialist artisans, yet were not connected closely enough for the workers to live nearby as is sometimes the case with specialists sponsored by chiefs.

Further evidence of specialization comes from the artifacts themselves, the quality of the chipped and ground stone, weaving, woodcarving, and metal-working industries, and the technical skill required for some. Polished obsidian mirrors, for example, are "technically difficult" (Oats and Oats 1976:98), yet this was carried out with skill and "without any scratches" (Gimbutas 1991:8). There is a subjective element to using "product quality" as evidence of specialization, but consider that archaeologists familiar with other Near Eastern sites are among the most generous in their praise of Çatal industries. David and Joan Oats state: "Specialization of labor is clearly evident at earlier seventh-millennium sites such as Beidha and Abu Hureyra, but the craftsmanship of Çatal attains an unusually high level, illustrated particularly among the luxury grave goods" (1976:97), and again, "there can be no doubt that specialization and even luxury craftsmanship in certain materials was an important feature of the Çatal economy" (1976:98). Yet Fairservis, one of the few to address the question in depth, takes a minimalist view of specialization here. He sorted out the materials used and the manufacturing processes required for the artifacts recovered (1975:224–233, Tables 4 and 5) and concludes:

> Of the twenty occupations represented at Çatal Hüyük which can be defined from the combination of materials used and the processes necessary to turn them into usable artifacts, there are none that do not fall within the normal capabilities of the various members of tribes found in various parts of the

world. Sex and age division of labor, lulls in subsistence activity, and the support of certain skilled members of the group on an individual basis make possible the elaboration in cultural style among some known groups which are on a par and indeed superior to that of Çatal Hüyük – all in an "uncivilized" context.
(Fairservis 1975:167)

This is an important caution. But while he shows that Çatal artifacts could be made without any techniques requiring lengthy specialized training, it is also clear that many items drew on more than routine skill, attention to detail, and effort. Mellaart observes that "[t]echnical competence was high, so high in fact that it was seldom equalled and rarely surpassed in Anatolia" (1963a:103). We might not postulate manufacturing quarters, where highly apprenticed and trained individuals produced their beads, chipped tools or hammered metal items, but it remains appropriate to conclude that the residents of the area excavated did not make all their own material goods through a domestic mode of production in which each family unit produced everything it needed.[15] The presence of finely made objects that could be prestige items indicates a degree of support for certain skilled individuals – probably part time unless their produce was also used by people in other parts of the settlement, or traded.

Hoards, residences, and regions

The other main approach to inferring status relations from artifacts is by demonstrating unequal distributions of high-quality items. This depends on relating artifacts to a distributional context, particularly burials, hoards, residences, and regions. Because of the great difference in size between Çatal Hüyük and all known sites in the region that might be contemporary, and because of the probable connections among these sites (discussed shortly under regional settlement patterns), it would not be surprising to find that high-quality crafts were concentrated at Çatal Hüyük. I have not encountered any clear evidence of it but this is likely enough a product of my limited knowledge of the region.

Hoards

Several hoards have been found, "caches" of tools and weapons interpreted as either votive deposits (Mellaart 1964:103, 107) or "capital" (1964:103), perhaps the wares of a trader or of an artisan, supplies meant for production, trade or future use. Most of the offerings are caches of large quantities of tools or weapons, often unused and buried beneath the floors of shrines. Other deposits are found beneath houses. Placement indicates that they may have been in bags, and deposits consist of used and unused tools, and often blanks, cores, and other unfinished materials, all of which affirm that recovery was intended. In both cases the fact of the deposits shows us that the items were "greatly prized" (Mellaart 1964:103), but none reaches the quality of certain weapons found in burials. There is little indication of the specific significance of these hoards, ritual or otherwise, which could aid the inference of status.

Residences

Houses were kept very clean and little was found in residences other than that included in burials. Even so, some variation in artifact inventories was found. Most statuettes were recovered from shrines, but some were from dwellings – typically associated with grain or legumes (Mellaart 1963a:82). Important examples include the group of white marble figures from house E,VI,25, and the well-known green slate plaque depicting a couple embracing to the left and a mother and child to the right (E,VI,30) (Mellaart 1963a:90–91). These are important (though perhaps more for their ritual than status value) and unevenly distributed.

Bialor found a distinctly uneven distribution of projectile points among the first season's inventory. In Level VI, nine points (including perhaps the finest piece in the assemblage) were found in House I, and in Level IV six came from the "Painted Room" (House I), while all fifteen from that level were uncovered in only five of the twelve rooms (Bialor 1962:78; 86). The same pattern is seen in other levels. In Level III two houses provided the bulk of the projectile points: eleven of which were found in House 4 which "proved to be a rich one in many respects, providing a necklace of fish vertebrae beads, a number of well-made pots, a red-painted bench" (Bialor 1962:90). These points were also of fine quality. Sling shot pellets were more widely distributed. It may be that certain people were hunters (warriors?), which although a specialization, would not necessarily carry ranking implications unless hunting was a sport or game, a luxury food. Overall, the uneven distribution of artifacts among dwellings does not point either toward ranking or away from it.

A regional economy?

There is reason to believe the residents of Çatal Hüyük were involved in extensive regional trade, and had at least indirect contacts with people as far away as the Levant.

> Apart from food, mud brick and plaster, salt, and some wood and reeds, the people of Çatal Hüyük had to import everything else they used from at least one day's walk away – the distance to the nearest hills. This included timber for their houses (oak and juniper), raw materials for their stone tools, weapons, beads, statuettes, paints and metals, shells and flint, fruit and berries from the hills, etc. They had, however, domestic cattle and thus a form of transport
> (Mellaart 1975:105)

Use of non-local materials is impressive (see Todd 1976:126 for a more detailed list), and some were used for central purposes. Add the craft specialization already inferred, and we appear to have a fairly complex economy. But common characterizations are distinctly speculative, including, I believe, claims that the prosperity of the site can be attributed to a prominent position in a trading network: "[M]uch of the raw material upon which the local technology depended was

obtainable within 20 miles of the site. Furthermore, all the artifacts identified ...
were to be found no more than 100 miles away" (Fairservis 1975:169).

We do not need to adopt this minimal view to recognize that there is little evidence
for how acquisition was organized. Far the strongest case for actual trading concerns
obsidian. Çatal Hüyük was located near several sources, and studies have shown that
the obsidian used at many Near Eastern sites came from central Anatolia.[16] If there
was an organized trading system, Çatal Hüyük is far the most likely candidate for its
center (due to its size and prosperity; it is not the closest contemporary settlement to
these sources). But was the trading process organized and centralized? I am in
agreement with Todd that "any discussion of the role of Çatal Hüyük in the obsidian
trade must be mainly hypothetical" (1976:128). If Çatal reaped the benefits of a high-
volume trading system, we do not know what the town received in return for all the
obsidian that would have flowed through it. There are exotic materials at the site, but
those which came from a great distance are not numerous enough to show that Çatal
was an economic center supporting specialist traders. Also important, there is little
indication that artifacts themselves were imported. We have only a collection of raw
materials, far weaker evidence of complex trade than if we had artifacts from those
regions of Palestine known to have used Anatolian obsidian. On the other hand, the
fact that these exotic materials were often used for ritual or finely made personal items
suggests that people of high status were involved in what exchange there was. In this
sense there is support for status differentiation, perhaps connected with ritual, but
any mention of entrepreneurial groups is more speculative.

Use of iconography to infer status

I have found nothing in the wall paintings or mobile art that could be considered an
overt representation of social inequality, no depictions of queens holding audience,
chiefs on stools surrounded by attendants, conquering heroes (or, for that matter, any
depictions of armed conflict). This is important and consistent with other lines of
evidence which give little hint of strong, overt expression of status or authority, but it
does little more than suggest that major status differentiation did not exist. Much of
the art was religious in content or purpose, and found in residences or shrines. Even
the shrines are not true "public spaces," so we would not expect these murals to be
prime locations for the expression (much less assertion) of status and power.[17]

Yet it may be possible to detect a more subtle expression of status in these works. If
inequality is pervasive, basic to people's understanding of the world, it may "come
out" in art even when this is not directly relevant to either the scene depicted or the
purpose of the work. Naturally, any such conclusions will be tentative, not to
mention easily missed by someone largely untrained in the interpretation of art, but I
believe the extensive corpus of Çatal Hüyük art does include hints of this sort. Here
are a few possibilities which attest to inequality, but which also work against the idea
of extensive hierarchy or centralized control of life:

1. A scene of a deer hunt (antechamber, shrine A.III.1) includes one human figure
much larger than the rest, "evidently the leader of the hunt" (Mellaart 1962:62;

plates 55 and 56, Mellaart 1967). This may be so. But I note that this person is dressed no differently than (at least some of) the others, and that the deer vary in size even more than the men.

2. In several lively scenes of the "Hunting Shrine" (F.V.1; see Mellaart 1966b:186–190) several of the men are dressed differently from the rest. Size differences are also noticeable and the more elaborately dressed men are the ones drawn larger. The smaller individuals are painted in monochrome while others are polychrome. But if there is any symbol of strength and power in these scenes it would be the animals, particularly the great bull dominating the mural on the north wall, which from a naturalistic perspective is way out of proportion to the little humans swarming about. The variation among the men is nonetheless significant, although it could indicate people from different clans or men's clubs rather than ranked statuses.

3. It has been suggested that the "hunting" scenes really depict rituals. This is plausible, and if true they are rites held outdoors and attracting wider participation than is possible in the shrines. Or they might be games – if such competition can be distinguished from rituals. Under this interpretation, differences among the figures may represent people from different villages, or some other social unit, participating together. They do not appear antagonistic. Whether hunts, ritual enactments or social events that do not fit in any such category, these scenes do indicate differentiation within the population.

4. A feature of early scenes especially (as in the Vulture Shrine, Level VII, 8) is that "no account is taken of corners and the entire wall-space is treated as one continuous field of decoration" (Mellaart 1964:64). This lack of enclosures is (as a very rough tendency) associated with egalitarian rather than hierarchical thinking.

5. No scene can reasonably be interpreted as organized warfare, torture, or conflict (Gimbutas 1991:x), typically among the activities powerful leaders like to brag about. While no argument from the negative is strong in archaeology, this does correlate with the limited evidence overall of highly organized activity, and of "governmental" kinds of institutions.

6. One small sculpture depicts a profusely corpulent female seated on a stool and 'supported' by a large animal on either side. While this is more often seen as a goddess than, say, a princess, there is something in the imagery of being elevated, and something of power in the association with dangerous wild animals. I am not aware of any use of stools as seats of power, or of the kind of political and status system with which these are associated, for this time period (unless that is what we have here), but it may nevertheless be the case that here we have art produced by a person who can conceive of inequality – even if only in the sense of humans and "higher beings."

Stamp seals
Not perhaps iconography in any strict sense, stamp seals represent a peculiarly important medium of expression. The stamp itself is just a small, simple clay object bearing a design. The design may or may not be simple as well, but is inevitably limited by having to fit within the available stamping surface. Yet each such design, limited though it may be compared to a nine-foot mural, had been chosen or even

contrived for repeated use; it is a "mark" or at the least a pattern someone wishes to make over and over again.

A number of stamp seals were uncovered. This is significant, but unfortunately, it is not clear what they were used for. It is not certain, as with seals from so many later Near Eastern sites, that they marked personal property, correspondence, or official documents. The motifs were not writing, nor even almost writing, but essentially designs – for example, spirals and "elaborate pseudo-meander patterns" (Mellaart 1962:56). The identification of these objects as stampers appears firm, but what they were meant to stamp, and why, is not; they "could have been used to stamp cloth as well as produce stored in sacks. No impression of such stamp-seals has ever been found on clay, but the fact that no two are alike and that they always occur singly in a house supports the idea that they were used to indicate ownership" (Mellaart 1962:56). Because they could have been for decoration (e.g. to decorate cloth), they are not unequivocal evidence of merchant activity, of a developed concept of private property, or of anything but a very early step toward writing. This does not mean they are unimportant socially – there are always social implications to decoration, and the seals may, in any case, carry more specific symbolic messages – only that if they hold any implications for status organization, these remain obscure.

Archaeological recognition of social stratification

I have not uncovered any direct evidence of stratification, any indication that the people of Çatal Hüyük experienced unequal access to food, protective devices or the tools for producing these necessities. Nor is there evidence of substantial differences in wealth, the kind of accumulation that would follow only from stratification. According to Lamberg-Karlovsky and Sabloff: "Evidence for class differentiation as well as differential accumulation of wealth comes from the graves of the dead associated with shrines. Unlike the bodies found under houses, the dead found in shrines were often buried with valuable objects" (1979:89). Although plausible, I believe this goes beyond the evidence, for the differences are not great and the artifacts in question seem to be prestige objects, not accumulated wealth. Of course my view also is subjective, and it is important to note that social stratification has also been suggested on indirect grounds.

This indirect evidence is basically extrapolation from what was found to what we might expect in other parts of the site. Mellaart speaks of the excavated area as the priestly quarter, and expects further excavation to uncover a workshop quarter and other major divisions which would be characteristic of stratification and even perhaps a market economy (1967:211). It is clear that not all of the site can be exactly like the sector excavated. The importance of agriculture compared to the quantity of implements found and even more so the disparity between highly developed crafts and almost non-existent evidence for their manufacture, argue both for specialization and that few if any residents of the excavated area were seriously involved in farming or craft production. Social stratification is not out of the question since the lack of positive evidence would make perfect sense if it turns out that all the households uncovered represent one stratum of a class society. And as long as we are leaving open the possibility that people of other strata lived elsewhere, we need not assume that this religious-ritual area represents the highest stratum.

These speculations can be tested with further excavation, perhaps *only* with further excavation, and the importance of these issues for understanding human history cannot be overestimated. But for the moment we must conclude that there is no solid evidence for stratification. True, craft specialists probably can be found elsewhere, but why assume they would represent a class?

Settlements and architecture

While our concern is with the site itself, clues to its place in the wider Neolithic world are also clues to status relations among those who lived at Çatal Hüyük. Some interesting suggestions emerge and I believe further insight would be possible given a fuller understanding of the regional archaeology than I have been able to muster. Study at the level of the settlement is also suggestive even though it raises more questions than it answers. Finally, information available on individual structures is nothing short of remarkable; yet here too, evidence of ranking is less than conclusive.

The Konya Plain and beyond

The Konya Plain is spotted with Neolithic sites, many contemporary with some phase of Çatal Hüyük. And while variation in size does not a hierarchy make, Çatal was so out of proportion (possibly the world's largest habitation in those days) as to demand more of an explanation than agrarian good fortune. But can we propose any direct testimony to ancient hierarchy on the Plain? On grounds of proximity alone we can rule out true isolation and there is much evidence (including Çatal's inventory of materials) for an extensive network of contacts, or at least wide-ranging travel about the Plain and nearby mountains. And if Angel (1971) is even roughly correct in his assessment of demographic trends, Çatal's population grew much faster than did the settlement – on which basis Mellaart postulates extensive emigration. "Many towns and villages would owe their origin to Çatal Hüyük's population explosion, and its culture, cults and language may have been widespread in southern Anatolia" (1975:100). This is obviously speculative, yet there is evidence of cultural traits common to these sites, and we might reasonably assume that innovations most often moved out from Çatal. Bialor (1962:109) found similar chipped-stone industries "spread out in the Konya Plain – Niğde (eastern end), Ilıcapınar (northern end) and Çatal Hüyük and Kerhane just to the north of it (toward the western end)," and Mellaart observes that: "its culture covers the entire Konya plain as well as a number of outlying areas: the Beyşehir-Seydişehir region, the sites in the Karaman area, and the region of the central Anatolian volcanoes" (1975:106). Isolating four groups of sites with affinities to Çatal Hüyük (based on a factor analysis of stone tools and pottery), Bartel found them to be spaced in a circular pattern with Çatal as the center, and uniformly within the circular region (Bartel 1972; see also Todd's summary,

1976:130). It is not clear how far we can go with this, but in locating settlements, people were apparently responsive to considerations of regional communication and interaction.

Çatal Hüyük may well have been the primate site of a regional hierarchy. Yet it seems rather a stretch to say it "was able to control the trade through its 'emporia' and colonies, drawn from its expanding population" (Mellaart 1975:106), that it "was the capital site of the Konya Plain, without any rivals" (Mellaart 1962:42), or that "the unusual size of Çatal Hüyük itself strongly suggests that it exercised some form of political control over its surrounding territory" (Oats and Oats 1976:98). Still, there is solid evidence for regional interaction, and it is easy enough to imagine a concentration of trade and luxury items at this large, comparatively urbane town. But that is an empirical question to be answered through study of the artifact inventories characterizing these other settlements and the rest of Çatal Hüyük itself. In addition, it may be that the exceptional ritual focus of the excavated area – the rich belief system, the extraordinary physical facilities and art devoted to religion and ritual, and possibly also the healing arts – not only served the whole site, but the entire region (Mellaart 1975:106).

Accepting tentatively that Çatal was part of a settlement hierarchy, it may be significant that there are no more than two levels. To the extent that we can relate this to the social order, it suggests a status system with personal ranking, but a level of complexity and centralization of authority somewhat short of a state system. I have advised using this line of inference with caution – not that number of levels is unimportant, but because of the indeterminant relationship between levels and configurations of social organization. Nevertheless, it does seem to lead us in the same direction as other lines of inference.

Other features of the built environment

We have no direct evidence for construction beyond the settlement, but Mellaart offers an interesting if circumstantial case for the use of large reed charnel houses. We can also presume some alteration of the landscape for agriculture, and despite intensive modern cultivation, evidence may yet remain of the former field systems, since the current land surface is probably higher than when the site was founded.[18] "The economy of Çatal Hüyük," Mellaart states, "was based on simple irrigation agriculture and cattle-breeding, trade and industry" (1975:98). This is significant, but he is not speaking of centrally coordinated capital projects, and Hans Helbaek, who may have been the first to suggest irrigation agriculture, believed it "took the form of uncontrolled flooding rather than proper canalization" (1964:123). Oats and Oats argue (based on the water requirements of the crops in question) that we need not presume irrigation of any sort (1976:96).

The site and its organization

One of the virtues of Mellaart's emphasis on horizontal exposure is that we have complete plans for areas of up to an acre for some levels. But at only about 4% of this large mound, this still limits what we can say about overall plan and organization. Keeping this in mind, one tentative observation is that Çatal Hüyük is not an especially complex settlement. All known structures have been identified as dwellings or shrines, which are similar in many ways. Building design and layout (structures clustered together with blank outer walls and roof entry only) has suggested defense, but Mellaart also remarks on the absence of streets or alleys, observing that "all communication was at roof level" (1975:100). It is interesting that the inhabitants were separated as much from each other as from the outside, hinting at possible divisions within the society for which we currently have no other evidence. The few small courtyards were usually ruined houses of the previous building level, not yet rebuilt.

> The main function of ... [the courts and courtyards found between two groups of Level VI buildings] were as repositories for household rubbish, food remains, etc. They also served as lavatories, but were not apparently used as a means of communication, for keeping domestic animals or for domestic tasks. No single oven, bin or storage space was found in them, nor do they communicate with each other or give access to a single building. (Mellaart 1963c:722)

Of course we do not know how much time people spent out of doors, or what important meeting places might be located elsewhere. Todd suggests the site may be comprised of "a number of major blocks, possibly with sizable open spaces between them," but none has been delimited in its entirety (1976:25). Neither the design of specific buildings nor the overall plan encourages communication despite the settlement's "agglomerate" character, and the apparent desire of the people to live close together. Renfrew concludes from this that Çatal Hüyük was lacking in the level of interaction one would expect of a true urban site (1984b:89–90). This must be tempered with the evidence for specialization (a very significant kind of interaction), but the architecture and settlement plan set limits to our ability to postulate a diverse and bustling city.

Another of the site's widely-noted features is the orderliness and standardization of its plan. Of one cluster of shrines and dwellings Mellaart observes that the "whole layout was carefully thought out and planned before building began" (1963b:26), and referring to the building unit of E VI he objects to the term agglutinative because it implies a haphazard lack of planning.

> On the contrary, the buildings were planned and it is very clear how they were planned, for outside each of the shrines there is at least one important dwelling, and sometimes more. Each of the four shrines is provided with its storeroom, often directly accessible from it, in the same way as the houses are normally provided with a secondary room for purposes of storage. (Mellaart 1963a:59)

Further, it is often the case that "lines of walls run straight for more than a single building, suggesting clearly that the entire plan was well laid out (even if less well executed)" (1963a:59). The most widespread conclusion is expressed by Oats and Oats: "The extraordinary standardization, indeed deliberate planning, seen in the architecture and furnishings of the houses, is also striking and suggests a high level of cohesion and cooperation within the community if not an organizing authority" (1976:97). Possibly. But however striking this standardization, it is better evidence of common ideas about what a house should be than of either coordinated planning or central direction. The point that larger areas exhibit planning is more germane, suggesting cooperation at the least (not surprising given contiguous buildings). But while we might detect an underlying design, Todd observes that adherence to such a plan was loose. "The plan of a building seems to be dictated by the shape of the immediately preceding structure in that position, and irregularities inevitably occurred during the rebuilding" (Todd 1976:27). This speaks of cohesion and cooperation and the sector may have been planned originally as a coherent block. But if the design and work were centrally directed, it is not clear from later rebuildings.

Residential architecture
The residential architecture of Çatal Hüyük is fairly standardized, even in specific details, but not without some variation. The single-story timber-framed houses were built of mudbrick (formed in a wooden mold squared with an adze [Mellaart 1967:55]), and had flat roofs "made of bundles of reeds with a thick mud cover on top and a mat below to prevent an incessant rain of bits of reeds falling on the floors" (Mellaart 1967:56). Houses and shrines had no other entrance than a hole in the roof reached with a ladder of squared timber against the south wall (where its diagonal mark is often found in the plaster), and which also allowed smoke from the hearth and lamps to escape. The main room of a house – rectangular and averaging about 25 square meters – was divided into a "kitchen" area along the south side (with built-in oven and hearth), a "sunken" area in the center, and mud platforms or benches along the east and north walls (Mellaart 1964:50) covered with reed or rush matting as a base for cushions, textiles or bedding. Carefully plastered, and often provided with rounded kerbs, these platforms "are the prototypes of the Turkish sofa (or divan) and served for sitting, working and sleeping" (Mellaart 1967:60). Assuming these were sleeping platforms, no house could have accommodated more than eight people. They clearly were not meant for extended families. Secondary rooms were a part of most houses. Used for storage, these auxiliary rooms were entered from the main room through low open doorways (never covered with doors), and some had separate entry-passages or light shafts. Houses and shrines were kept very clean; "remains of meals such as broken bones are a rarity" (Mellaart 1967:62).

Scale, prominence, energy expenditure
While no dwelling was unusually prominent or of a different scale, houses did vary in size. "The minimum requirement," Mellaart observes, "is a single room with two platforms and wooden ladder, hearth and oven (e.g. room 6 [Level VII]), but most houses are larger or better appointed" (1964:50). Typical was a plan of either 6 × 4 meters or 5 × 5 meters, and while "smaller or larger houses are uncommon" (Mellaart 1975:100), they do "range from small ones with a floor space of 11.25

square meters to huge ones with areas of 48 square meters" (1967:67). With the largest over four times the area of the smallest, and nearly twice the average, this is a significant range. But some variation might relate to family size, as larger dwellings have more platforms, possibly indicating more people sleeping there. Further, people may have had little choice about the size and shape of their dwellings once the pattern had begun. Yet there must have been some reason for the size differential when first established, and in any event buildings did not always follow exactly the plan of the previous level. This argument from necessity can only be taken so far, for surely the people would have been aware of the differences and counted them as significant. The wall painting interpreted as a town with an erupting volcano in the background (Mellaart 1964:55, 56; Pl. VIa) shows rooms or buildings of varying size. Since the town plan – if that is what it is – is somewhat schematic, it is all the more significant that this internal characteristic would be prominent. If we are on the right track with this interpretation, and if the whole town or a cross-section is represented, it suggests not just residential variation within one area, but a section of town in which nearly all buildings are smaller than elsewhere.

Variation in the Plans of Residences
Building plans varied little either within a level or over time, but there were differences (these are not "tract houses"), some of which correlate with size (e.g. a small house with fewer platforms than a larger house). The more extensive concern internal features (Todd 1976:27), and more variation is found in early levels, after which the internal equipment becomes quite standardized.

As with size, once plans were set there was little opportunity for change; Mellaart states: "The structure of the city did not allow for individual rebuilding; this was done *en bloc*, and old house walls were used as foundations for the new" (1975:101). Shrines often follow a similar plan although internal features differ from houses and from each other. Apart from the house–shrine distinction there is little evidence of specialized activity, and there is no variation in residence plans that would indicate ranking among those living in this part of town.

Aspects of residential construction
Residences and shrines of Çatal Hüyük are well made, carefully finished, and scrupulously clean. All are plastered inside "with a white or creamy clay (*ak toprak*), still widely used by present day villagers, and the plaster ... was smoothed with polishers in white or green limestone" (Mellaart 1962:48). Several other special features add to the impression of care, order, and neatness.

> These are the vertical wooden posts of squared timber, plastered and painted red and the horizontal panelling of the walls. These are characteristic features of every dwelling or shrine so far found at Çatal Hüyük and with the division of the room into its component functional apartments and the "built-in furniture" they give the architecture of Çatal Hüyük an ordered neatness rarely paralleled.
> (Mellaart 1963a:59–60)

Under most circumstances such a list would almost certainly indicate high-status dwellings, but the problem here is that all buildings are so characterized. Could it be that we are not seeing the whole picture? Do these houses represent the basic standard of living for the Neolithic residents of Çatal Hüyük, a high-status neighborhood of a more diverse town, or perhaps even a mid-status area of a town yet more remarkable than we now suspect? This cannot be answered without further excavation, but the large number of shrines edges me toward the view that this is a special area, for this ratio of ritual structures seems unlikely to have characterized an entire settlement of 32 acres.

Shrines are distinctive primarily in architectural and decorative features. Specific criteria for distinguishing shrines from houses are: "the presence of wall-paintings of an elaborate nature that have obvious ritual or religious significance; plaster reliefs showing deities, animals or animal heads; horns of cattle set into benches; rows of bucrania and the presence of groups of cult statues found in the main room; ex-voto figures stuck into the walls; human skulls set up on platforms, etc." (Mellaart 1967:78). But in plan and construction they are much like ordinary dwellings. The similarity of design, including built-in furniture, indicates that shrines, while obviously special, may have been residences as well, an idea reinforced by the fact that kitchen features were not just "mock-ups" of a functioning house; in at least one shrine Mellaart found used cooking pots (1966b:178). But whether they were buildings devoted entirely to the specialized purpose of performing ritual (which may include healing), or houses as well, it is clear that there were people in town who were ritual specialists, and that this was viewed as an important and distinctive function. There is good reason to single out the functionaries of shrines as people of importance and prestige, of a higher rank than others.

Change in residential architecture over time
Conservatism was the rule, and the few recognizable changes in architecture are not easily related to status. In early levels contiguous buildings tended to share walls, while later on each was separate even though still close together (Mellaart 1966b: 168). It may be that early levels took more coordination but it is not safe to infer a reduced level of organization in later periods. Individual structures were rebuilt at different times within a building level, a practice made easier by the free-standing approach to construction. Change can also be seen in construction details. Early houses had an extensive wood-beam framework, and mudbrick was used to fill in. At first beams were often rounded, while later on people took the trouble to square them (Mellaart 1966b:168). This is a fine example of the attention to finish and detail characteristic of Çatal Hüyük, but as a feature of all known buildings it does not reveal growing differentiation. In later levels, walls were entirely of mudbrick, but the reduced use of wood could have an ecological as well as social basis (local deforestation, perhaps) and in any case this too is characteristic of all contemporary buildings. As one final observation, early on (Levels XI and XII) the "arrangement of platforms is less stereotyped, but round hearths and oval ovens show no appreciable change" (Mellaart 1966b:169).

Non-residential construction

No monumental or corporate labor construction has been found at Çatal Hüyük, and there is little chance of anything coming to light in future excavation unless it was built in an early period, and the mound subsequently rose around it, finally to leave no trace on the surface. It has been suggested that a defensive wall may have enclosed the town. If the numerous clay balls recovered are weapons (e.g. slingstones) and meant for battle, not just hunting, this might suggest the need for defense. Protection, in fact, is the most common suggestion for rooftop entry of houses – and is a reason offered by contemporary villagers whose homes boast the same feature. Altogether this is not much as evidence of either real or perceived need for protection, and no trace of such a wall has yet been found. A wall around a town of this size, however, would be a major construction project indeed.

The question of public architecture is a little more complicated, for it is entirely possible that additional types of structures may yet be found. For the moment, though, shrines and charnel houses are the only candidates. There is some justification for viewing the shrines as "public" structures, although they were likely residences as well. In addition, one of the murals can be interpreted as representing an elaborate reed charnel house. This, too, is plausible given the burial evidence, even though no such structure has been found. It may be that the concept of public activity and building was not well developed. What evidence there is of centralized, coordinated or even informal social activity is of a ritual nature. I tentatively inferred a status of ritual specialist with economic implications (access to the products of craft specialists), based on artifactual evidence. The limited architectural evidence generally confirms this, but otherwise adds little. We have no evidence of leaders organizing major public works, no projects of any sort meant to display their own status, and little to suggest coordination of economic activity. Shrines are associated with store-room granaries, but so are most residences, and there is no hint of a redistribution system. There may well have been redistribution within Çatal Hüyük, or even throughout the region, but if so, it was either centered in another part of town or did not involve actual mobilization of goods.

Access patterns and status

The shrines, which come the closest of any structures yet uncovered to representing public architecture, were of limited size. To the extent that they were the centers of worship and ritual, such activities took place in closed settings, with limited participation. If the wall paintings of festivals, games or rituals depict physical, earthly events that people of the town attended, rituals performed in the shrines would be distinctly exclusive by contrast. But several were functioning at any one time (up to fifteen in one case), reducing the sense of restriction and exclusivity, as would the view that healing and death rituals were primary functions.

Social inequality at Neolithic Çatal Hüyük?

There is no single line of evidence that conclusively demonstrates ranking at Çatal Hüyük; in each case I have felt constrained to emphasize the tentative nature of my conclusions. Yet most of this evidence points us in the same direction, offering a pattern of consistency which encourages a firmer conclusion overall. That is, I believe we can accept with confidence the basic conclusion that social relations at Çatal Hüyük were characterized by significant structural inequality.

What this evidence does not suggest, is a great regard for personal status differentiation. The exceptional stability of the social order – with most patterns of material culture persisting century after century – reinforces the view that status rivalry, personal aggrandizement, and expanding leadership or economic control could not have been characteristic of Çatal social organization. And there is little in the way of evidence for wealth accumulation, social strata, or differential access to basic resources. It may be that intensive study of the excavated portion of this large site is like looking at the corner of a picture through a high-powered loupe. But while I would dearly love to view the rest of the picture, current evidence in itself does not point toward social stratification at Çatal Hüyük.

There is reason to think status was hereditary. There are few reliable ways of inferring the distinction between ascription and achievement, further compounded at this site by the understated expression of ranking in general. But burials indicate that families were of central social importance, and the recovery of child (even infant) burials conforming to the pattern tentatively identified as high status, indicates that whatever status this marked, it was inherited. Further, while limited by being an argument from the negative, there is no indication of competition or rivalry. Another important feature of the status system is that the higher statuses were associated with the religious-ritual system, itself of exceptional importance to the people of Çatal Hüyük. Even if I am on the wrong track altogether – and there really was no institutionalized inequality – the religious statuses, priests, healers, shamans or whatever, were the most distinctive in status-role attributes.

In sum, there is good evidence for social inequality during the Neolithic. At Çatal Hüyük this seems to have been a fairly simple ranking, possibly hereditary (and with kinship broadly important to the social order), and probably not involving social stratification or much personal aggrandizement. The higher statuses seem to have a strong religious connection, and women appear to be as well-represented among the high statuses as men.

Gimbutas (1991:viii) seems to be on firm ground including Çatal Hüyük among her group of largely classless societies. It is also the case that direct evidence for warfare is completely lacking. Whether Çatal's culture and society was "mother/women-centered" is less clear, although also possible. Gerda Lerner observes that more extreme claims have often been made for the site; in particular it has been judged an example of a matriarchy. But this requires uncritical acceptance of some of Mellaart's more speculative conclusions, as well as a "blurring of the distinction between male–female egalitarian relationships and matriarchy" (1986:34). Lerner's own conclusion is that Çatal provides us with "hard evidence of the existence of some sort of alternative model to that of patriarchy" (1986:35). This is similar to what Gimbutas is saying, and is, I believe, compatible with my findings. Çatal Hüyük was almost certainly not an egalitarian society, either in the literal sense or in Fried's sense, but what ranking there was appears to cross-cut gender lines.

Ultimately Gimbutas's full model of a "Civilization of the Goddess" also depends on how we define "civilization" and the extent to which the religion practiced at Çatal was really goddess-centered, but it is clear that the culture of Çatal Hüyük at least approaches civilization in its sophisticated artistic and aesthetic sensibility, and its appreciation for the cultivation of thought and expression (even though lacking in writing as such). It was also comparatively wealthy, yet not, apparently, deeply divided by this fact, or characterized by extensive personal dominance and submission.

These conclusions must be recognized as tentative as well as limited. More insight into the status organization of Çatal Hüyük will certainly come to light from first-hand study of the original materials and excavation records, from further excavation, and also from other approaches to analysis. A more thorough study of the economy could well lead to conclusions which confirm, refine or challenge my picture of the social order. And much could be gained from a contextual approach which emphasizes Çatal Hüyük as a unique human "event" (if I may so describe 800 years of vibrant town life). There is certainly potential for an interpretive approach which takes fuller advantage of the extraordinary evidence for thought and meaning preserved at Çatal, this unique glimpse into the Neolithic mind which I have hardly begun to explore.

NOTES

1 The present study of past society

1. Leach has recently been cited with approval by Bhattacharya (1989) who said that while archaeologists undertake cultural reconstruction with their data, this "culture" "has little or no information for a social anthropologist" (p. 12). Bhattacharya's argument overall, however, is more of an historical-contextual objection to social archaeology, like those discussed below.

2. Watson argues that in attempting to retrieve the humanity of the cultural past, Hodder "has brought himself – and, perhaps, a certain number of his archaeological colleagues as well – to the brink of a serious skeptical crisis about any meaningful accessibility to the prehistoric human past" (Watson and Fotiadis 1990:621). This is true. However these scholars (see also Tilley, ed. 1990 and Miller 1987) are introducing archaeology to a movement that has been developing in other fields for much longer. These are issues we must face, and the epistemological questions in particular are crucial. A skeptical crisis may be unnerving, but for those areas of processual archaeology that turn out to have been inadequate, it will at least have been better to go through such a crisis than continuing, as they say, to live in bliss. In the meantime, it may be inevitable that we direct – fritter away? – some of our talents to, in Watson's evocative expression, "the intricate labyrinths of symbolic-structuralist mind-games" (Watson and Fotiadis 1990:621).

3. To avoid getting too far off the subject, I have left out several important qualifiers discussed in chapter 7.

2 Social theory and social life

1. See Possehl 1990:261–262; 269–270 for a discussion of the rise of Harappan civilization, and H. Wright 1986:358 who comes to the same conclusion from a comparative study of the rise of the state in Mesopotamia, Mesoamerica, and the central Andes as well.

2. For example, Schmandt-Basserat (1992) has put forward a sustained argument that writing was not a sudden "invention" but the result of thousands of years of manipulating symbolism from clay tokens ("counters") to clay impressions which she identifies as precursors to cuneiform.

3. For Shanks and Tilley it is all for the worse. Their objection is not the "knee-jerk" reaction of some anthropologists, for whom the word evolution "is as obnoxious . . . as the word *rex* was to the Romans" (Hallpike 1989). Yet they seem more intent on making evolutionary theory *seem* obnoxious than showing it to be wrong. Thus "theories of social evolution in practice have always been riddled with ethnocentric evaluations" (Shanks and Tilley 1987b:155). Or consider the even firmer expression of Miller and Tilley: "Some societies develop to the status of civilizations and reach the top of the league while others are relegated to the lower divisions of bands and chiefdoms. To use such a framework is not a normatively neutral process. It is to measure, to compare, to order the sequences according to definite criteria, time and place, and in doing so to pass judgment. It seems preferable to grant to all *Homo sapiens sapiens* the abilities and characteristics we would wish granted to

ourselves" (Miller and Tilley 1984a:2). To the hardened relativist, passing judgment is the ultimate sin (except when it is a relativist passing judgment on someone else for making a judgment). But the deepest problem here is to insist that measuring and comparing is also judgment of worth, moral judgment, not just judgment as discernment. What would it mean to grant others the same characteristics as ourselves? Are we to conclude, for example, that societies have not actually developed from simple to complex, that they are all virtually identical, and when we say otherwise we are just archaeologists from complex societies using social theory to puff ourselves up? Shanks and Tilley's objection to models from other disciplines is primarily that, as a result, "views of the past are thoroughly embedded in the present" (1987b:137). As with the ethnocentrism argument, this point gains much of its apparent force from their assumption that archaeological data have little influence on archaeological conclusions, the extreme "presentism" I have already rejected.

4. Another approach would be to consider how our social models developed, an aspect of what I have called "observation and analysis in ethnography."

5. The blanket idea that a contextual archaeology rules out cross-cultural methodology is itself ambiguous, for the contextual approach is a methodology meant to apply regardless of the culture. We could even argue that contextual archaeology is actually a middle range theory, a set of programmatic statements attempting to make cross-culturally valid generalizations about how to connect static archaeological data with a living past.

6. Binford replies that denial of human intentionality was never critical to the New Archaeology. It was argued that "apparent free will and volitional actions by individuals was not the explanation for long-term historical process. Intentional action was never denied; it was only suggested that human actions could be explained as manifestations of other causal forces, and it was maintained that intentional acts were not *the* causal force standing behind history" (Binford 1989:58). Determinism, closely interwoven with reductionism, naturalism, and materialism, infect much of twentieth-century thought, and no one school or movement can take the blame for work that grows from these presumptions. Tim Ingold relates this to the current neo-evolutionary paradigm in biology and the idea of cultural inheritance in the study of society. Even in biology, he argues, it is misleading to eliminate the organism as a real entity, however characteristic of the population thinking of the neo-Darwinian synthesis (Ingold 1990:208). And if non-human organisms are legitimately viewed as effective agents (even in the genesis of organic form), how much more should human agency be recognized, for "the genesis of social form lies in the transformative potentials of the field, constitutive of persons as intentional agents, that intervene between genes or culture and manifest social behavior" (Ingold 1990:221). While I follow Binford and Ingold as far as agreeing that determinism is neither inherent in, nor unique to, processual archaeology, I understand why Hodder associates the two since the New Archaeology can be most congenial to the mind already clouded with these ideas (which includes most scholars alive today, including those, like me, who are disturbed by these assumptions).

7. Bettinger uses "theories of limited sets," or "limited theories" for those like middle range theory and optimal foraging theory that "are practical and meant for application in the real world" (1991:vi). They contrast with general theories, or theories of general sets, an example being what he calls neo-Darwinism. He also observes that "limited theories are no less 'theoretical' than theories of general sets – they are simply less general" (1991:vi).

8. Of course, neither can we predict a specific behavior from a detailed knowledge of the specific historical context.

3 Inequality and social life

1. This typology reflects the fact that Berreman has substantially more interest in social stratification than non-stratified social inequality. Non-stratified forms of hierarchy,

though, are actually quite varied, as later sections of this chapter make clear.

2. Service (1975) used the Cherokee as an example of a state evolving from a chiefdom, but the society from which the Cherokee state developed did not fit his chiefdom definition since it "differed from other chiefdoms in those years in that it lacked permanent authority offices inherited by primogeniture" (p. 142).

3. Gilbert (1943) suggested that membership in the inner council (p. 322) and white chief of the nation were hereditary ranks, but this refers to the time of European-inspired centralization, and King (1979:xi) shows that the one person actually to inherit his father's position was not universally thought the most appropriate.

4. This point is very important, and for greater depth it is worth considering another, more substantive example: "suppose we feed gas to a burner, and mix air with it. If we mix too much air with the gas and hold a glowing splint over the burner, it will not light. Gradually increasing the proportions of gas to air – a continuous process – we will reach a point at which, suddenly, a flame appears – a qualitatively new phenomenon. Once again we see that to discover (or postulate) a continuous transition between one extreme and another does not for a moment rule out the possibility of qualitatively new phenomena distinguishing one extreme from the other" (MacKay 1974:74).

5. One caveat is that Hawaiian society was clearly stratified, and it may be that Marquesan society was as well. However this affects the actual character of social life, it does not seem to override the achieved–ascribed distinction.

6. As Fried notes, distinguishing power and authority is not easy, and his own contribution is helpful although far from universally followed. "Authority is taken here to refer to the ability to channel the behavior of others in the absence of the threat or use of sanctions. Power is the ability to channel the behavior of others by the threat or use of sanctions. Authority and power may go together or separately" (Fried 1967:13).

7. Polanyi himself refers to Richard Thurnwald "whom we follow closely on the subject" (1944:15, Thurnwald 1932: xii, 106–108).

8. Davenport (1969:5) notes that not all of the islands would be subject to reallocation on change of a high chief. That some districts were free of this, and that such a thing was carefully noted indicates that the process was taken seriously.

9. Price reiterated essentially the same position in a 1987 paper, where she said, "the transition between ranked society and stratified/state institutions is analyzed as a quantitative continuum rather than as a rubicon." She also noted that she and Morton Fried had "gone around in circles" over this on several occasions, to no avail in either case (Price 1987).

10. One reviewer of this work suggested, based on neo-marxist-influenced work, that valuables can indeed be essential resources, and concluded that my distinction between ranking and stratification is overdrawn. However, what this work actually shows is that valuables are extremely important for "social reproduction." Essential resources are not those essential for reproducing the social order, but essential for maintaining the lives of individuals. Valuables are not among these, however important they are to those of high status in maintaining social distinctions, whether stratified or simply ranked.

11. As they point out, there is some uncertainty as to how stratification is best defined, but my argument does not assume Fried's definition is the better, or that Feinman and Neitzel's observations have no bearing on economic differentiation (thus on stratification if so defined). It is merely that to evaluate Fried's distinction, one must use his definitions. Yet something may in fact be said on the relative value of these definitions. Feinman and Neitzel's definition of stratification, when applied to real societies does not elucidate anything particularly distinctive about them, as these authors are at great pains to point out. Fried's definition (as I will show shortly) does draw attention to significant qualitative differences among societies.

12. Earle's extensive familiarity with Hawaii also influences the way he and Johnson look at chiefdoms generally.

13. It may be that Renfrew's group-oriented and individualizing chiefdoms can also be related to the distinction between ranking and stratification (Renfrew 1974), although Drennan notes that an emphasis on the individual can be a kind of status rivalry among chiefs. Those chiefdoms he studied in pre-Hispanic America that were more individualizing were the ones, contrary to Renfrew's expectation, that did not develop into states (Drennan 1991:283).

4 Mortuary data as evidence of ranking, Part 1

1. As among the Tikopia (Firth 1936: 269, 1939:345, 1959:269), Easter Islanders (Metraux 1940:115–117), Tahitians (Ferdon 1981:172–173), Nootka (Sapir 1921:366, Koppert 1930:111–112), Tlingit (Krause 1956:157–158, Emmons 1907:345), Natchez (Swanton 1911:138) and Omaha (O'Shea 1981:43).

2. Kent suggests a third possibility, that men attain leadership status through hunting success, "and because they are better hunters, they may have more access to meat, and therefore better dentition" (1991:942). In this case the state of one's dentition would be a side effect, irrelevant to leadership, and the apparent contradiction of dental health being based on status in what was thought an egalitarian society "may not be a contradiction after all, since health may not be based on status, but instead on hunting skill, in a still essentially egalitarian society" (Kent 1991:943). Hewlett and Walker note, however, that while this is indeed a possibility, their data focused on the lineage-based leaders (Aka *kombeti* and Mbuti *kapita*) not the great-hunter kind of leader (*tuma*), and they disagree "about the importance of hunting as a determinant of the high social status and good dentition of *kombeti* and *kapita*" (Hewlett and Walker 1991:944).

3. This is clear in records for the Tahitians (Oliver 1974:101), Arawak (Steward 1948:24, Rouse 1948:533), Natchez (Swanton 1911:138, Spencer *et al.* 1965:410), groups of the Cauca-Atrato River area of Western Colombia (Steward and Faron 1959:220), and the Uraba (Steward and Faron 1959:222).

4. A canoe *is* an energy-expensive bit of material culture, however, and may be even more important for its cultural associations.

5 Mortuary data as evidence of ranking, Part 2

1. Even among the small sample I studied, it was a characteristic of high status burial among the Tongans (Davidson 1979:102; Renfrew 1984a: 212), Tahitians (Oliver 1974:101, 507–509, 960), Natchez (Swanton 1911) and Nore (Steward and Faron 1959).

2. It is mentioned for example, in descriptions of Hawaii (Bellwood 1979:358), Tahiti (Ferdon 1981:173), the Shilluk (Westermann 1912:136), Arawak (Steward 1948:24, Rouse 1948:532), Natchez (Swanton 1911:141–143), Cuna (Steward and Faron 1959:225), Chibcha (Steward and Faron 1959:214), and the Catio, Nore, and other groups of the Cauca-Atrato River region of Western Colombia (Steward and Faron 1959).

3. In his essay *The Domestication of Europe* Hodder describes the adoption of agriculture as a social-symbolic process in which "[t]he natural (wild) is made cultural (domesticated, agricultural)" (1990b:18). Domus refers to the home as a focus of thought and the discourse of power; "it was through the domus that the origins of agriculture were thought about and conceived" (p. 38). In the same purposely imprecise and flexible way, agrios refers to "the outside" (p. 85), to "field" and to "the wild" (p. 86), a conceptual focus somewhat in opposition to the domus, and one which becomes more important later in the Neolithic.

4. This example "of the poetic nature of material culture," whatever it says about inferences

from a change from collective to individual burial, does not "throw doubt on the usual assumption that variations in social ranking can be monitored using archaeological evidence" (Hodder 1990b:309). Nor (as far as I can tell) does anything else Hodder has ever said.

5. It is probable that the following did not place many items in high-status graves, even though some included human sacrifices: the Shilluk (Westermann 1912:136, Seligman and Seligman 1932), Tikopia (Firth 1936), Tahitians (Oliver 1974, Ferdon 1981:173), Natchez (Swanton 1911:141–143, Spencer *et al.* 1965:418), and Chibcha (Steward and Faron 1959:214).

6. High-status burials received different items from those used for everyone else in each of these cases: Hawaii (Bellwood 1979), Tikopia (Firth 1936:180, 1959:129), Tahiti (Oliver 1974), Shilluk (Westermann 1912:136), Natchez (Swanton 1911:141–143, Spencer *et al.* 1965: 418), Arawak (Steward 1948:24, Rouse 1948:532), Cuna (Steward and Faron 1959:225), Chibcha (Steward and Faron 1959:214), Catio, Nore, and other groups of Western Colombia (Steward and Faron 1959), Pawnee, Arikara, and the Omaha (O'Shea 1981:41,44,46,49).

7. I found evidence for the concentration of exotics among those of high rank for the Tikopia (Firth 1959:109, 129), Arawak (Rouse 1948: 527), Cuna (Steward and Faron 1959), Chibcha (Steward and Faron 1959:213), Pawnee (O'Shea 1981:44), Arikara (O'Shea 1981:46), Omaha (O'Shea 1981:49), and the modern traditional village of Hasanabad (Watson 1979a:229–230).

8. In a reply Shay concludes: "The difference in terms of funerary goods is not so great that it cannot be accounted for by the variations in positions of status that exist even in an egalitarian society" (1989:85). Even this is but one part of a long-standing and complicated argument. Kenyon (the excavator) postulated different ethnic groups using the cemetery, an idea which, interestingly, has been widely accepted. And then there are the disputes about dating which seem ever to plague the Jericho excavations. Palumbo (1987:49) notes that others (e.g. Dever) have had different ideas about which burials are contemporary.

6 The form and distribution of artifacts

1. Sources: Natchez, Swanton 1911:61, 106; Arawak, Rouse 1948:525, 527, 534; Cuna, Steward and Faron 1959:225; Chibcha, Catio, Nore, Steward and Faron 1959:213–215, 220; Tikopia, Firth 1940:25; Tahitians, Oliver 1974:72, 154, 732–733 and Ferdon 1981:172; Shilluk, Seligman and Seligman 1932.

2. In each of these cases those of high rank used high-quality versions of otherwise common items: Tahiti (Oliver 1974:171–172, 207), the Natchez (Swanton 1911:56, 60–61), Arawak (Steward 1948:25), Chibcha (Steward and Faron 1959:220), and the modern traditional village Watson calls Hasanabad (1979a: 229–230).

3. This question of original intent is of great interest, for example, in Dead Sea Scrolls scholarship. Protection from loss through capture is a commonly cited reason for the scrolls' deposition, but it is conceivable that they represent ritual disposal of sacred manuscripts worn from use, rather than primarily acts of hiding. There are many scholars in this field with strongly held views, but these views differ widely, and it remains unclear who is responsible, and how likely they would have been to follow standard manuscript disposal proscriptions.

4. Although the purpose of pottery types is not always clear, "functional differences" would imply different activities, and possibly different lifestyles (as London argues for second-millennium Palestine [1989:37]). Yet even when variation among artifacts may be explained as functional differences – a proximate cause – this does not rule out status inequality – an antecedent cause – in that the different activities represent specializations with status implications.

5. As Tilley observes, "the archaeological pursuit of signs is no easy business" (1989:191) even apart from this question, for an object "has no ultimate or unitary meaning that can be held to exhaust it. Rather, any object has multiple and sometimes contradictory meanings" (p. 191).
6. This point is discussed more fully under regional settlement patterns in the following chapter.

7 Status, settlements, and structures

1. Many archaeologists have grown discontent with spatial models (Wagstaff 1987:29) in recent years. Central-place theory in particular requires assumptions (e.g. market-based economies) unlikely to be met in archaeological examples (Hodges 1987:119–120). But much of Kowalewski's analytical approach can be used as though central places were simply higher-level sites in a hierarchy, nodes of varying importance in a network, without making economic assumptions (e.g. profit maximization and cost minimization) typically associated with central-place theory as derived from Cristaller.
2. Findlow and Goldberg (1983) elaborate a similar model for measuring the strength of political administration using the degree to which settlements cluster around centers – a more gradual "drop off" indicating weaker control. This model, too, makes assumptions about the expected distribution of the population in the absence of central control – assumptions which are more likely to be valid when conceived as relative tendencies than predictable patterns.
3. They define the social integrative facility as "a structure or prepared space socially acknowledged as a context for integration of individuals above the household level" (Adler and Wilshusen 1990:133). The peoples represented in their ethnographic sample (listed on p. 134) include the Mandan, Maidu, and Yurok of North America; the Bororo, Jivaro, and Yanamamo of South America; the Arapesh, Etoro, and Tsembaga Maring of New Guinea; and the Dogon, Fang, and Tallensi of Africa.
4. Among the following, chiefs lived in houses representing notably greater energy: The Natchez (Swanton 1911:59, Spencer *et al.* 1965:412), Carib (Bennett 1949:16, Rouse 1948), Arawak (Rouse 1948:525), Chibcha (Steward and Faron 1959:214), Tahitians (Oliver 1974:1162), and the Tikopia (Firth 1936:58), although to a much smaller degree among the latter two.
5. Actually, many sites (and regions, "culture areas," even eras of time) display an easily recognized uniformity in architectural plan and style. But if there *are* variations we cannot always rule out the possibility that they reflect some non-status-based creativity or experimentation.
6. Swanton 1911, Steward and Faron 1959:227 and 214, Firth 1936, and Steward and Faron 1959:222 respectively.

8 Çatal Hüyük: a ranked Neolithic town in Anatolia?

1. The site derives its name "from a road fork at the northern end" of the great double mound (Mellaart 1967:27). Hüyük is Modern Turkish for "mound." Pronounced roughly as "*Ch*atal Ho*y*ok," in some recent publications it is spelled "Çatal Höyük" (Gorny 1989:78), but I have retained the spelling found in the excavation reports which remains in wide use among prehistorians.
2. Carbon 14 samples for Levels II through X give dates from about 5,700 BC to 6,300 BC. One date for Level XII of about 6,000 BC is lower than six of the seven dates available for VIII through X and generally considered anomalous. Todd adds roughly 200 years to the date for Level X for a more likely date for Level XII. But these are not calibrated, and while rather a rough measure I have "added" 1,000 years to the C 14 dates to arrive at approximate calendar dates.

3. *Early Anatolia* 1956, quoted in Oats and Oats 1976:61. See Todd for a history of the excavation of Neolithic sites in Turkey (1976:1–6), and Mellaart for a recounting of surveys of the region and of his impressions on first reaching the site "[o]n a cold November day in 1958, just before nightfall" (1967:27–30).

4. Excavation has not yet taken us to the ground level, and there may be five meters of cultural deposits *below* the present ground level. No sounding has reached virgin soil, although even these five meters appear to bring the cultural deposits below the present water table.

5. Some, as with three adjoining walls of the "Second Shrine" (E,VI,10), to roof level, a height of 9 feet (2.7 meters) or more (Mellaart 1963a:70).

6. Fairservis sees civilization as primarily a state of intellectual development, more or less an intellectual liberation from the material world.

7. Mellaart considers a population of 5,000–6,000 "in its heyday" (e.g. Level VI and possibly others) a conservative estimate (1975:99). But Fairservis believes this is high, suggesting instead "something less than 3,000" (1975:158). As he points out, an estimate like Mellaart's assumes the shrines were regularly inhabited (reasonable enough, although it means there were many more burials elsewhere) and that the entire mound was inhabited at the same density as the area excavated (also plausible, but untested, and leaving no room for workshops, a central plaza, or public architecture of any sort). These estimates are for the main mound. It is generally assumed that the site's other mound, Çatal Hüyük West, was established around the time Çatal Hüyük East was abandoned, but to my knowledge this has not been demonstrated.

8. This may be significant in light of another osteological observation. Angel noted the curiously high proportion of femurs with "a special backward direction of the lesser trochanter" (1971:92) which would affect control of the hip joint. "Extra posterior development of the lesser trochanter ... adds a little leverage in quick turning and poising as in dancing or in the animal games shown in the frescoes" (p. 94).

9. Parents with considerable material wealth or possessions could include some of these in the grave of a child they loved quite apart from whether high status was inherited, but they could not legitimately "pass on" the representations of a status – say of priest or healer – that one of them had achieved.

10. Interestingly, it was found in a house burial (E VIA, 29), while many of the finest items were recovered in shrine burials.

11. Several other Level VIII and VII burials were similarly positioned (Mellaart 1966b:182).

12. In Shrine E VI, 7 the "central part of the room was covered with fine matting, made of a marsh grass laid on a bedding of strewn rushes" (Mellaart 1963a:75). This required skill and hard work – but given the quality of some of the other items produced at the site, it may, alternatively, have been a normal floor covering.

13. The daggers can be addressed with the production step measure, for the fine pressure flaking of at least one surface represents a considerable amount of careful, skilled work applied *after* they were already well-made and workable tools. The flint used on these tools was probably more difficult to obtain than obsidian; that used for the "ceremonial" flint dagger found in Shrine VI A, 29 may have been imported from Syria (Mellaart (1975:103).

14. This point is emphasized by Bialor (1962:69) and is certainly significant – particularly the lack of chipped axes, adzes, picks, and hoes. But Bialor studied only the finds from the first season and no sickles had yet been found (Mellaart 1961:7). Others have remarked on the lack of agricultural implements, but it is not always clear whether they are aware that some agricultural tools were found in later seasons. Further, Bialor's argument is based in part on the lack of microliths, a nearly universal component of early Near Eastern harvesting tools. But Mellaart notes that curved sickles of wood (or antler) have been found (1975:104), and it may just be that the people did not make stone sickles.

15. Mellaart's suggestion that priests and priestesses, rather than weaving their own cloth "went to the bazaar and utilized the handiwork of others" (1967:211) is a possibility. Both

the quality of cloth and the absence of production tools argue for specialization, but bazaars have not been found. Just what *was* the town plan? It would be a wonderful thing to undertake further excavation now after thirty years of accumulated questions and speculations (not to mention technical advances in excavation), and I would strongly advocate tackling new areas rather than extending the earlier work.

16. "Obsidian from the Acigöl area has been found as far south as Byblos on the Lebanese coast, and that from Çliftlik reached Beidha near Petra in southern Jordan" (Todd 1976:127) to mention just two examples.

17. Not only were the images produced indoors in small, private or semi-public space, but they were not placed where they would be most easily seen. A number of paintings were on lower wall panels (Mellaart 1963a:61), and covered over not long after they were painted, possibly within a year. This is not art meant to be shown off to the masses.

18. This may be due to flood deposits, as tentatively identified within the settlement. These could preserve field markings and other signs of human activity outside the site itself and it is my hope that renewed exploration would consider a selected study of the land adjacent to the mound.

REFERENCES

Abrams, Elliot M., 1989, "Architecture and Energy: An Evolutionary Perspective," in Michael B. Schiffer (ed.), *Archaeological Method and Theory, Volume I*, Tucson, University of Arizona Press, 47–87.

Adler, M. A. and R. H. Wilshusen, 1990, "Large-Scale Integrative Facilities in Tribal Societies: Cross-Cultural and Southwestern United States Examples," *World Archaeology*, 22(2), 133–146.

Aleskshin, V. A., 1983, "Burial Customs as an Archaeological Source," *Current Anthropology*, 25(5), 674–679.

Angel, J. Lawrence, 1971, "Early Neolithic Skeletons from Çatal Hüyük: Demography and Pathology," *Anatolian Studies*, 21, 77–98.

Arnold, Dean E., 1984, "Social Interaction and Ceramic Design: Community-Wide Correlations in Quinua, Peru," in Prudence M. Rice (ed.), *Pots and Potters: Current Approaches in Ceramic Archaeology*, Los Angeles, University of California Los Angeles, Institute of Archeaology Monograph XXIV, 133–161.

Arnold, Jeanne E. and Anabel Ford, 1980, "A Statistical Examination of Settlement Patterns at Tikal, Guatemala," *American Antiquity*, 45, 713–726.

Bard, Kathryn A., 1989, "The Evolution of Social Complexity in Predynastic Egypt: An Analysis of the Naqada Cemeteries," *Journal of Mediterranean Archaeology*, 2(2), 223–248.

Bartel, Brad, 1972, "The Characteristics of the Çatal Hüyük Supracommunity," *American Journal of Archaeology*, 76, 204–205.

1982, "A Historical Review of Ethnological and Archaeological Analyses of Mortuary Practice," *Journal of Anthropological Archaeology*, 1, 32–58.

Bellwood, Peter, 1979, *Man's Conquest of the Pacific*, New York, Oxford University Press.

Bennett, W. C., 1949, "Habitations," in Julian H. Steward (ed.), *The Comparative Ethnology of South American Indians, Handbook of South American Indians, Vol. 5*, Bureau of American Ethnology Bulletin 143, 1–20.

Berreman, Gerald D., 1981, "Social Inequality: A Cross-Cultural Analysis," in Gerald D. Berreman (ed.), *Social Inequality: Comparative and Developmental Approaches*, New York, Academic Press, 3–40.

Beteille, Andre, 1981, "The Idea of Natural Inequality," in Gerald D. Berreman (ed.), *Social Inequality: Comparative and Developmental Approaches*, New York, Academic Press, 59–80.

Bettinger, Robert L., 1991, *Hunter-Gatherers: Archaeological and Evolutionary Theory*, New York, Plenum Press.

Bhattacharya, D. K., 1989, "Terracotta Worship in Fringe Bengal," in Ian Hodder (ed.), *The Meanings of Things: Material Culture and Symbolic Expression*, London, Unwin Hyman, 12–22.

Bialor, P. A., 1962, "The Chipped Stone Industry of Çatal Hüyük," *Anatolian Studies*, 12, 67–110.

Binford, Lewis R., 1968, "Methodological Considerations of the Archaeological Use of

Ethnographic Data," in Richard B. Lee and Irven DeVore (eds.), *Man the Hunter*, Chicago, Aldine Publishing Company, 268–273.

1971, "Mortuary Practices: Their Study and Their Potential," in James A. Brown (ed.), *Approaches to the Social Dimensions of Mortuary Practices*, Memoirs of the Society for American Archaeology No. 25, 6–29.

1981, *Bones: Ancient Men and Modern Myths*, New York, Academic Press.

1983, *Working at Archaeology*, New York, Academic Press.

1986, "In Pursuit of the Future," in David J. Meltzer, Don D. Fowler, and Jeremey A. Sabloff (eds.), *American Archaeology Past and Future: A Celebration of the Society for American Archaeology 1935–1985*, Washington, Smithsonian Institution Press, 459–479.

1987, "Data, Relativism and Archaeological Science," The Huxley Memorial Lecture 1986, *Man* (n.s.), 22, 391–404.

1989, "The 'New Archaeology,' Then and Now," in C. C. Lamberg-Karlovsky (ed.), *Archaeological Thought in America*, Cambridge, Cambridge University Press, 50–62.

Bonnano, A., T. Gouder, C. Malone, and S. Stoddart, 1990, "Monuments in an Island Society: The Maltese Context," *World Archaeology*, 22(2), 190–205.

Bradley, Richard, 1984, *The Social Foundations of Prehistoric Britain: Themes and Variations in the Archaeology of Power*, London, Longman Group Ltd.

1990, *The Passage of Arms: An Archaeological Analysis of Prehistoric Hoards and Votive Deposits*, Cambridge, Cambridge University Press.

1991, "The Pattern of Change in British Prehistory," in Timothy K. Earle (ed.), *Chiefdoms: Power, Economy, and Ideology*, Cambridge, Cambridge University Press, 229–262.

Braun, David P., 1979, "Illinois Hopewell Burial Practices and Social Organization: A Reexamination of the Klunk-Gibson Mound Group," in David S. Brose and N'omi Greber (eds.), *Hopewell Archaeology: The Chillicothe Conference*, Kent, Ohio, The Kent State University Press, 67–79.

Brown, James A., 1981, "The Search for Rank in Prehistoric Burials," in Robert Chapman, Ian Kinnes, and Klavs Randsborg (eds.), *The Archaeology of Death*, Cambridge, Cambridge University Press, 25–37.

Buikstra, Jane E., 1981, "Mortuary Practices, Palaeodemography and Palaeopathology: A Case Study From the Koster Site (Illinois)," in Robert Chapman, Ian Kinnes, and Klavs Randsborg (eds.), *The Archaeology of Death*, Cambridge, Cambridge University Press, 123–132.

Burnham, Harold B., 1965, "Çatal Hüyük – The Textiles and Twined Fabrics," *Anatolian Studies*, 15, 169–174.

Carneiro, Robert L., 1981, "The Chiefdom: Precursor of the State," in Grant D. Jones and Robert R. Kautz (eds.), *The Transition to Statehood in the New World*, Cambridge, Cambridge University Press, 37–39.

Chapman, Robert, 1981, "Archaeological Theory and Communal Burial in Prehistoric Europe," in Ian Hodder, Glynn Isaac, and Norman Hammond (eds.), *Pattern of the Past: Studies in Honor of David Clarke*, Cambridge, Cambridge University Press, 387–411.

1987, "Mortuary Practices: Society, Theory Building and Archaeology," in A. Boddington, A. N. Garland, and R. C. Janaway (eds.), *Death, Decay, and Reconstruction: Approaches to Archaeology and Forensic Science*, Manchester, Manchester University Press, 198–213.

Chapman, Robert and Klavs Randsborg, 1981, "Approaches to the Archaeology of Death," in Robert Chapman, Ian Kinnes, and Klavs Randsborg (eds.), *The Archaeology of Death*, Cambridge, Cambridge University Press, 1–24.

Childe, V. Gordon, 1951, *Social Evolution*, London, Watts.

Clark, J. G. D., 1952, *Prehistoric Europe, The Economic Basis*, London, Methuen.

Clark, Grahame (J. G. D.), 1957, *Archaeology and Society*, New York, Barnes and Noble Books (third edn.; first edn. 1939).

Clarke, David L., 1977, "Spatial Information in Archaeology," in D. L. Clarke (ed.), *Spatial Archaeology*, New York, Academic Press, 1–32.

1978, *Analytical Archaeology*, New York, Columbia University Press (second edn., revised by Robert Chapman).

Cliff, Maynard B., 1988, "Domestic Architecture and Origins of Complex Society at Cerros," in Richard R. Wilk and Wendy Ashmore (eds.), *Household and Community in the Mesoamerican Past*, Albuquerque, University of New Mexico Press, 199–225.

Cohen, Mark Nathan, 1989, "Paleopathology and the Interpretation of Economic Change in Prehistory," in C. C. Lamberg-Karlovsky (ed.), *Archaeological Thought in America*, Cambridge, Cambridge University Press, 117–132.

Conrad, Geoffrey W., 1978, "Models of Compromise in Settlement Pattern Studies: An Example from Coastal Peru," *World Archaeology*, 9, 281–298.

Cook, Anita Gwynn, 1987, "The Middle Horizon Ceramic Offerings from Conchopata," *Nawpa Pacha 22–23* (1984–1985), 49–90.

Coontz, Stephanie and Peta Henderson, 1986, "Introduction: 'Explanations' of Male Dominance," in Stephanie Coontz and Peta Henderson (eds.), *Women's Work, Men's Property: The Origins of Gender and Class*, London, Verso, 1–42.

Cordell, Linda S. and Fred Plog, 1979, "Escaping the Confines of Normative Thought: A Reevaluation of Puebloan Prehistory," *American Antiquity*, 44, 405–429.

Cordy, Ross H., 1981, *A Study of Prehistoric Change: The Development of Complex Societies in the Hawaiian Islands*, New York, Academic Press, Inc.

Costin, Cathy Lynne and Timothy Earle, 1989, "Status Distinction and Legitimation of Power as Reflected in Changing Patterns of Consumption in Late Prehispanic Peru," *American Antiquity*, 54(4), 691–714.

Crabtree, Pam J., 1990, "Comment on Gary S. Webster: Labor Control and Emergent Stratification in Prehistoric Europe," *Current Anthropology*, 11(4), 347.

Creamer, Winifred and Jonathan Haas, 1985, "Tribe Versus Chiefdom in Lower Central America," *American Antiquity*, 50(4), 738–754.

Dalton, George, 1968, "Introduction," in George Dalton (ed.), *Primitive, Archaic and Modern Economies: Essays of Karl Polanyi*, Boston, Beacon Press, ix–liv.

Davenport, William, 1969, "The Hawaiian Cultural Revolution: Some Political and Economic Considerations," *American Anthropologist*, 71, 1–20.

Davidson, Janet M., 1979, "Samoa and Tonga," in Jesse D. Jennings (ed.), *The Prehistory of Polynesia*, Cambridge, MA, Harvard University Press, 82–109.

de Montmollin, Olivier, 1989a, *The Archaeology of Political Structure: Settlement Analysis in a Classic Maya Polity*, Cambridge, Cambridge University Press.

1989b, "Land Tenure and Politics in the Late/Terminal Classic Rosario Valley, Chiapas, Mexico," *Journal of Anthropological Research*, 45(3), 293–314.

Dempsey, James, 1955, *Mission on the Nile*, London, Burns and Oates.

Dever, William G., 1987, "The Middle Bronze Age: The Zenith of the Urban Canaanite Era," *Biblical Archaeologist*, 50(3), 148–177.

1990, *Recent Archaeological Discoveries and Biblical Research*, Seattle, University of Washington Press.

1993, "Further Evidence on the Date of the Outer Wall at Gezer," *Bulletin of the American Schools of Oriental Research*, Number 289, 33–54.

Drennan, Robert D., 1991, "Pre-Hispanic Chiefdom Trajectories in Mesoamerica, Central America, and Northern South America," in Timothy K. Earle (ed.), *Chiefdoms: Power, Economy, and Ideology*, Cambridge, Cambridge University Press, 263–287.

Drucker, Philip, 1939, "Rank, Wealth, and Kinship in Northwest Coast Society," *American Anthropologist*, 41, 55–65.

1951, *The Northern and Central Nootkan Tribes*, Washington, DC, US Government Printing Office.

Earle, Timothy K., 1977, "A Reappraisal of Redistribution: Complex Hawaiian Chiefdoms," in Timothy K. Earle and Jonathon E. Ericson (eds.), *Exchange Systems in Prehistory*, New York, Academic Press, 213–229.

1978, *Economic and Social Organization of a Complex Chiefdom: The Halelea District, Kaua'i Hawaii*, Ann Arbor, Anthropological Papers, Museum of Anthropology, University of Michigan, No. 63.

1987, "Specialization and the Production of Wealth: Hawaiian Chiefdoms and the Inka Empire," in Elizabeth Brumfiel and Timothy K. Earle (eds.), *Specialization, Exchange and Complex Societies*, Cambridge, Cambridge University Press, 64–75.

1989, "The Evolution of Chiefdoms," *Current Anthropology*, 30(1), 84–88.

1991a, "The Evolution of Chiefdoms," in Timothy K. Earle (ed.), *Chiefdoms: Power, Economy, and Ideology*, Cambridge, Cambridge University Press, 1–15.

1991b, "Property Rights and the Evolution of Chiefdoms," in Timothy K. Earle (ed.), *Chiefdoms: Power, Economy, and Ideology*, Cambridge, Cambridge University Press, 71–99.

Emmons, George Thornton, 1907, "The Chilkat Blanket," *American Museum of Natural History, Memoirs 3, Part 4*, 329–404.

1916, *The Whale House of the Chilkat*, New York, American Museum of Natural History.

Fairservis, Walter A., Jr., 1975, *The Threshold of Civilization: An Experiment in Prehistory*, New York, Charles Scribner's Sons.

Feinman, Gary M., 1990, "Comment on Gary S. Webster: Labor Control and Emergent Stratification in Prehistoric Europe," *Current Anthropology*, 11(4), 348–349.

1991, "Demography, Surplus, and Inequality: Early Political Formations in Highland Mesoamerica," in Timothy K. Earle (ed.), *Chiefdoms: Power, Economy, and Ideology*, Cambridge, Cambridge University Press, 229–262.

Feinman, Gary and Jill Neitzel, 1984, "Too Many Types: An Overview of Sedentary Prestate Societies in the Americas," in Michael B. Schiffer (ed.), *Advances in Archaeological Method and Theory, Volume 7*, New York, Academic Press, Inc., 39–102.

Feldman, Robert A., 1987, "Architectural Evidence for the Development of Nonegalitarian Social Systems in Coastal Peru," in Jonathan Haas, Shelia Pozorski, and Thomas Pozorski (eds.), *The Origin and Development of the Andean State*, Cambridge, Cambridge University Press, 9–14.

Ferdon, Edwin N., 1981, *Early Tahiti as the Explorers Saw It 1767–1797*, Tucson, The University of Arizona Press.

Ferguson, Yale H., 1991, "Chiefdoms to City-States: The Greek Experience," in Timothy K. Earle (ed.), *Chiefdoms: Power, Economy, and Ideology*, Cambridge, Cambridge University Press, 169–192.

Findlow, Frank J. and Neil J. Goldberg, 1983, "Some Simple Measures for the Study of Prehistoric Political Organization," in Elisabeth Tooker (ed.), *The Development of Political Organization in Native North America*, Washington, DC, American Ethnological Society, 214–226.

Finkelstein, Israel, 1988, *The Archaeology of the Israelite Settlement*, Jerusalem, Israel Exploration Society.

Firth, Raymond, 1929, *Primitive Economics of the New Zealand Maori*, London, George Routledge and Sons.

1936, *We, The Tikopia*, London, Allen and Unwin, 2nd edn., 1957.

1939, *Primitive Polynesian Economy*, London, George Routledge, second edn., 1965.

1940, *The Work of the Gods in Tikopia*, London, London School of Economics and Political Sciences.

1947, "Bark-Cloth in Tikopia, Solomon Islands," *Man*, 47, 69–72.

1957, "A Note on Descent Groups in Polynesia," *Man*, 57, 4–7. (Reprinted in Nelson Graburn [ed.], 1971, *Readings in Kinship and Social Structure*, New York, Harper and

Row, 195–200.)

1959, *Social Change in Tikopia: Restudy of a Polynesian Community After a Generation*, London, Allen and Unwin.

1970, *Rank and Religion in Tikopia: A Study of Polynesian Paganism and Conversion to Christianity*, Boston, Beacon Press.

Flannery, Kent V., 1976, "The Early Mesoamerican House," in Kent V. Flannery (ed.), *The Early Mesoamerican Village*, New York, Academic Press, 16–24.

Flannery, Kent V. and Michael D. Coe, 1968, "Social and Economic Systems in Formative Mesoamerica," in Sally Binford and Lewis Binford (eds.), *New Perspectives in Archaeology*, Chicago, Aldine Publishing Company, 267–283.

Fleming, Andrew, 1973, "Tombs for the Living," *Man*, 8(2), 177–193.

Folan, William J., Ellen R. Kintz, Laraine A. Fletcher, and Burma H. Hyde, 1982, "An Examination of Settlement Patterns at Coba, Quintana Roo, Mexico, and Tikal Guatemala: A Reply to Arnold and Ford," *American Antiquity*, 47, 430–436.

Ford, Anabel and Jeanne E. Arnold, 1982, "A Reexamination of Labor Investments at Tikal: Reply to Haviland and Folan, Kintz, Fletcher, and Hyde," *American Antiquity*, 47, 436–440.

Fortes, Meyer, 1953, "The Structure of Unilineal Descent Groups," reprinted in Nelson Graburn (ed.), *Readings in Kinship and Social Structure*, New York, Harper and Row, 1971, 163–173.

Fortes, M. and E. E. Evans-Pritchard (eds.), 1940, *African Political Systems*, London, Oxford University Press.

Freeman, Leslie G., 1968, "A Theoretical Framework for Interpreting Archaeological Materials," in Richard Lee and Irven DeVore (eds.), *Man the Hunter*, Chicago, Aldine Publishing Company, 262–267.

Fried, Morton H., 1960, "On the Evolution of Social Stratification and the State," in Stanley Diamond (ed.), *Culture and History: Essays in Honor of Paul Radin*, New York, Columbia University Press. Reprinted in Morton H. Fried (ed.), *Readings in Anthropology Volume 1*, New York, Thomas Y. Crowell Company, 462–476.

1967, *The Evolution of Political Society: An Essay in Political Anthropology*, New York, Random House.

Gearing, Fred, 1962, "Priests and Warriors: Social Structures for Cherokee Politics in the 18th Century," The American Anthropological Association, Memoir 93, *American Anthropologist*, 64, No. 5, Part 2.

Gibson, D. Blair and Michael N. Geselowitz, 1988, "The Evolution of Complex Society in Late Prehistoric Europe: Toward a Paradigm," in D. Blair Gibson and Michael N. Geselowitz (eds.), *Tribe and Polity in Late Prehistoric Europe: Demography, Production, and Exchange in the Evolution of Complex Social Systems*, New York, Plenum Press, 3–37.

Gilbert, William Harlen, Jr., 1943, "The Eastern Cherokees," *Smithsonian Institute Bureau of American Ethnology Bulletin 133*, Anthropological Papers No. 23, Washington DC, US Government Printing Office, 169–414.

Gilman, Antonio, 1981, "The Development of Social Stratification in Bronze Age Europe," *Current Anthropology*, 22, 1–23.

1989, "Marxism in American Archaeology," in C. C. Lamberg-Karlovsky (ed.), *Archaeological Thought in America*, Cambridge, Cambridge University Press, 63–73.

Gimbutas, Marija, 1991, *The Civilization of the Goddess: The World of Old Europe*, San Francisco, Harper San Francisco, ed. by Joan Marler.

Goldman, Irving, 1970, *Ancient Polynesian Society*, Chicago, The University of Chicago Press.

Goldstein, Lynne, 1981, "One-dimensional Archaeology and Multi-Dimensional People: Spatial Organization and Mortuary Analysis," in Robert Chapman, Ian Kinnes, and Klavs Randsborg (eds.), *The Archaeology of Death*, Cambridge, Cambridge University

Press, 53–69.

Goodman, Alan H. and George J. Armelagos, 1988, "Childhood Stress and Decreased Longevity in a Prehistoric Population," *American Anthropologist*, 90(4), 936–944.

Goody, Jack, 1982, *Cooking, Cuisine and Class: A Study in Comparative Sociology*, Cambridge, Cambridge University Press.

Gophna, Ram and Juval Portugali, 1988, "Settlement and Demographic Processes in Israel's Coastal Plain from the Chalcolithic to the Middle Bronze Age," *Bulletin of the American Schools of Oriental Research*, 269, 11–28.

Gorny, Ronald L., 1989, "Environment, Archaeology, and History in Hittite Anatolia," *Biblical Archaeologist*, 52(2 + 3), 78–96.

Gould, Richard A., 1978, "Beyond Analogy in Ethnoarchaeology," in Richard A. Gould (ed.), *Explorations in Ethnoarchaeology*, Albuquerque, University of New Mexico Press, 249–293.

Gregory, C., 1980, "Gifts to Men and Gifts to Gods: Gift Exchange and Capital Accumulation in Contemporary Papua," *Man* (n.s.), 15(4), 628–652.

Grove, David C., 1981, "The Formative Period and the Evolution of Complex Culture," in Jeremy A. Sabloff (ed.), *Supplement to the Handbook of Middle American Indians, Volume 1, Archaeology*, Austin, University of Texas Press, 373–391.

Haas, Jonathan, 1981, "Class Conflict and the State in the New World," in Grant D. Jones and Robert R. Kautz (eds.), *The Transition to Statehood in the New World*, Cambridge, Cambridge University Press, 80–104.

1982, *The Evolution of the Prehistoric State*, New York, Columbia University Press.

1987, "The Exercise of Power in Early Andean State Development," in Jonathan Haas, Shelia Pozorski, and Thomas Pozorski (eds.), *The Origin and Development of the Andean State*, Cambridge, Cambridge University Press, 31–35.

Hallpike, C. R., 1989, "Review of Ernest Gellner: Plough, Sword, and Book: The Structure of Human History, 1988," *Man* (n.s.), 24, 691–692.

Harris, Marvin, 1968, *The Rise of Anthropological Theory: A History of Theories of Culture*, New York, Thomas Y. Crowell Company.

Hastorf, Christine A., 1990, "The Effect of the Inca State on Sausa Agricultural Production and Crop Consumption," *American Antiquity*, 55(2), 262–290.

1991, "Gender, Space, and Food in Prehistory," in Joan M. Gero and Margaret W. Conkey (eds.), *Engendering Archaeology: Women and Prehistory*, Oxford, Basil Blackwell, 132–159.

Helbaek, Hans, 1964, "First Impressions of the Çatal Hüyük Plant Husbandry," *Anatolian Studies*, 14, 121–123.

Helms, Mary W., 1979, *Ancient Panama: Chiefs in Search of Power*, Austin, University of Texas Press.

Hendon, Julia A., 1991, "Status and Power in Classic Maya Society: An Archaeological Study," *American Anthropologist*, 93(4), 894–918.

Herr, Larry G., 1988, "Tripartite Pillared Buildings and the Market Place in Iron Age Palestine," *Bulletin of the American Schools of Oriental Research*, 272, 47–67.

Hewlett, Barry S. and Phillip L. Walker, 1991, "Social Status and Dental Health Among the Aka and Mbuti Pygmies," *American Anthropologist*, 93(4), 943–944.

Hodder, Ian, 1984, "Burials, Houses, Women and Men in the European Neolithic," in Daniel Miller and Christopher Tilley (eds.), *Ideology, Power and Prehistory*, Cambridge, Cambridge University Press, 51–68.

1985, "Postprocessual Archaeology," in Michael B. Schiffer (ed.), *Advances in Archaeological Method and Theory, Volume 8*, 1–25.

1987a, "Converging Traditions: The Search for Symbolic Meanings in Archaeology and Geography," in J. M. Wagstaff (ed.), *Landscape and Culture: Geographical and Archaeological Perspectives*, Oxford, Basil Blackwell, Ltd., 134–145.

1987b, "Forward," in Michael Shanks and Christopher Tilley, *Reconstructing Archaeology: Theory and Practice*, Cambridge, Cambridge University Press, xv–xvi.

1990a, "Comment on Gary S. Webster, Labor Control and Emergent Stratification in Prehistoric Europe, 1990," *Current Anthropology*, 31(4), 350.

1990b, *The Domestication of Europe: Structure and Contingency in Neolithic Societies*, Oxford, Basil Blackwell.

1991a, "Interpretive Archaeology and its Role," *American Antiquity*, 56(1), 7–18.

1991b, *Reading the Past: Current Approaches to Interpretation in Archaeology*, second edn., Cambridge, Cambridge University Press (first edn. 1986).

Hodges, Richard, 1987, "Spatial Models, Anthropology and Archaeology," in J. M. Wagstaff (ed.), *Landscape and Culture: Geographical and Archaeological Perspectives*, Oxford, Basil Blackwell, Ltd., 118–133.

Hole, Frank, 1968, "Evidence of Social Organization in Western Iran: 8000–4000 BC," in Sally Binford and Lewis Binford (eds.), *New Perspectives in Archaeology*, Chicago, Aldine Publishing Company, 245–266.

1979, "Rediscovering the Past in the Present: Ethnoarchaeology in Luristan, Iran," in Carol Kramer (ed.), *Ethnoarchaeology: Implications of Ethnography for Archaeology*, New York, Columbia University Press, 192–218.

Hole, Frank and Robert F. Heizer, 1973, *An Introduction to Prehistoric Archaeology*, third edn., New York, Holt, Rinehart and Winston, Inc.

Howell, P. P. and W. P. G. Thomson, 1946, "The Death of a Reth of the Shilluk and the Installation of His Successor," *Sudan Notes and Records*, 27, 4–85.

Humphreys, S. C., 1981, "Introduction: Comparative Perspectives on Death," in S.C. Humphreys and Helen King (eds.), *Mortality and Immortality: The Anthropology and Archaeology of Death*, London, Academic Press, 1–13.

Huntington, Richard and Peter Metcalf, 1979, *Celebrations of Death*, Cambridge, Cambridge University Press.

Ingold, Tim, 1990, "An Anthropologist Looks at Biology," *Man* (n.s.), 25(2), 208–229 (The 1989 Curl Lecture of the Royal Anthropological Institute).

Jacobsen, T. W. and Tracy Cullen, 1981, "A Consideration of Mortuary Practices in Neolithic Greece: Burials From Franchthi Cave," in S. C. Humphreys and Helen King (eds.), *Mortality and Immortality: The Anthropology and Archaeology of Death*, London, Academic Press, 79–101.

Johnson, Allen W. and Timothy Earle, 1987, *The Evolution of Human Society: From Foraging Group to Agrarian State*, Stanford, California, Stanford University Press.

Jones, Livingston French, 1914, *A Study of the Tlingets of Alaska*, New York, Revell.

Kassam, Aneesa and Gemetchu Megersa, 1989, "Iron and Beads: Male and Female Symbols of Creation. A Study of Ornament Among Booran Oromo," in Ian Hodder (ed.), *The Meanings of Things: Material Culture and Symbolic Expression*, London, Unwin Hyman, 23–32.

Keegan, William F. and Morgan D. Maclachlan, 1989, "Evolution of Avunculocal Chiefdoms: A Reconstruction of Taino Kinship and Politics," *American Anthropologist*, 91, 613–630.

Kent, Susan, 1991, "Cause and Effect of Dental Health, Diet, and Status Among Foragers," *American Anthropologist*, 93(4), 942–943.

Kenyon, Kathleen M., 1974, *Digging Up Jerusalem*, New York, Praeger Publishers.

Keswani, Priscilla Schuster, 1989, "Dimensions of Social Hierarchy in Late Bronze Age Cyprus: An Analysis of the Mortuary Data from Enkomi," *Journal of Mediterranean Archaeology*, 2(1), 49–86.

King, Duane H., 1979, "Introduction," in Duane H. King (ed.), *The Cherokee Indian Nation: A Troubled History*, Knoxville, The University of Tennessee Press, ix–xix.

King, Thomas F., 1978, "Don't That Beat the Band?: Nonegalitarian Political Organization in

Prehistoric Central California," in Charles L. Redman, William T. Langhorne, Jr., Mary Jane Berman, Nina M. Versaggi, Edward V. Curtin, and Jeffrey C. Wanser (eds.), *Social Archaeology: Beyond Subsistence and Dating*, New York, Academic Press, 225–248.

Kipp, Rita Smith and Edward M. Schortman, 1989, "The Political Impact of Trade in Chiefdoms," *American Anthropologist*, 91(2), 370–385.

Kirch, Patrick V., 1991, "Chiefship and Competitive Involution: The Marquesas Islands of Eastern Polynesia," in Timothy Earle (ed.), *Chiefdoms: Power, Economy, and Ideology*, Cambridge, Cambridge University Press, 119–145.

Kirchhoff, Paul, 1955, "The Principles of Clanship in Human Society," in Morton Fried (ed.), 1959, *Readings in Anthropology, Vol. II*, New York, Thomas Y. Crowell, 260–270.

Knapp, A. Bernard, 1988, "Ideology, Archaeology, and Polity," *Man* (n.s.), 23(1), 133–163.

1989, "Complexity and Collapse in the North Jordan Valley: Archaeometry and Society in the Middle-Late Bronze Ages," *Israel Exploration Journal*, 39(3–4), 129–148.

1990, "Comment on Gary S. Webster, Labor Control and Emergent Stratification in Prehistoric Europe, 1990," *Current Anthropology*, 31(4), 351.

Knight, Vernon James, Jr., 1990, "Social Organization and the Evolution of Hierarchy in Southeastern Chiefdoms," *Journal of Anthropological Research*, 46(1), 1–23.

Kohl, Philip L., 1989, "The Use and Abuse of World Systems Theory: The Case of the 'Pristine' West Asian State," in C. C. Lamberg-Karlovsky (ed.), *Archaeological Thought in America*, Cambridge, Cambridge University Press, 218–240.

Koppert, Vincent Aloysius, 1930, *Contributions to Clayoquot Ethnology*, Washington, DC, Catholic University of America.

Kosso, Peter, 1991, "Method in Archaeology: Middle-Range Theory as Hermeneutics," *American Antiquity*, 56(4), 621–627.

Kowalewski, Stephen A., 1990, "The Evolution of Complexity in the Valley of Oaxaca," *Annual Review of Anthropology*, 19, 39–58.

Kramer, Carol, 1979a, "Introduction," in Carol Kramer (ed.), *Ethnoarchaeology: Implications of Ethnography for Archaeology*, New York, Columbia University Press.

1979b, "An Archaeological View of a Contemporary Kurdish Village: Domestic Architecture, Household Size, and Wealth," in Carol Kramer (ed.), *Ethnoarchaeology: Implications of Ethnography for Archaeology*, New York, Columbia University Press, 139–163.

Krause, Aurel, 1956, *The Tlingit Indians: Results of a Trip to the Northwest Coast of America and the Bering Straits*, trans. Erna Gunther, Seattle, University of Washington Press for The American Ethnological Society.

Lamberg-Karlovsky, C. C. and Jeremy A. Sabloff, 1979, *Ancient Civilizations: The Near East and Mesoamerica*, Prospect Heights, IL, Waveland Press, Inc. (1987 reprint edn).

Larson, Lewis H., Jr., 1971, "Archaeological Implications of Social Stratification at the Etowah Site, Georgia," in James A. Brown (ed.), *Approaches to the Social Dimensions of Mortuary Practices*, Memoirs of the Society for American Archaeology No. 25, 58–67.

Leach, Edmund, 1973, "Concluding Address," in Colin Renfrew (ed.), *The Explanation of Culture Change: Models in Prehistory*, Pittsburgh, University of Pittsburgh Press, 761–771.

Lee, Richard B., 1981, "Politics, Sexual and Nonsexual, in an Egalitarian Society: the !Kung San," in Gerald D. Berreman (ed.), *Social Inequality: Comparative and Developmental Approaches*, New York, Academic Press, 83–102.

Lerner, Gerda, 1986, *The Creation of Patriarchy*, Oxford, Oxford University Press.

Levy, Janet E., 1979, "Evidence of Social Stratification in Bronze Age Denmark," *Journal of Field Archaeology*, 6, 49–56.

1982, *Social and Religious Organisation in Bronze Age Denmark: An Analysis of Ritual Hoard Finds*, Oxford, British Archaeological Reports, BAR International Series 124.

Lightfoot, Kent G. and Gary M. Feinman, 1982, "Social Differentiation and Leadership Development in Early Pithouse Villages in the Mogollon Region of the American

Southwest," *American Antiquity*, 47, 64–86.

London, Gloria, 1989, "A Comparison of Two Contemporaneous Lifestyles of the Late Second Millennium B. C.," *Bulletin of the American Schools of Oriental Research*, 273, 37–55.

MacKay, Donald M., 1974, *The Clockwork Image*, Downers Grove, Illinois, InterVarsity Press.

Maclachlan, Morgan D. and William F. Keegan, 1990, "Archeology and the Ethno-Tyrannies," *American Anthropologist*, 92, 1011–1013.

Magness, Jodi, 1990, "Some Observations on the Roman Temple at Kedesh," *Israel Exploration Journal*, 40(2–3), 173–181.

Maisels, Charles Keith, 1993, *The Near East: Archaeology in the 'Cradle of Civilization'*, London, Routledge.

Marcus, George E., 1983, "'Elite' as a Concept, Theory, and Research Tradition," in George E. Marcus (ed.), *Elites: Ethnographic Issues*, Albuquerque, University of New Mexico Press, A School of American Research Book, 7–27.

Marcus, Joyce, 1976, *Emblem and State in the Classic Maya Lowlands*, Washington, DC, Dumbarton Oaks.

Martinez, Navarrete, 1990, "Comment on Gary S. Webster: Labor Control and Emergent Stratification in Prehistoric Europe," *Current Anthropology*, 31(4), 352–353.

McAnany, Patricia A., 1989, "Stone-Tool Production and Exchange in the Eastern Maya Lowlands: The Consumer Perspective from Pulltrouser Swamp, Belize," *American Antiquity*, 54(2), 322–346.

McGuire, Randall H., 1983, "Breaking Down Cultural Complexity: Inequality and Heterogeneity," in Michael B. Schiffer (ed.), *Advances in Archaeological Method and Theory, Volume 6*, New York, Academic Press, Inc., 91–142.

Mellaart, James, 1961, "Çatal Hüyük Excavations, 1961," *Archäolgischer Anzeiger*, 1–11.

  1962, "Excavations at Çatal Hüyük: First Preliminary Report, 1961," *Anatolian Studies*, 12, 41–65.

  1963a, "Excavations at Çatal Hüyük, 1962: Second Preliminary Report," *Anatolian Studies*, 13, 43–103.

  1963b, "Excavations at Çatal Hüyük, 1962: Summary of Results," *Archäologischer Anzeiger*, 19–32.

  1963c, "Excavations at Çatal Hüyük, 1963: Summary of Results," *Archäologischer Anzeiger*, 722–740.

  1964, "Excavations at Çatal Hüyük, 1963: Third Preliminary Report," *Anatolian Studies*, 14, 39–119.

  1966a, "Excavations at Çatal Hüyük, 1965," *Archäologischer Anzeiger*, 1–15.

  1966b, "Excavations at Çatal Hüyük, 1965: Fourth Preliminary Report," *Anatolian Studies*, 16, 165–191.

  1967, *Çatal Hüyük: A Neolithic Town in Anatolia*, New York, McGraw-Hill Book Company.

  1975, *The Neolithic of the Near East*, New York, Charles Scribner's Sons.

Metcalf, Peter, 1981, "Meaning and Materialism: The Ritual Economy of Death," *Man*, 16, 563–578.

Metraux, Alfred, 1940, *Ethnology of Easter Island*, Honolulu, Bernice P. Bishop Museum.

Michels, Joseph W., 1979, *The Kaminaljuyu Chiefdom*, The Pennsylvania State University Press Monograph Series on Kaminaljuyu.

Miller, Daniel, 1987, *Material Culture and Mass Consumption*, Oxford, Basil Blackwell.

Miller, Daniel and Christopher Tilley, 1984a, "Ideology, Power and Prehistory: An Introduction," in Daniel Miller and Christopher Tilley (eds.), *Ideology, Power and Prehistory*, Cambridge, Cambridge University Press, 1–15.

  1984b, "Preface," in Daniel Miller and Christopher Tilley (eds.), *Ideology, Power and*

Prehistory, Cambridge, Cambridge University Press, vii.

Moore, Jerry D., 1981, "Chimu Socio-Economic Organization: Preliminary Data from Manchan, Casma Valley, Peru," *Nawpa Pacha 19*, 115–128.

Morris, Ian, 1989, "Circulation, Deposition and the Formation of the Greek Iron Age," *Man* (n.s.), 24(3), 502–519.

Moseley, Michael Edward, 1975, *The Maritime Foundations of Andean Civilization*, Menlo Park, California, The Benjamin/Cummings Publishing Company.

Murray, Tim and Michael J. Walker, 1988, "Like WHAT? A Practical Question of Analogical Inference and Archaeological Meaningfulness," *Journal of Anthropological Archaeology*, 7, 248–287.

Oats, David and Joan Oats, 1976, *The Rise of Civilization*, Lausanne, Elsevier Phaidon.

Oberg, Kalervo, 1955, "Types of Social Structure Among the Lowland Tribes of South and Central America," *American Anthropologist*, 57, 472–489.

Okauchi, Mitsuzane, 1986, "Mounded Tombs in East Asia from the 3rd to 7th Centuries AD," in Richard J. Pearson, Gina Lee Barnes, and Karl L. Hutterer (eds.), *Windows on the Japanese Past: Studies in Archaeology and Prehistory*, Ann Arbor, Center for Japanese Studies, the University of Michigan, 127–148.

Oliver, Douglas L., 1974, *Ancient Tahitian Society*, Honolulu, The University of Hawaii Press.

Orme, Bryony, 1981, *Anthropology for Archaeologists: An Introduction*, Ithaca, New York, Cornell University Press.

O'Shea, John, 1981, "Social Configurations and the Archaeological Study of Mortuary Practices: A Case Study," in Robert Chapman, Ian Kinnes, and Klavs Randsborg (eds.), *The Archaeology of Death*, Cambridge, Cambridge University Press, 39–52.

   1984, *Mortuary Variability: An Archaeological Investigation*, Orlando, Academic Press.

Palumbo, Gaetano, 1987, "'Egalitarian' or 'Stratified' Society? Some Notes on Mortuary Practices and Social Structure at Jericho in EB IV," *Bulletin of the American Schools of Oriental Research*, 267, 43–59.

Parker Pearson, Michael, 1982, "Mortuary Practices, Society and Ideology: An Ethnoarchaeological Study," in Ian Hodder (ed.), *Symbolic and Structural Archaeology*, Cambridge, Cambridge University Press, 99–113.

   1984a, "Economic and Ideological Change: Cyclical Growth in the Pre-state Societies of Jutland," in Daniel Miller and Christopher Tilley (eds.), *Ideology, Power and Prehistory*, Cambridge, Cambridge University Press, 69–92.

   1984b, "Social Change, Ideology and the Archaeological Record," in Matthew Spriggs (ed.), *Marxist Perspectives in Archaeology*, Cambridge, Cambridge University Press, 59–71.

Patrik, L. E., 1985, "Is There an Archaeological Record?," in Michael B. Schiffer (ed.), *Advances in Archaeological Method and Theory, Volume 8*, New York, Academic Press, 27–62.

Patterson, Thomas C., 1989, "History and the Post-Processual Archaeologies," *Man* (n.s.), 24, 555–566.

Pearson, Richard, Jon-wook Lee, Wonyoung Koh, and Anne Underhill, 1989, "Social Ranking in the Kingdom of Old Silla, Korea: Analysis of Burials," *Journal of Anthropological Archaeology*, 8(1), 1–50.

Peebles, C. S., 1971, "Moundville and Surrounding Sites: Some Structural Considerations of Mortuary Practices II," in James A. Brown (ed.), *Approaches to the Social Dimensions of Mortuary Practices*, Memoirs, Society for American Archaeology No. 25, 68–91.

Peebles, Christopher S. and Susan M. Kus, 1977, "Some Archaeological Correlates of Ranked Societies," *American Antiquity*, 42, 421–448.

Peregrine, Peter, 1991, "Some Political Aspects of Craft Specialization," *World Archaeology*, 23(1), 1–11.

Plog, Fred and Steadman Upham, 1983, "The Analysis of Prehistoric Political Organization," in Elisabeth Tooker (ed.), *The Development of Political Organization in Native North America*, 1979 Proceedings of The American Ethnological Society, 199–213.

Polanyi, Karl, 1944, *The Great Transformation*, reprinted in George Dalton (ed.), 1968, *Primitive, Archaic and Modern Economies: Essays of Karl Polanyi*, Boston, Beacon Press, 3–25.

1957, "The Economy as an Instituted Process," reprinted in George Dalton (ed.), 1968, *Primitive, Archaic and Modern Economies: Essays of Karl Polanyi*, Boston, Beacon Press, 139–174.

1960, "On the Comparative Treatment of Economic Institutions in Antiquity with Illustrations from Athens, Mycenae, and Alalakh," reprinted in George Dalton (ed.), 1968, *Primitive, Archaic and Modern Economies: Essays of Karl Polanyi*, Boston, Beacon Press, 306–334.

1966, "Redistribution: The State Sphere in Eighteenth-Century Dahome," reprinted in George Dalton (ed.), 1968, *Primitive, Archaic, and Modern Economies: Essays of Karl Polanyi*, Boston, Beacon Press, 207–237.

Possehl, Gregory L., 1990, "Revolution in the Urban Revolution: The Emergence of Indus Urbanization," *Annual Review of Anthropology*, 19, 261–282.

Pozorski, Shelia, 1987, "Theocracy vs. Militarism: The Significance of the Casma Valley in Understanding Early State Formation," in Jonathan Haas, Shelia Pozorski, and Thomas Pozorski (eds.), *The Origin and Development of the Andean State*, Cambridge, Cambridge University Press, 15–30.

Pozorski, Thomas, 1980, "The Early Horizon Site of Huaca De Los Reyes: Social Implications," *American Antiquity*, 45, 100–110.

1982, "Early Social Stratification and Subsistence Systems: The Caballo Muerto Complex," in Michael E. Moseley and Kent C. Day (eds.), *ChanChan: Andean Desert City*, Albuquerque, University of New Mexico Press, 225–253.

Pozorski, Thomas and Shelia Pozorski, 1987, "Chavin, the Early Horizon and the Initial Period," in Jonathan Haas, Shelia Pozorski, and Thomas Pozorski (eds.), *The Origin and Development of the Andean State*, Cambridge, Cambridge University Press, 36–46.

Price, Barbara J., 1978, "Secondary State Formation: An Explanatory Model," in Ronald Cohen and Elman R. Service (eds.), *Origins of the State: The Anthropology of Political Evolution*, Philadelphia, Institute for the Study of Human Issues, 161–186.

1987, "Analysis of the Ranking–Stratification Transition," Paper presented at the "Morton Fried in Anthropological Perspective" session of the 86th Annual Meeting of the American Anthropological Association, Chicago, Illinois, November 20, 1987.

Quilter, Jeffrey, 1990, "Cerro de Media Luna: An Early Intermediate Period Site in the Chillon Valley, Peru," *Nawpa Pacha 24*, [1986], 73–98.

Radcliffe-Brown, A. R., 1950, "Introduction," in A. R. Radcliffe-Brown and Daryll Forde (eds.), *African Systems of Kinship and Marriage*, London, Oxford University Press, 1–85.

Randsborg, Klavs, 1981, "Burial, Succession and Early State Formation in Denmark," in Robert Chapman, Ian Kinnes, and Klavs Randsborg (eds.), *The Archaeology of Death*, Cambridge, Cambridge University Press, 105–121.

1982, "Rank, Rights and Resources– – An Archaeological Perspective from Denmark," in Colin Renfrew and Stephen Shennan (eds.), *Ranking, Resource and Exchange: Aspects of the Archaeology of Early European Society*, Cambridge, Cambridge University Press, 132–139.

Redman, Charles L., 1978, *The Emergence of Civilization: From Early Farmers to Urban Society in the Ancient Near East*, San Francisco, W. H. Freeman and Company.

Renfrew, Colin, 1972, *The Emergence of Civilization: The Cyclades and the Aegean in the Third Millennium BC*, London, Methuen and Co., Ltd.

1973a, *Before Civilization: The Radiocarbon Revolution and Prehistoric Europe*, New York,

Alfred A. Knopf.

1973b, "Monuments, Mobilization, and Social Organization in Neolithic Wessex," in Colin Renfrew (ed.), *The Explanation of Culture Change: Models in Prehistory*, Gerald Duckworth and Company, Ltd., 539–558.

1974, "Beyond a Subsistence Economy: The Evolution of Social Organization in Prehistoric Europe," in Charlotte B. Moore (ed.), *Reconstructing Complex Societies: An Archaeological Colloquium*, Supplement to the Bulletin of the American Schools of Oriental Research No. 20, 69–95.

1978, "Space, Time and Polity," in J. Friedman and M. J. Rowlands (eds.), *The Evolution of Social Systems*, Pittsburgh, University of Pittsburgh Press, 89–112.

1982, "Socio-Economic Change in Ranked Societies," in Colin Renfrew and Stephen Shennan (eds.), *Ranking, Resource and Exchange: Aspects of the Archaeology of Early European Society*, Cambridge, Cambridge University Press, 1–8.

1984a, *Approaches to Social Archaeology*, Cambridge, MA, Harvard University Press.

1984b, "Trade as Action at a Distance," in Colin Renfrew, *Approaches to Social Archaeology*, Cambridge, MA, Harvard University Press, 86–134.

1986, "Introduction: Peer Polity Interaction and Socio-Political Change," in Colin Renfrew and John F. Cherry (eds.), *Peer Polity Interaction and Socio-Political Change*, Cambridge, Cambridge University Press, 1–18.

Renfrew, Colin (ed.), 1973, *The Explanation of Culture Change: Models in Prehistory*, Gerald Duckworth and Company, Limited.

Rice, Prudence M., 1981, "Evolution of Specialized Pottery Production: A Trial Model," *Current Anthropology*, 22, 219–240.

1989, "Ceramic Diversity, Production, and Use," in Robert D. Leonard and George T. Jones (eds.), *Quantifying Diversity in Archaeology*, Cambridge, Cambridge University Press, 109–117.

Rouse, Irving, 1948, "The Arawak," in Julian Steward (ed.), *Handbook of South American Indians, Volume 4*, Bureau of American Ethnology Bulletin 143, 507–546.

Royce, Charles C., 1887, "The Cherokee Nation of Indians," in J. W. Powell (ed.), *Fifth Annual Report of the Bureau of Ethnology 1883–1884*, Washington, Government Printing Office, 121–378.

Rupp, David W., 1988, "The 'Royal Tombs' at Salamis (Cypris): Ideological Messages of Power and Authority," *Journal of Mediterranean Archaeology*, 1(1), 111–139.

Ryder, M. L., 1965, "Report of Textiles from Çatal Hüyük," *Anatolian Studies*, 15, 175–176.

Sahlins, Marshall D., 1958, *Social Stratification in Polynesia*, Seattle, University of Washington Press Monograph 27, The American Ethnological Society.

1960, "Political Power and the Economy of Primitive Society," in Gertrude Dole and Robert L. Carneiro (eds.), *Essays in the Science of Culture in Honor of Leslie White*, New York, Thomas Y. Crowell Company, 390–415.

Salmon, Merrilee H., 1982, *Philosophy and Archaeology*, New York, Academic Press.

Sanders, William T., 1974, "Chiefdom to State: Political Evolution at Kaminaljuyu, Guatemala," in Charlotte B. Moore (ed.), *Reconstructing Complex Societies*, Supplement to the Bulletin of the American Schools of Oriental Research No. 20, 97–122.

Sanders, William T., Jeffrey R. Parsons, and Robert R. Santly, 1979, *The Basin of Mexico*, New York, Academic Press.

Sanders, William T. and Barbara J. Price, 1968, *Mesoamerica: The Evolution of a Civilization*, New York, Random House.

Sanders, William T. and David Webster, 1988, "The Mesoamerican Urban Tradition," *American Anthropologist*, 90(3), 521–546.

Sapir, Edward, 1921, "Vancouver Island Indians," in James Hastings (ed.), *Encyclopedia of Religion and Ethics, Volume 12*, New York, Charles Scribner's Sons, 591–595.

Saxe, Arthur A., 1971, "Social Dimensions of Mortuary Practices in Mesolithic Populations from Wadi Halfa, Sudan," in James A. Brown (ed.), *Approaches to the Social Dimensions of Mortuary Practices*, Memoirs of the Society for American Archaeology No. 25, 39–57.

Schiffer, Michael B., 1976, *Behavioral Archaeology*, New York, Academic Press.

1988, "The Structure of Archaeological Theory," *American Antiquity*, 53(3), 461–485.

Schmandt-Basserat, Denise, 1992, *Before Writing: Volume 1: From Counting to Cuneiform*, Austin, University of Texas Press.

Seligman, Charles and Brenda Seligman, 1932, "The Shilluk," in *Pagan Tribes of the Nilotic Sudan*, London, George Routledge and Sons, 37–105.

Service, Elman R., 1971, *Primitive Social Organization*, second edn., New York, Random House (first edn. 1962).

1975, *Origins of the State and Civilization: The Process of Cultural Evolution*, New York, W. W. Norton and Company, Inc.

Settegast, Mary, 1987, *Plato Prehistorian: 10,000 to 5,000 BC in Myth and Archaeology*, Cambridge, MA, The Rotenberg Press.

Shanks, Michael, 1992, *Experiencing the Past: On the Character of Archaeology*, London, Routledge.

Shanks, Michael and Christopher Tilley, 1987a, *Reconstructing Archaeology: Theory and Practice*, Cambridge, Cambridge University Press.

1987b, *Social Theory and Archaeology*, Cambridge, Polity Press.

Sharer, Robert J. and Pamela Hearne, 1988, "Panama's River of Gold," *Archaeology*, 41(2), 54–57.

Shay, Talia, 1989, "The Intermediate Bronze Period: A Reply to G. Palumbo," *Bulletin of the American Schools of Oriental Research*, 273, 84–86.

Shennan, Stephen, 1986, "Central Europe in the Third Millennium BC: An Evolutionary Trajectory for the Beginning of the European Bronze Age," *Journal of Anthropological Archaeology*, 5, 115–146.

Sherratt, Andrew, 1982, "Mobile Resources: Settlement and Exchange in Early Agricultural Europe," in Colin Renfrew and Stephen Shennan (eds.), *Ranking, Resource, and Exchange: Aspects of the Archaeology of Europe*, Cambridge, Cambridge University Press, 13–26.

Sillen, Andrew, Judith C. Sealy, and Nikolaas J. Van der Merwe, 1989, "Chemistry and Paleodietary Research: No More Easy Answers," *American Antiquity*, 54(3), 504–512.

Spaulding, Albert C., 1968, "Explanation in Archaeology," in Sally Binford and Lewis R. Binford (eds.), *New Perspectives in Archaeology*, Chicago, Aldine Publishing Co., 33–39.

Spencer, Robert F., Jesse D. Jennings, *et al.* (eds.), 1965, *The Native Americans*, New York, Harper and Row Publishers.

Spriggs, Matthew (ed.), 1984, *Marxist Perspectives in Archaeology*, Cambridge, Cambridge University Press.

Steponaitis, Vincas P., 1978, "Location Theory and Complex Chiefdoms: A Mississippian Example," in Bruce D. Smith (ed.), *Mississippian Settlement Patterns*, New York, Academic Press, 417–453

1991, "Contrasting Patterns of Mississippian Development," in Timothy K. Earle (ed.), *Chiefdoms: Power, Economy, and Ideology*, Cambridge, Cambridge University Press, 193–228.

Steward, Julian H., 1948, "The Circum-Caribbean Tribes: An Introduction," in Julian Steward (ed.), *Handbook of South American Indians, Volume 4*, Bureau of American Ethnology Bulletin 143, 1–41.

Steward, Julian H. and Louis C. Faron, 1959, *Native Peoples of South America*, New York, McGraw-Hill.

Swanton, John R., 1911, *Indian Tribes of the Lower Mississippi Valley and Adjacent Coast of the Gulf of Mexico*, Smithsonian Institution Bureau of American Ethnology Bulletin 43, Washington, DC, US Government Printing Office.

1946, *The Indians of the Southeastern United States*, Smithsonian Institution Bureau of American Ethnology Bulletin 137, Washington, DC, US Government Printing Office.

Tainter, Joseph A., 1977, "Modeling Change in Prehistoric Social Systems," in Lewis R. Binford (ed.), *For Theory Building in Archaeology*, New York, Academic Press, 327–352.

1978, "Mortuary Practices and the Study of Prehistoric Social Systems," in Michael B. Schiffer (ed.), *Advances in Archaeological Method and Theory, Volume 1*, New York, Academic Press, 105–141.

Tainter, Joseph A. and Ross H. Cordy, 1977, "An Archaeological Analysis of Social Ranking and Residence Groups in Prehistoric Hawaii," *World Archaeology*, 9, 95–112.

Thomas, Julian, 1990, "Monuments From the Inside: The Case of the Irish Megalithic Tombs," *World Archaeology*, 22(2), 168–178.

1991, "Reading the Neolithic," *Anthropology Today*, 7(3), 9–11.

Thurnwald, Richard, 1932, *Economics in Primitive Communities*, Oxford, Oxford University Press.

Tilley, Christopher, 1989, "Interpreting Material Culture," in Ian Hodder (ed.), *The Meanings of Things: Material Culture and Symbolic Expression*, London, Unwin Hyman, 185–194.

1991, *Material Culture and Text: The Art of Ambiguity*, London, Routledge.

Tilley, Christopher (ed.), 1990, *Reading Material Culture: Structuralism, Hermeneutics and Post-Structuralism*, Oxford, Basil Blackwell.

Todd, Ian A., 1976, *Çatal Hüyük in Perspective*, Menlo Park, CA, Cummings Publishing Company.

Topic, John and Theresa Topic, 1987, "The Archaeological Investigation of Andean Militarism: Some Cautionary Observations," in Jonathan Haas, Shelia Pozorski, and Thomas Pozorski (eds.), *The Origin and Development of the Andean State*, Cambridge, Cambridge University Press, 47–55.

Trigger, Bruce G., 1978a, "The Archaeology of Government," in Bruce G. Trigger, *Time and Traditions: Essays in Archaeological Interpretation*, New York, Columbia University Press, 153–166.

1978b, "The Determinants of Settlement Patterns," in Bruce G. Trigger, *Time and Traditions: Essays in Archaeological Interpretation*, New York, Columbia University Press, 167–193.

1980, *Gordon Childe: Revolutions in Archaeology*, New York, Columbia University Press.

1989a, *A History of Archaeological Thought*, Cambridge, Cambridge University Press.

1989b, "History and Contemporary American Archaeology: A Critical Analysis," in C. C. Lamberg-Karlovsky (ed.), *Archaeological Thought in America*, Cambridge, Cambridge University Press, 19–34.

Trinkaus, K. Maurer, 1984, "Mortuary Ritual and Mortuary Remains," *Current Anthropology*, 25(5), 674–679.

Tschopik, H., 1950, "An Andean Ceramic Tradition in Historical Perspective," *American Antiquity*, 15, 196–218.

Tuggle, H. David, 1979, "Hawaii," in Jesse D. Jennings (ed.), *Prehistory of Polynesia*, Cambridge, Harvard University Press, 167–199.

Upham, Steadman, Kent G. Lightfoot, and Gary M. Feinman, 1981, "Explaining Socially Determined Ceramic Distributions in the Prehistoric Plateau Southwest," *American Antiquity*, 46, 822–833.

Wagstaff, J. M., 1987, "The New Archaeology and Geography," in J. M. Wagstaff (ed.), *Landscape and Culture: Geographical and Archaeological Perspectives*, Oxford, Basil Blackwell Ltd., 26–36.

Wailes, Bernard, 1990, "Comment on Gary S. Webster: Labor Control and Emergent Stratification in Prehistoric Europe," *Current Anthropology*, 31(4), 354–355.

Walker, Phillip L. and Barry S. Hewlett, 1990, "Dental Health, Diet and Social Status Among

Central African Foragers and Farmers," *American Anthropologist*, 92(2), 383–398.

Wallerstein, Immanuel, 1974, *The Modern World-System: Capitalist Agriculture and the Origins of the European World-Economy in the Sixteenth Century*, New York, Academic Press, Inc.

Wason, Paul K., n.d., "The Significance of Social Types for the Archaeological Study of Ranking," Unpublished manuscript in the possession of the author.

Watson, Patty Jo, 1979a, *Archaeological Ethnography in Western Iran*, Viking Fund Publications in Anthropology #57, Tucson, University of Arizona Press.

1979b, "The Idea of Ethnoarchaeology: Notes and Comments," in Carol Kramer (ed.), *Ethnoarchaeology: Implications of Ethnography for Archaeology*, New York, Columbia University Press, 277–287.

Watson, Patty Jo and Michael Fotiadis, 1990, "The Razor's Edge: Symbolic-Structuralist Archaeology and the Expansion of Archaeological Inference," *American Anthropologist*, 92(3), 613–629.

Watson, Patty Jo, Steven A. LeBlanc, and Charles L. Redman, 1984, *Archaeological Explanation: The Scientific Method in Archaeology*, New York, Columbia University Press.

Webb, Malcom C., 1987, "Broader Perspectives on Andean State Origins," in Jonathan Haas, Shelia Pozorski, and Thomas Pozorski (eds.), *The Origin and Development of the Andean State*, Cambridge, Cambridge University Press, 161–167.

Webster, Gary S., 1990, "Labor Control and Emergent Stratification in Prehistoric Europe," *Current Anthropology*, 31(4), 337–366.

Westermann, Diedrich, 1912, *The Shilluk People, Their Language and Folklore*, Philadelphia, Board of Foreign Missions of the United Presbyterian Church of NA.

White, J. P., 1985, "Digging Out Big-Men?," *Archaeology in Oceania*, 20, 57–60.

Wilkinson, Richard G. and Richard J. Norelli, 1981, "A Biocultural Analysis of Social Organization at Monte Alban," *American Antiquity*, 46, 743–758.

Willey, Gordon R., 1953, *Prehistoric Settlement Patterns in the Viru Valley, Peru*, Washington, Bureau of American Ethnography, Bulletin 155.

1976, "Foreword" to Joyce Marcus, *Emblem and State in the Classic Maya Lowlands*, Washington, Dumbarton Oaks, ix–xv.

Wilson, Woodrow, 1898, *The State: Elements of Historical and Practical Politics*, revised edn., Boston, D.C. Heath and Co., Publishers.

Wittfogel, Karl A., 1957, *Oriental Despotism: A Comparative Study of Total Power*, New Haven, Yale University Press.

Wright, G. A., 1978, "Social Differentiation in the Early Natufian," in Charles L. Redman *et al.* (eds.), *Social Archaeology: Beyond Subsistence and Dating*, New York, Academic Press, 201–223.

Wright, Henry T., 1986, "The Evolution of Civilizations," in David J. Meltzer, Don D. Fowler and Jeremey A. Sabloff (eds.), *American Archaeology Past and Future: A Celebration of the Society for American Archaeology 1935–1985*, Washington, Smithsonian Institution Press, 323–365.

Wylie, Alison M., 1985, "The Reaction Against Analogy," in Michael B. Schiffer (ed.), *Advances in Archaeological Method and Theory, Volume 8*, New York, Academic Press, 63–111.

Zaccagnini, Carlo, 1990, "The Transition from Bronze to Iron in the Near East and in the Levant: Marginal Notes," *Journal of the American Oriental Society*, 110, 493–502.

INDEX

Abrams, Elliot 134, 146–147
acephalous local group 43–44
achieved ranking, *see* ranking achieved or
  non-hereditary
Adler, M. A., and R. H. Wilshusen 134, 147
Alekshin, V. A. 100
analogy, ethnographic, 12, 15–16, 26–30; *see also*
  ethnographic analogy
Andes 17, 34, 48, 119, 146–47, 150
Angel , J. Lawrence 157–158, 161, 171
Arawak 77, 87, 89–90, 94, 96, 97, 99, 105–106,
  112, 117, 134, 137, 139–141
archaeological correlates 2, 11–14, 22, 25–26,
  30–35, 40; based on artifacts 103–126, 163 171;
  the built environment 127–152, 171–177;
  mortuary 67–102, 156–163
archaeological inference 2–5, 7, 11–14, 16, 18–23,
  27–29, 32–35, 37–39, 68; *see also* archaeological
  correlates
archaeological record 2, 4, 9, 11, 20, 23–26, 28,
  30–33, 66, 70–71, 110; mortuary activity and
  70 –71; physical model 30–32; textual model
  30–31
architecture, as evidence of status 12, 29–30, 130,
  133, 134–152; access patterns and status
  149–152, 177; and artifact distributions
  111–112; at Çatal Hüyük 162–163; in stratified
  societies 124–125, 135–136
Arikara (Plains Indian) 68, 84, 94, 96, 98–99
aristocracy 48–49; *see also* ranking, hereditary
Arnold, Dean 115
Arnold, Jeanne and Anabel Ford 138–139
artifacts 20–21, 23–24, 33, 89, 93, 101, 114, 150;
  at Çatal Hüyük 154, 160–162, 163–168, 170,
  172, 177; distributions as evidence of status
  93–98, 101–102, 108–116, 125–126, 142; nature
  of as evidence of status 68, 83, 93–98, 103–108,
  114–116
ascription, *see* ranking, hereditary or ascribed
Aspero, Peru, site of 146, 150
authority 37–38, 40, 42–43, 47m 49–51, 54–55,
  59, 65–66, 80, 95, 99, 104, 107–108, 128–131,
  146–148; Fried's definition of 42
Aymara 34

band society 18, 40–42, 47–48, 129
Bantu 74
Bard, Kathryn 93
Bartel, Brad 70, 171
basic resources 37–38, 57–58, 61–63, 119–121,
  123–125, 133, 135; at Çatal Hüyük 178
Bellwood, Peter 89, 94
benefits, of leadership activity 56, 65–66, 107,
  168
Bennett, W. C. 137
Berewan 81–83
Berreman, Gerald 19, 36–39, 42, 46, 58
Beteille, André 36
Bettinger, Robert L. 23
Bhattacharya, D. K. 5
Bialor, P. A. 165, 167, 171
big-man society 13, 43–45, 53, 62, 81, 100–101
Binford, Lewis 4, 22–24, 28, 31, 35, 67, 70–71,
  87, 94, 100
Bonnano, A. 150
Booran Oromo 115
Bradley, Richard 16, 50, 83, 104, 107, 109–111,
  115
Braun, David P. 73, 76, 97, 100, 104
bridging arguments 20, 25–26, 33; *see also*
  middle-range theory
Britain, Bronze Age 111; Modern and Victorian
  68–69
Bronze Age, Anatolia 153; Britain 111; Cyprus
  90; Denmark 109; Europe 65, 90–98, 106, 110,
  130–131; Germany 111; Near East 83;
  Palestine 101, 106, 115, 141, 146, 150
Brown , James A. 49, 73, 78, 80, 100, 104
Buikstra, Jane E. 72
burials 6, 20, 22–23, 27, 33, 103–105, 123, 145,
  151–152; at Çatal Hüyük 156–163, 164, 166,
  167, 177–178; compared with hoards 67–102;
  compared with residential context 111;
  evidence of inequality 67–102;
Burnham, Harold B. 156, 165

Caballo Muerto, Peru, site of 149
cannibalism 50
Carib 137, 139
Carneiro, Robert L. 56
caste 1, 38–39
Çatal Hüyük 13–14, 26; access patterns and
  status 177; architecture, non-residential 172,
  177; art, iconography and status 153–154;
  168–170; artifact distributions by residence
  167; case study 156–179; characterizations of
  154–155; craft specialization and status
  164–166; dating of 153; demography of 157;
  elite and sumptuary items 163–164; evidence
  for a regional economy 167–168; grave

NEW STUDIES IN ARCHAEOLOGY

Series editors

Colin Renfrew, *University of Cambridge*
Jeremy Sabloff, *University of Pittsburgh*
Clive Gamble, *University of Southampton*